THE
EUREKA!
ENIGMA

7 KEYS TO REALIZING YOUR DREAMS

Ron G Holland - The Trilogy

Talk & Grow Rich

Turbo Success

The Eureka! Enigma

THE
EUREKA!
ENIGMA

7 KEYS TO REALIZING YOUR DREAMS

RON G HOLLAND

New York

The Eureka! Enigma
7 Keys to Realizing Your Dreams

ISBN 978-1-60037-527-9 (PB)

ISBN 978-1-60037-595-8 (HC)

Library of Congress Control Number: 2009901358

Cover Design by: Tony Laidig
www.thecoverexpert.com

tony@thecoverexpert.com

MORGAN · JAMES
THE ENTREPRENEURIAL PUBLISHER

Morgan James Publishing, LLC
1225 Franklin Ave., STE 325
Garden City, NY 11530-1693
Toll Free 800-485-4943
www.MorganJamesPublishing.com

In an effort to support local communities, raise awareness and funds, Morgan James Publishing donates one percent of all book sales for the life of each book to Habitat for Humanity. Get involved today, visit **www.HelpHabitatForHumanity.org**.

To the memory of Alan Turing – the genius behind the legend

and

With love to my very beautiful and extremely talented daughter
Kay, who truly is the light of my life

ACKNOWLEDGMENTS

The Eureka! Enigma took over four years to write and has been through many iterations. My mastermind group of about twenty special guys and girls gave no end of valuable feedback, criticism, constructive thought, stimulation and encouragement. Edited by John Parker and Molly Castelazo, polished by David Noble and Peter Brown and the final read through was completed by the very diligent and courageous code breaker, Bob Morey. A big thank you, to all of you! An extra big thank you to my wife Elisabeth, for her patience and support while the book was being written. A final thank you goes to Tony Sale who spent valuable time with me at Bletchley Park explaining exactly how the Enigma machine and the Colossus computer works, which helped me create the analogy that I have used in this codebook.

Contents

ABOUT THE AUTHOR

Ron G Holland is a seasoned entrepreneur, age 60, and has been written up as Britain's Leading Motivational Speaker, Top Biz Guru and the Entrepreneur's Entrepreneur. He gives numerous seminars and presentations and has been interviewed by TV, radio and the press on four continents. He specializes in raising equity funding for early stage and start-up companies.

Ron has been at the bleeding edge of personal development and self-help for over thirty years. He is the author of many business books, manuals and audio programs including *Talk & Grow Rich* and *Turbo Success* and *The Eureka! Enigma*. His first book, *Debt Free with Financial Kung Fu* was published in 1977 and his audio programs, including *Escape From Where I Am* are in every prison library in the UK, and have been highly acclaimed.

FOREWORD

THE EUREKA! ENIGMA

Do you want to advance in life? Get ahead in the game? Then this practical codebook – designed in the real world for real people – is for you. Learn how to unlock the secrets of your mind and *impressively* increase your usable brain power. First things first. Why is this codebook called *The Eureka! Enigma*? Let's start with Eureka!…

Eureka!

Eureka! comes from the Greek word *heureka,* meaning *I have found it!* It is an expression of delight at an unexpected discovery or the answer to a seemingly unsolvable problem.

The legendary origins of "Eureka!" as a triumphant cry of success lie with the Greek philosopher Archimedes. He was asked by King Hiero to test the purity of his gold crown, but Archimedes had no idea how to begin such a task. Despairing at his inadequacy, he sought the comfort of a warm bath. Plunging in, he noticed for the first time how the quantity of water that simultaneously splashed out of the tub as he got in it equated to the volume of his own body. This led him to conceive of the notions of volume and density – if the King's purportedly gold crown had been alloyed with baser metals it would have to be larger in volume than a real gold crown of the same weight, gold being a denser, heavier metal. The Archimedes Principle was absolutely watertight (unlike his bath!) and, according to Vitruvius, *"when the idea flashed across his mind the philosopher jumped out of the bath exclaiming 'Eureka! Eureka!' and ran home without dressing, to try the experiment."*

The crucial point in relation to what you are about to learn in this codebook is that Archimedes did not make his discovery by careful deductive reasoning alone. He'd done all the thinking, but it was the Eureka! moment that finally freed the logjam in his mind.

In other words, it wasn't while he was working on the problem – while he was in his lab – that Archimedes came up with his Eureka! It was when he had relaxed and let his mind wander – thinking about other things, while his biocomputer subconsciously worked on the problem – that he found his solution. The point here is that the brain is an extremely powerful biological computer (biocomputer) – if you let it do its work.

Do you ever feel like Archimedes before his Eureka! moment? Like the answer is in your mind, but it's stuck and can't get out? That brings me to the second part of this codebook's title...

Enigma

Enigma originated from the Greek word *ainigma* meaning riddle or obscure statement. The modern English use, which describes a person, thing or situation that is mysterious, puzzling or ambiguous, dates from the seventeenth century.

Perhaps the most famous enigma was the code used by Germany in World War II to encrypt their messages – troop movement orders, battle plans, and other crucial and top secret information – so that if the messages were intercepted by the Allies all they would see was meaningless jumbled-up Enigma code. When Germany received the encoded message at the other end of the line, they used another Enigma machine to decode it – to translate the meaningless jumbled-up Enigma code into a real, absolutely vital message.

When the Allies were able to build their own decoding machine (which they achieved, under the guidance of mathematical genius Alan Turing, working with Allied Intelligence at Bletchley Park in Buckinghamshire, England), they were able to crack the Enigma code, decode Germany's messages and help win the war.

Turning Enigmas into Eurekas!

This codebook is about doing the same thing the Allies did, but in your brain. If you're like most people, the messages moving around the one hundred billion neurons in your brain are encoded, so that when you receive those messages, they're jumbled-up Enigma code. But what if you could decode those messages – translate Enigma code into Eurekas! that will allow you to achieve your dreams?

Here's the secret: you can. And the best part is you don't need to be a mathematical genius like Alan Turing to do it. To decode your Enigma code, all you have to do is learn to program your brain to be its very own personal decoder. That's what this codebook is about – finding the *keys* and developing programs that will help you interpret and understand your Enigma code and turn it into Eurekas!

The Eureka! Enigma

The Eureka! Enigma is the third book in a series that began in 1981 with *Talk & Grow Rich: How to Create Wealth Without Capital*, which showed readers how to stop their jumbled internal dialogue and instead find brilliant ideas – Eurekas! It then showed how to turn those ideas into money.

The second book, *Turbo Success: How to Reprogram the Human Biocomputer*, was published in 1993. This volume delved much more deeply into how the mind works and again taught readers how to understand the workings of their brains and to come up with invaluable Eurekas!

Nearly thirty years after the initial book, I'm still talking about Eurekas! Yet after writing and speaking a great deal about both books, I was one day struck, as if for the first time, by what seemed to be a mind-boggling and glaring enigma. Namely, why is it that some people come up with ideas and others don't? Furthermore, why do some people get ideas and *actually* turn them into money, while others, though they may experience brilliant Eurekas! fail to make a dime?

Out of those questions, this codebook was born. I will show you not only how to generate Eurekas! but how to actually turn those brilliant ideas into success. Two assertions underlie this codebook:

1) Codes and problems exist to be cracked and solved. If your mind feels like an enigma, this codebook will help you to unravel your mind's secrets and break the frustrating, coded language cluttering your head. I'll teach you how to understand your mind and use it – how to harness, control and enhance your positive thoughts in order to achieve your personal goals.

2) You have unique hidden qualities that need to be nurtured, brought out into the fore and eventually celebrated when you truly recognize your full potential.

The Eureka! Enigma is about Eurekas! – about generating creative ideas and solutions to all kinds of problems with infallible regularity. It is about creating **Eurekas! on Demand** – being able to come up with incredible thoughts whenever you want to. (Now that's a powerful concept!) It will teach you how to create a *Big Idea,* the one that will be life-changing and wealth-creating. Perhaps, most importantly, it is about turning those totally intangible ideas and dreams into luxurious reality, today.

More than anything, *The Eureka! Enigma* is about mind power, creating happiness, health, peace of mind, successful relationships, well-being and accomplishing your own personal dreams – whatever they are. Whoever you are and wherever you are, this codebook will help you to crack the code of your own mind and release your mind's hidden power to help you maximize your potential.

Who This Codebook Is For

Are you young or old, male or female, unemployed or unemployable, self-employed, or working for someone else? Whoever you are, wherever you are on the ladder of success, this codebook will help you move onward and upward in life, to meet your goals, material or intangible. This codebook is a business book, designed to help you make money. But it's also more than that – it's designed to help you accomplish *all* your goals and dreams, whether you aim to make millions of dollars, climb Mt. Everest, patent an invention, achieve success in the arts or perhaps create a charitable or non-profit enterprise, or some other project close to your heart.

The Mission of This Codebook

The mission of this codebook is to equip you with the skills, knowledge, methods, inspiration and courage to increase exponentially the capacity and *output* of your mind and ultimately help you to discover serenity and success in all those areas of your life where these things may have eluded you so far. This codebook will have a *profound impact* on your life – it is designed to!

Finally, the further aim is to attract philanthropists, donors, sponsors and benefactors to help set up a Foundation for the study of positive thinking, whole-brain thinking and goal accomplishment that will ultimately lead all human beings, no matter what race or creed or where they are on the planet, to be able to access *and* harness the secrets of successful living. Go to www.eureka-enigma.com for further information.

THE FIRST KEY

CRACKING THE CODE

Left to its own devices the human mind can be likened to an *Enigma* machine. Properly programmed it can be likened to a *Colossus* computer.

- Ron G Holland

Enigma: To solve an enigma it helps to know precisely what that enigma is. Here are two related enigmas for you: why is it so difficult to get your mind to perform and start delivering solutions to every-day problems, creative ideas and **Eurekas! on Demand** that will get you ahead in life? And why is it that the more we put ourselves under pressure to perform, the worse things become?

Eureka! There is a definitive way of making the mind perform because the mind is like a computer – a human biocomputer. To operate it at optimum levels we must treat it like a computer and program it like one – but we need to be taught how!

MY EUREKA! MOMENT

As a young man, my initial incentive for making lots of money was driving, but not in the everyday sense. I had an insatiable appetite for all things fast, particularly cars and motorcycles – powerful pieces of machinery, beautifully streamlined and *seriously* expensive. To make sufficient money to pay for my passion meant getting into business and that brought with it a regular host of problems needing solutions. This necessity in turn led to my life-long quest for practical mind power to uncover the secrets of success.

My love affair with speed continues to this day; my current pet project is a V8 Puma-powered, nitro-methane-guzzling drag bike that, when completed, will produce well in excess of 1,000 BHP. Puma Engineering has already produced one of the fastest motorcycle engines in the world, a four-cylinder, fire-breathing monster, which has run a breath-taking standing-start quarter mile in 5.8 seconds, with a terminal speed approaching 250mph. Exciting! I always say, "Fear not death, but rather an inadequate life!" My drag bike is actually only a flying test bed for the real project – cracking the current motorcycle land speed record of 360mph. I don't see this as unrealistic; I pride myself on having accomplished practically every other goal I have set for myself, and this is simply another. I think it's important in life to feel you are always moving forward somehow, though perhaps not necessarily at 360mph!

Apart from the pleasure of talking about my hobby, I mention the bike project because it was this interest that quite by chance set me on the road to an even more exciting creative idea – the culmination of a thirty-year quest to solve *The Eureka! Enigma*.

Bletchley, near Milton Keynes in Bedfordshire, is a quiet backwater of rural England. The prettier parts would not look out of place in an Agatha Christie novel and, when visiting the engineering workshops there to check on my beloved motor bikes I would not have been surprised to see Miss Marple appear in one of the leafy country lanes pedaling her own more leisurely machine – now there's a lady who's solved some enigmas in her time!

One day, arriving in Bletchley too early for my meeting with my chief mechanic Roger Forsythe, I decided to pull into a nearby café and relax with a coffee and newspaper for half an hour. I pondered on the café's name: why I wondered, was it called *The Enigma Tavern?* Then it dawned on me: I was no more than two minutes from Bletchley Park which, during World War II, was the top secret *Station X* where Allied code breakers had worked day and night to crack Germany's codes – which they called Enigma. I can honestly say I felt a tingle down my spine at the realization. Bletchley Park was also the site of Colossus, the world's first semi-programmable computer. Colossus versus Enigma was a legendary struggle, the most exciting and important code-breaking story ever. And what had I been trying to do all these years? Crack the code of the human brain! Call it melodramatic, but I experienced a powerful sense of purpose at that moment, a feeling of destiny; I had been led to *The Enigma Tavern* that day for a reason other than coffee and a sticky bun. Although I didn't fully realize it at the time, there was thundering towards me – with as much velocity as my V8 Puma – one enormous, ground-shaking, turn-your-life-around Eureka!

My clarity and intensity of thought increased as I drove off from *The Enigma Tavern*. Two minutes later I arrived at Bletchley Park, where I had the extremely good fortune to meet Tony Sale – the man who had just finished twelve years of painstaking work rebuilding the *Colossus* computer, a perfect working rebuild of the original machine deliberately destroyed at the end of World War II on the order of Winston Churchill. Tony gave me a complete guided tour, and I have to confess I was like a kid on his first trip to Disneyland! Needless to say, I was now going to be three hours late, not half an hour early, for the meeting with my engineers and my magnificent V8 Puma. My mind, though, was buzzing at a phenomenal rate; faster than even my beloved thirty-foot long, cigar-shaped streamliner could ever skim over Utah's Bonneville Salt Flats.

ALAN TURING – THE GENIUS BEHIND THE LEGEND

Tony Sale was most amenable and gave me a fascinating three-hour history lesson on the Colossus computer and the Enigma machine.

Let's take a closer look at the Enigma encrypting machine itself, which was used by Germany to scramble and disguise their radio communications. In appearance, the device was somewhat unremarkable, resembling one of the clunky typewriters common to the period. It comprised a series of rotor wheels and interchangeable electric plug positions. In selecting a set of positions on the machine there were sixty possible wheel orders and 17,576 ring settings for each wheel order that allowed the machine to create a mind-boggling 159,000,000,000,000,000,000 permutations of keys. Each day German radio operators would change the permutations by altering the Enigma's rotors and plug settings. A message sent via the Enigma encryption machine, when first intercepted by British intelligence might resemble this:

BTHMZYSHRUHFKSPOEHETYSGEHYFLPOEMNCGAEQ-IZMCNHFYEHSOPSLSMSNDHTQPRTHSGXZLMVNF-HYURHGSFETAPLSHNBHSXHAYWTQABX

Where to start?! There was rather limited success in deciphering these messages until a new arrival began to tip the balance for the boffins at Bletchley Park. Cambridge University mathematics luminary Alan Matheson Turing was at first regarded by many among the resident code breakers as merely an eccentric figure, a moody reticent character with a brilliant reputation and not much else. Some feared there may be less to him than his reputation suggested – a sphinx without a secret. Undeniably, his behavior was odd – chaining his coffee-mug to the radiator and cycling around Bletchley wearing a gas mask. (The latter habit turned out to be an inventive way to counter a hay-fever allergy). It's now thought that Turing may have suffered from Asperger's syndrome, a mild form of autism often found in gifted individuals.

Turing was born in 1912. As a young man Turing quickly became the leading light among a talented Oxbridge set, contributing to significant advances in philosophy, mathematics, cryptanalysis and biology. But it was in World War II, during the Allies' darkest days that Turing's extraordinary mental abilities proved indispensable as he took on the challenge of cracking the seemingly unbreakable Enigma and Lorenz codes. As German U-boat torpedoes destroyed Allied ships, men and vital supplies – and with the outcome of the war hanging in the balance – behind the closed doors of Bletchley, Turing's team conducted a relentless battle to unlock the Enigma code and turn the tide of the war.

Turing had in fact already created the world's first computer – a computer in his mind – to help him solve a mathematical problem.

This cerebral computer, detailed in Turing's published theories, paved the way towards the production of the first physical computers.

When he arrived at Bletchley and started work on cracking the Enigma code, Turing came up with a radical approach; where others had attempted to find the *key* to cracking the code, Turing worked in reverse, creating his own formula for quickly finding millions of *non-solutions*. Using a mechanical calculating device – known as a Bombe – that Turing and his colleagues designed, he could eliminate one million wrong answers every eighteen hours. Later, Turing created an absolutely brilliant algorithm that enabled him to reduce the number of potential *keys* from 159,000,000,000,000,000,000,000 down to 150,000,000 – still a daunting number, but certainly a lot closer to the ultimate solution.

Turing had at his disposal thirty-six *Letchworth bombes* (made in the town of Letchworth), each with its own unique name, including; Victory, Otto, Agnus Dei – and Eureka. Once set in motion, these bombes worked flat out, ticking away, day and night, week after week, producing millions of non-solutions. Using this *deductive* process of elimination, Turing was eventually able to find the *actual keys* to the Enigma code. Working with a hand-picked team and a staff of over 7,000 code breakers, Turing was able to replicate the continually-changing settings of the Enigma machine and decipher Germany's messages.

At the time Turing was at Bletchley Park, engineer Tommy Flowers was building the world's first semi-programmable computer, which was aptly named Colossus. Built in London's Dollis Hill Post Office Research Station, Colossus was a gigantic machine, filling a room sixteen feet long, ten feet deep and eight feet high. It used multiple electronic valves (vacuum tubes) for high speed digital computing and could read and check five thousand characters per second, a phenomenal feat at the time. This machine was instrumental in cracking the Lorenz cipher, a code even more sophisticated than the Enigma.

All the time I was talking to Tony Sale and furthering my investigations about Enigma and Colossus, the one thought that kept gnawing away inside my cranium was, "When you are cracking astronomical numbers, dealing with staggeringly vast data-banks of information, the human mind can never do the work quickly enough, accurately enough, if at all – the *only* solution is a computer – ergo: the brain *must be* a human biocomputer."

COMPUTERS AND BIOCOMPUTERS – A POWERFUL ANALOGY

MY EUREKA! *The mind, left to its own devices is like an Enigma machine, but properly programmed it becomes like a Colossus computer that can solve major problems.* Wow!

Both computers and biocomputers are capable of completing complex tasks. They can select, correlate, compile and process data at high speeds and solve difficult problems by virtue of:

a)   Having input and output

b)   Having stored information and instructions that we call programs

The similarities between computers and biocomputers by no means end there. Most computers come with pre-bundled software – your new PC, for example, may include Windows Vista. Your biocomputer equivalent to Vista is whatever cultural and environmental *software* you had installed early on in life. Our hardware, if you like, is the brain. Computers can multi-task to a degree, but the biocomputer does so at a fantastic level – via the autonomic nervous system it allows you to breath, pump blood and regulate its pressure, ride a bicycle, chew gum and talk to your friends and *at the same time* it is carrying out literally trillions of computations simultaneously, helping towards your problem solving.

You can increase your computer's memory by adding RAM. The memory in our biocomputer grows stronger by synaptic connections. For example, from the time my little girl Kay was born, I did all I could to help create new neuronal pathways for her. On outings, I'd point out colorful billboards and unusual architecture, encourage her to look up, look around, to be aware of and enjoy her surroundings. I'd even take food cartons from the refrigerator and together we'd examine and marvel at the colors, shapes, textures *and* tastes. In spare moments I'd teach her how to clip out magazine pictures, make funny paper hats and carve apples into star and moon shapes. I would always be on the lookout for new ways to stimulate Kay's mind, stimulating and creating thousands of new neuronal pathways. My wife Elisabeth and I have always encouraged her to dance, sing, paint, draw, write, color, use scissors and other tools, play music, attend ballet and swim. She could sew, cut out butterfly, crocodile and elephant shapes and had her own portfolio of over 200 incredible paintings and drawings all before she was four. It's easy to see that her *brain wiring* is completely different from a little girl who had followed different pursuits. Indeed, children born in poorer countries are less likely to receive the quality and depth of varied stimulation, input and nurturing – deprivation that dramatically inhibits a child's internal wiring and ability to process and deliver useable output. I have long recognized and seen the tangible evidence that the human biocomputer benefits enormously from creative stimulation and the *input* of positive software.

BESPOKE SOFTWARE IS PIVOTAL

If our physical brains are our biocomputer hardware; then our skills, aptitudes, experiences, values, and habits form part of our software. For every task we accomplish we have a software program in our biocomputer. Software is collected subconsciously as we read, watch TV, converse, study, listen or think.

So why do biocomputers suffer from software problems? Are they inherent or self imposed? There is pre-loaded software in our biocomputer from the day we are born – very soon, culture, language and family all begin programming us. We are inputted with software for speaking English, Russian, Chinese or whatever language (mixed parenting may provide software for more than one language) and an ethics and beliefs program derived from our particular nation or community. We might call these basic skills software, equipping us to deal with and relate to the world as we grow up.

But many of us may also receive negative software whereby we are programmed to limit our expectations: "Only clever people can be lawyers / doctors / real estate millionaires / entrepreneurs. . ." the negative software says. The parents and teachers inputting this kind of software may be genuinely trying to guide us, to protect us from disappointment. They program with the best of intentions – but we all know where that particular road leads. Your early upbringing doesn't have to be abusive or even unhappy for you to have been inputted with negative software. Tolstoy wasn't telling the whole story when he famously said, "All happy families are alike, but unhappy ones are all different in their unhappiness." On the contrary, happy families can differ widely in terms of the software they provide.

So the answer isn't to blame the family (who probably did their best), but to blame the outdated software, and then replace it. I think that negative programming is like Spyware on a conventional PC – often it is not obvious; it just sits there undetected until the time is right, and then it *pops up,* usually at the most inconvenient time, to do its worst!

And, as in conventional PCs, sometimes good biocomputer software gets corrupted, i.e. software is placed by well-meaning parents or good teachers and other *safe* mediums, but nevertheless holds a completely erroneous message that will not serve our best interests.

WE'RE DROWNING IN NUMBERS!

It's worth talking a little more about numbers. A billion is now widely accepted as a *thousand* million, though for decades the British billion was traditionally a *million* million. To get some idea of how big a billion actually is, it would take you your entire lifetime to count to it, assuming that you started the day you were born. Most people can't comprehend these mind-boggling figures – they just make us dizzy, but you'll see where I'm going with all this, in a millionth of a second.

The human biocomputer consists of some major hardware components, including the right and left hemispheres; Reticular Activating System (RAS); Corpus Callosum and at the very least one hundred billion (100,000,000,000) cells known as neurons. Each neuron is connected in some way to every other cell by an intricately complex series of synapses, some one hundred trillion (100,000,000,000,000) of them. Some cells have as many as ten thousand connections either directly or indirectly to other cells, each looking like a demented spider, whose legs are also connected to millions upon millions more demented spiders. Each time you have a thought it is shot down those spider legs in the form of a chemical and electrical message.

But that's not all! What really kicks the numbers through the stratosphere, is the vast amount of permutations that information creates within the biocomputer. The *American Heritage Dictionary* consists of around 750,000 words and we have an average vocabulary of 40,000 words that form part of the human biocomputer program. When you speak, these tens of thousands of words are instantly accessed and arranged by your biocomputer, with the number of possible permutations running into multiple billions. We store an alphabet of twenty-six letters. Not an impressively big number – and any three letters can only be arranged six different ways, e.g. fox, ofx, oxf, fxo, xfo, xof. But what about a larger combination of letters? The phrase *How to Reprogram the Human Biocomputer* contains just thirty-three letters. Care to guess at the number of possible permutations of those letters? It's a staggering 8,600,000,000,000,000,000,000,000,000,000,000,000. (Don't test it out right now!) Consider how many permutations of letters, words, pictures and concepts, your biocomputer has at its command. It's billions! Countless billions!

To add dramatically to the numbers involved, your biocomputer also stores a far larger amount of data in the form of pictures. Any estimate is tricky because of the subtle variations of visual images, but you certainly have millions of pictures stored in your brain – scientists estimate some twenty-two million (22,000,000) images are stored in every single biocomputer in its lifetime. I have never counted them, but I can recollect many of the millions of images, some in full color and intricate detail of various events I have experienced in my own life. I also have an equal number of pictures that I have created in my own imagination – many of which came to pass at a later date!

Your brain is about three pounds of blood and tissue, "a computer made of meat" as Professor Marvin Minsky aptly described it. Every second your biocomputer takes in and stores more information than all the world's computers put together. It receives information from 250,000 temperature sensors, 600,000 touch sensors and over 260,000,000 light sensors distinguishing between over 1,000,000 shades of color; it can see a candle in the dark at a distance of over 14 miles. Its 10,000,000 olfactory cells can sniff out one molecule of odor-causing substance in one part per trillion of air, smelling beautiful perfumes and fragrances as well as sickly bogs, foul chemicals and acrid smoke. It can help you bake a delicious cake, navigate winding mountain roads, play chess, read a map and complete complex business transactions. According to some neuroscientists, the human biocomputer has a capacity equal to about 100,000 gigabytes – 500 times more than a conventional computer and 20 times more than the world's largest and most powerful supercomputer. (Makes the latest offering from Intel seem a bit lame, doesn't it!)

When pictures *and* words join up in your brain, it's no longer *billions* of possible permutations, but *trillions* heaped upon many more *trillions*. In actual fact, your biocomputer's capabilities far surpass any supercomputer's capability and will remain so for the foreseeable future, providing – and this is the *key* – that it has the *appropriate* software installed.

Hot Tip! Until now we had absolutely no idea how to harness *and* use all the unbelievable supercomputing power of our brains, but the good news is that all the *keys* to unlocking this computing power are detailed in this codebook.

DISCOVER THE KEYS THAT CRACK YOUR PERSONAL CODE

Remember the time you lost your house keys? As you stood on the doorstep, wondering how to get into your home, did you ask to borrow your neighbor's keys? Of course not – any door lock might have thousands of combinations of notches and someone else's key wouldn't open up your home. Your human biocomputer likewise has only one *combination* to open it. Other people's solutions won't ever be exactly right for you – they won't let you in. This is where many self-help systems lose the plot; they don't take account of your unique traits and the way you are wired up. That's why you'll need to learn specific techniques for finding your own unique *key.*

The *key* to unlocking your biocomputer can be compared to the computer password you use on your personal computer at the office and at home. No *key* means NO unlocking the computer – and we all know how frustrating that is!

Turing's challenge was to unlock the Enigma code; yours is to unlock your biocomputer – to crack your brain's Enigma code and translate that code into Eurekas! that will allow you to achieve your dreams. Like the Enigma code, your biocomputer has billions of possible permutations. You have billions of neurons and their *infinite* inter-connections facilitate your incredible internal databanks of words, pictures and concepts – it's a phenomenal powerhouse just waiting to be unlocked and turned **ON!**

Some of the *keys* in this book will unlock some biocomputers – other *keys* will unlock others. But you have to try them out to see which work for you; it's up to you to discover what your own *keys* – or combinations of *keys* – are!

YOUR BIOCOMPUTER OUTPUT WILL MAKE OR BREAK YOU

Conventional computer output – shown on your computer screen as words, pictures, bar charts, graphics or figures – is easy to evaluate. You can see with your own eyes if the *output* you have created is the *output* that you want. The *output* of the human biocomputer, in contrast, is solutions, thoughts, ideas, hunches, dreams, consciousness and habits. An average person's thoughts might equate to about five hundred words a minute. This thought-flow (roof brain chatter, internal dialogue), which is incessant, contains a high percentage of aimless, un-useable, negative material – *Enigma Output.*

Check this out, the *Enigma Output* of a typical biocomputer (maybe yours?):

"I feel tired. I feel hungry. I feel sexy. I wonder what's for dinner tonight. How does everyone else have a credit card except me? Should I paint the wall white or red? Another McDonalds has opened on Main Street. I wonder if Fred will call me. I'll take the dog for a walk when I get home. If the Repo man comes to repossess my car, I'll probably end up in jail. I think I need to relax. I'm so bored. I wonder if Anne will phone me. I'm so depressed. I think I'll run away. I'm cold. I'm hot. I've got a headache. I'll text Jill. I think I'll have pizza tonight. How do other people pay for their groceries? That woman's fat. I think I'll watch The Sopranos tonight. I'm so tired. What is the matter with me? I'm going home. I feel hungry again. You're not going to believe this – I feel sexy again!"

Not exactly inspiring, is it? Yet it's not untypical. When James Joyce used the stream-of-consciousness technique to write *Ulysses*, he was hailed a literary genius. But when you and I experience this kind of stream of consciousness – this kind of internal dialogue – on a daily basis, we are likely to wash up in a sea of failure.

Sure, we all need time to *free-associate,* as psychologists call it, but we must find a way to limit this kind of *biocomputer anarchy* and replace it with positive *Colossus Output*. What you see in the example of *Enigma Output* is a biocomputer that is failing to produce even the simplest of meaningful ideas, let alone Eurekas! and is at the complete mercy of its Enigma machine. Maybe you recognize yourself. A useful exercise to conduct over the next few weeks would be to start recording your own internal dialogue on paper. Carry a notebook around with you and try to capture as much of your biocomputer *output* as practically possible: negative thoughts, positive thoughts and any ideas or Eurekas! Aim for an absolutely verbatim version of what's in your head; no-one else need read it. (Think of it as therapy, but without the $150 an hour fee!) When you read your own biocomputer output you'll be amused, intrigued, maybe shocked. Maybe it will be a wake-up call that will help you crack your own code!

What might usable *Colossus Output* look like? Here are a few examples of Eureka! moments:

- ➢ **Eureka!** "An apple just hit me on the head. Why did it fall downwards and not sideways or up? It must be connected to the large mass of the earth and the tiny mass of the apple." – *Isaac Newton on discovering the Laws of Gravity*

- ➢ **Eureka!** "Start your own motorcycle business. Go immediately to Chessington Road and find an empty shop." – *Ron Holland's first major money-making idea*

- ➢ **Eureka!** "Why not carbonize cotton? The end result could be an incandescent light bulb." – *Thomas Edison's solution for creating an electric light bulb, which actually worked*

- ➢ **Eureka!** "Write a book called *The Eureka! Enigma*, it will transform the way people think." – *Another Ron Holland money-making idea*

- ➢ **Eureka!** "Why has that Petri dish gone moldy? It must be the mold killing the bacteria. AHAH! Penicillin!" – *Alexander Fleming on discovering the world's first antibiotic*

You too can achieve this kind of *Colossus Output* – outstanding creativity, million dollar ideas and solutions to everyday problems – by cracking your own code and switching your own biocomputer from *Enigma* mode to *Colossus* mode.

BE VITALLY AWARE OF YOUR BIOCOMPUTER OUTPUT

Decades of research and observation have shown me that there are **six distinct groups** of people when it comes to Eurekas! and the level of meaningful output from their human biocomputers.

People in **group one** get little *output*, other than *Enigma Output*. They're not aware of *output* and don't use their biocomputers to any meaningful degree. Frighteningly, the vast majority of the population fits into this group. Oblivious to the fact they have neck-top computers, they fail to switch them **ON** and use them. These people operate on the *eat when hungry, sleep when tired* mind.

People in **group two** get some positive *output* as a result of the work or activities they are engaged in, but because they are not consciously aware of how they receive *output,* they have no conscious way of improving or increasing it. Many in this group vaguely aspire to attain and achieve in some way, but lack usable mental tools to do so. They haven't accepted the fact that they could control their own minds and destinies.

People in **group three** are individuals who have consciously tried to solve problems, create success and escape mediocrity in their lives and have used their biocomputers to do so. They may produce some small degree of usable *output* and even occasional Eurekas! In search of tools for success they may invest heavily in self-help books, audio programs, seminars and training but their progress is limited and haphazard. Those in this group get regular hunches and inspirations but hardly ever follow through on them. They feel that, despite their efforts, things never quite *gel* for them; and continue to live their lives in quiet desperation and frustration.

People in **group four** are those who are successful, high-achievers. Perhaps as much as fifty percent of those in this group are very successful intuitively and the remaining fifty percent have got where they are through hard work, deliberately engaging their imaginations, regularly practicing the principles of success. These fifty percent know what it is they are doing, and as a result receive *Colossus Output.* They tend to get lots of creative ideas and act on those ideas immediately – and that has the habit of kicking the biocomputer into overdrive so it delivers even more creative ideas. These people are at the top of their game, or heading that way, and earn way above average incomes. Many live lifestyles of the rich and famous. I suspect the majority of my readers will come from groups three and four. Between us, we desperately need to educate groups one and two. Those in groups five and six are taking care of themselves – magnificently!

People in **group five** apply success principles intuitively. They often have tremendous faith in themselves and believe in old-fashioned values like perseverance, creativity, and industry. Many in this group achieve extraordinary results (Big Eurekas!) and enter the history books as geniuses. Those in this group follow their instincts, act on their *Colossus Output,* Eurekas! and even those ideas that seem small and insignificant at the time. This group includes iconic figures such as Bill Gates, Ruth Handler, Richard Branson, Edison, Madonna, and Einstein. Yet there doesn't seem to be any evidence that they're aware of how they succeed; therefore they cannot necessarily articulate the process to others.

People in **group six** are aware of exactly how they program their biocomputers and consciously *input* them to obtain optimum results as and when required. They don't get just a single Eureka! now and then, but a continuous flow of usable ideas, solutions, creative *output,* enabling them to develop their projects and deal creatively with daily events and their own ever-evolving ideas, businesses and lifestyles. *Colossus Output* is the only thing they know, demand and accept. Those in group six always know what to do next, are never stuck long for an answer and are seldom bored. They are always ahead of the game; what I would call a new, rare breed of *Super Genius.* They could, if so inclined, articulate their success process and teach others precisely how they solve problems, create brilliant ideas and tap into their creativity to generate **Eurekas! on Demand,** but invariably are too busy creating success and happiness in their own lives to have sufficient time to share that knowledge.

THINKING VERSUS NON-THINKING

When Bill Gates was once asked by his mother what he was doing in his bedroom for hours on end, he famously retorted, "Thinking – you ought to try it sometime!" It must have paid off, as he ended up richer than the Sultan of Brunei and Croesus combined; but I wonder how much thought Gates gave to his flippant answer. Exactly what kind of thinking does Bill indulge in? Obviously, we all think, all the time, about something. But if we don't do enough correct thinking, we will never achieve our goals. Yet how can you define correct and incorrect thinking? The *American Heritage Dictionary* definition of thinking is: the act or practice of one that thinks, thought, a way of reasoning, judgment...

To *my* way of thinking, this is not good enough! Personally I think this is a gross understatement, as I consider the most extraordinary powerful thinking is done by the biocomputer - when we are not-thinking. We have all had the experience of having someone's name on the tip of the tongue and not being able to recall it. Hours later, when the biocomputer has finished its computerized labor, invariably after a period of relaxation and non-thinking – the name just *pops out*. What the biocomputer has done is sifted through the *filing cabinets* of the mind containing all the people's names you know, sorted through its *picture carrousel* of all the thousands of images it has with its highly sophisticated *face recognition software* and eventually comes up with a match – a solution to that name you couldn't remember. This is the biocomputer working at its very minimal capacity, but imagine being able to harness the biocomputer to *pop-out* all sorts of elegant solutions to all manner of difficult problems.

Well, that's exactly what you can do – when the biocomputer is programmed correctly. Both Oriental and Western philosophies have claimed that only one-eighth of everything is visible. This applies particularly to the operation of the biocomputer. Apart from being invisible, a lot of what goes on in our biocomputers is involuntary – not just the autopilot biological functions of heart, respiration, blinking, etc, but also the involuntary, un-programmed biocomputer has an enigmatic tendency to drift, and a great preponderance to think negatively and churn out *Enigma Output!*

All my research leads me to believe that conscious thought is only a tiny amount of what we do, the vast majority of supercomputing remains hidden in the depths of the biocomputer, just waiting to be turned **ON.** Most of our big ideas come when we are not thinking, as a direct result of computerized labor, in the form of Eurekas!

There is simply *no way* the human biocomputer can *consciously* assimilate, organize and deliver a workable solution to every problem it is fed – it needs non-thinking time to carry out its computerized labor. Be serious about work but equally serious about relaxation (non-thinking), which is when your biocomputer has *time to process* the *input,* solve problems and produce Eurekas!

These days I am more and more inclined to *let the biocomputer do the work* especially when writing a book or taking on a new client by deliberately invoking its powers. I know that through *conscious thinking* I may be able to come up with ten options and maybe one or two solutions to a specific problem. I also know that when I properly harness the biocomputer, this number catapults into trillions of computations and options – without even trying, and then comes up with just the perfect *solution* for a specific problem, in the form of a Eureka!

Bill Gates should have told his mother, he was programming his biocomputer - which is probably nearer the truth. I've often wondered how much he knows about personally *inputting* bespoke software. After much reasoning I've come to the conclusion that it must be an *immeasurable* amount – because I see tangible evidence of his *Colossus Output* in every computer in every country in the world!

Input = Output (For the Time Being at Least)

If you want your biocomputer to perform like a computer, you will have to start using it like a computer. This requires a degree of mental realigning that not everyone is prepared to make. But again, our simple analogy serves us well: *input* will equal *output* – for the time being at least – until an overwhelming body of evidence forces us to turn the formula on its head, a little later on. If you are willing to apply yourself seriously, and follow the correct techniques, the rewards are out there - waiting for you. I can't say exactly what those rewards will be because they are personal to you, but you will have to be *crystal clear* about them. Whatever your own ambitions though, I am sure you could use more wealth, now and into the future. *The Eureka! Enigma* will get it for you, together with everything else on your wish list. Let's find out how…

COAXING YOUR BIOCOMPUTER TOWARDS COLOSSUS OUTPUT

My favorite anecdote at my seminars is about how I made my first fortune; well it would be wouldn't it! As a young man in my early twenties I had left the construction industry and started my own retail motorcycle empire in South London. I had seven shops and at that time, like thousands of other small and medium size business owners, I didn't understand the difference between cashflow and profit. I spent money as though it grew on trees and, sure enough, I suddenly found myself in trouble, with seven *empty* motorcycle shops and no funds to replenish stock. Meanwhile, debts were stacking up and the prospect of an appearance at the bankruptcy court loomed large.

I needed more stock to make sales and more sales to buy stock – it was a classic Catch 22 situation. I tried all the banks and many venture capital companies for extra funding but got short shrift. Time was running out. Intuitively, I tried something else: I began to *visualize* what I really wanted to accomplish. I *pictured* in my mind's eye my shops so full of motorcycles that the doors wouldn't close. It was a joyful *image,* which I would hold in my mind for about five minutes, twice a day for about three days. I am the first to confess I didn't quite know what I was doing or even what to expect. On the third day, a *small still voice* popped into my head and instructed me: "You don't need money! Go out and buy all the motorcycle papers, then phone all the classified advertisers. If they have a motorcycle for sale, tell them to bring it in; offer our showroom, finance and insurance facilities and our first-class sales people. Sell their bikes for them and take a realistic commission."

I acted on this idea immediately and made literally hundreds of phone calls. Nothing happened. I thought the idea was a flop. Yet on the following Saturday, a few motorcycles started to arrive. Monday saw a few more, and by the end of the first month of telephone canvassing we had all seven shops stocked to capacity. The business went from strength to strength. We had a method of replenishing stock on tap, without the need for any capital. Though completely legal and ethical, it was like we'd got something for nothing; *motorbikes* and *money* flooded in, manna from heaven – Ooh-la-la!

There are various levels of Eureka! experience. You may get a major Eureka! or a number of smaller ideas. Often, I have had one Big Idea, which, to build to a successful outcome needs hundreds, if not thousands, of further ideas along the way. Some small, some large and indeed some more full-blown, jumping-out-of-the-bath Eurekas! were needed to carry the day. These days I am significantly more interested in the overall volume of

Output, than how large or magnificent a single Eureka! may be. I have found countless times that, to succeed you need to be tapping into a *constant source* of smaller creative ideas – workable solutions *and* Eurekas! Anyone running their own business knows that solving problems on a *daily* basis is what keeps it afloat. I often say, "You *can't* expect Eurekas! daily - but you *can* and *should* expect smaller ideas hourly!"

Note carefully that I *intuitively* visualized my showroom full of motorcycles and three days later came up with a Eureka! which I followed through to the letter. The truth is that at the time, I never *really* made the connection between the visualization and the *popping out* of the idea – it just happened. It took years of soul searching and research, and years as an entrepreneur and self-help author to *establish* the connection and the truly awesome significance of it. In making this discovery, I finally unraveled the secret of why the biocomputer sometimes delivers on cue and sometimes it doesn't.

COMPUTERS CAN'T THINK IN PICTURES, BUT BIOCOMPUTERS CAN!

Your biocomputer really does have a phenomenal *three-dimensional-capacity* for concepts. It has the innate ability to process *words* and *pictures* and *concepts.* It can create Eurekas! for you – *bespoke solutions* if you like – that will propel you toward genius, fame and fortune, very quickly, if that's what you want. Conventional computers can't think in pictures, despite what you see in recent developments in face recognition software (which, incidentally I was heavily involved in fifteen years ago) and other incredible image related software, all of which have to be converted into 1s and 0s in order to be processed. Biocomputers don't have to do this, and it's the incredibly powerful genetic analog-digital algorithms that allows the human biocomputer to exceed any supercomputer that exists in the world today – we'll talk more about these later.

Some will argue that using the analogy of the computer / brain is old hat, but in actual fact nothing could be further from the truth. The more we understand computers and the brain the more we can see similarities, so much so that the next generation of computers will be neural, optical, DNA and quantum – ideas that have already received billions of dollars in investment. Both computers and brains seem almost too complex to even contemplate but given that so many people have a good vocabulary connected to computers it makes sense to make loose comparisons. I am neither a brain scientist nor a computer programmer, but I do know what the word *analogy* means. It simply means an explanation or illustration that uses a *comparison* with something similar and that is all I am doing here. That comparison could be accurate or vague or anywhere in between - don't get hung up on it. So to pre-empt all those that will say "the brain doesn't work like this" or "a computer doesn't work like that" or "this is totally non-scientific" – stop! If I had used the internal combustion engine / mind analogy, surely you wouldn't be disappointed if when I said, "I am now firing on all eight" only to discover when you got home that you didn't have *eight pistons on connecting rods belting up and down* but all you had was a hundred billion neurons. All I am trying to do is simplify, in layman's terms what we have to do in order to get the mind working at some meaningful level of efficiency. To make this analogy work, literary license has been used *throughout* the codebook! And to be honest, this is for my own benefit as much as anyone else's. I have been left high and dry by numerous self-help books that got me all excited but didn't articulate to my satisfaction at least, what I *really* had to do to access the remaining 90% of my mind. I am sure I have now done that and I am passing on to you what I have learned over a thirty-year period – I hope you will use it!

SCIENTIFIC KEYS

Dr. William Bergquist, a mathematician who specializes in a computer language known as APL has predicted the development of what he calls, "The Bifurcated computer" which will combine both analog and digital functions in one machine. Bergquist maintains that such a computer will function similarly to the two halves of the human brain.

Cracking Your Code

Another awe inspiring Eureka! for this codebook came after discovering what an incredible number of permutations the Enigma machine could create. All human biocomputers are wired up *differently;* their hundred billion cells and trillions of synapses are all connected in a *different* web-like fashion. In our formative years – indeed whilst we are in the womb growing from zero to a *hundred billion* brain cells in nine months – a lot depends on the stimulus, education, culture, environment, accidental drops on our heads, and other *input* we receive as young children. All this *input* becomes our inherent makeup and dictates the exact pattern of our own internal wiring, the neuronal pathways and synaptic connections created in our biocomputers.

But think how many biocomputers there are – approximately six billion worldwide, and counting! That's six billion *different* wiring systems and six billion personal codes. Only *one* of them is your *unique* code. We must crack our individual code in order to get the *Colossus Output* we desire. The fundamental purpose of this codebook is to show you *exactly* how to crack it; and what follows in the next six chapters are literally hundreds more *keys* to be used individually or as a *combination* to unlock your own biocomputer! Unlocking it will have the combined effect of brilliantly reducing *Enigma Output* and dramatically increasing *Colossus Output.*

What Exactly Can You Expect From Following a Specific Success Philosophy?

My research led me to interview hundreds of seminar attendees as they were leaving other speakers' seminars. I asked, "What was that particular seminar all about?" The attendees – of the same seminar – answered, "Passion," "Doing your own thing," "Going for it!" "Business management," and "Strategy." To hear them speak, you'd think they had all been to different seminars!

I believe every seminar leader and self-help author should start off by declaring what their seminar or book is all about and *exactly* what you can expect from following their prescribed formula. I hope everyone reading this codebook comes up with only one answer to the question "What is *The Eureka! Enigma* all about?" Allowing for individual phrasing, the answer should be:

"How to utilize your mind at maximum efficiency, by programming it or inputting information in a specific way to enable it to function like a computer, a human biocomputer. By unlocking your mind with your own unique combination of keys, you will start generating a never-ending supply of creative ideas, Eurekas! and solutions to all your problems. This Colossus Output, in turn, will allow you to accomplish all your goals and objectives and live a healthy, happy, successful and fulfilled life."

Highlight the foregoing paragraph and refer to it should you ever lose your way or vision. For once you know the overall purpose of your mission or philosophy, the path will always be clear, and you can soon get back on track and move forward again.

!!! Left to its own devices the human mind can be likened to an *Enigma* machine.

!!! Properly programmed the human mind can be likened to a *Colossus* computer.

CRACK THE CODE!

- ❖ The human mind is a vast supercomputer – a biological computer - a human biocomputer.

- ❖ Each biocomputer is wired up *differently* from any other on the planet.

- ❖ We have to crack our own *unique* code from billions upon billions of permutations. Computerized labor is the *key* to cracking the code.

- ❖ The human biocomputer has an *over-abundance* of hardware.

- ❖ The human biocomputer has a *vast* shortage of *appropriate* software.

- ❖ Become acutely aware of your own *output*. Aim and work to *immensely* increase and improve it.

- ❖ Input = Output – for the time being at least!

- ❖ The Biocomputer is highly adept at thinking in words *and* pictures *and* concepts.

- ❖ Left to its own devices, your biocomputer is an Enigma machine.

- ❖ Properly programmed your biocomputer becomes a Colossus computer and you too will receive prodigious *Colossus Output* and **Eurekas! on Demand**.

- ❖ Your biocomputer will perform like a computer – when you program it like one.

THE SECOND KEY

SOFTWARE FOR
THE BRAIN

Human biocomputers are all much alike in terms of hardware. It is the software – or lack of it – that makes each one perform, or not.

– Ron G Holland

Enigma: Is there any way we can control our thoughts? Can we increase our creativity and problem-solving ability? What is it that is all in the mind? Why is it some people flourish with no conscious effort, succeed in everything they do, almost intuitively; while others, no matter how hard they strive, the more they seem to struggle?

Eureka! The truth is as profound as it is simple. It is the deliberate, conscious use of specific appropriate programming that will turn your life around and transform valueless Enigma Output into powerfully augmented Colossus Output, and **Eurekas! on Demand**. Let's find out how!

NON-RELEVANT HARDWARE

For all intents and purposes the hardware in your biocomputer is irrelevant. This realization finally dawned on me after a number of minor Eureka! experiences. The biggest occurred during a routine visit to a London computer store. Browsing for my annual upgrade, I was targeted by an enthusiastic young salesman who sensed I had money to burn – and he wasn't wrong. His spiel lasted a full half hour – minimum! It went something like this: "This computer has 800 zillion megabytes of RAM, its Pentium motherboard can waffle, zap and zing and if you want to multi-task, you jack up the hard-drive. The screen has at least 2.5 billion colors and 1040 pixies." I was tempted to ask if the pixies were sitting on toadstools – but as I knew he meant pixels, the tiny shapes that make up the images on screen – asking about the pixies would have been facetious. And of course, I've exaggerated his jargon for impact! We become victims of information overload and computer retailers in particular seem desperate to convince us that there is great diversity in the product, particularly the *hardware*. This is not so. I have been told dozens of times, by people who *really* know, that most computers are fundamentally the same; what makes the distinctive difference is the software. To paraphrase Alan Turing's powerful message, "The computer, machine or calculator doesn't matter; it is only the *output* that counts." And *output* is determined by *software*.

In the previous chapter we touched briefly on the general hardware of the brain and its physical makeup – but our focus on hardware ends there. Increasing numbers of self-help books devote far too much space to the topic of the physical brain, the hardware. I read one recently where every other word was akin to presynaptic membrane, dopamine receptor, neuromodulator or adenosine monophosphate molecules. While neuroscientists obviously need to know all this scientific, biological stuff, non-specialists like you and I definitely do not. Memorizing a complex scientific vocabulary won't help you operate your biocomputer any more than knowing the technical specification of every component in your PC will help you churn out a blockbuster novel or create a business plan for the purpose of raising a few million dollars.

It seems some authors have fallen into the same trap as the *sales monster* I met in the store – blinding us with science. This codebook is concerned solely with those components of the brain that are instrumental in generating Eurekas! and providing practical *output* we can use in the real, often cruel world. Seasoned entrepreneurs know that time is money, and so is energy. Studying uses both resources – we must be efficient in both regards as we study the human biocomputer.

RELEVANT HARDWARE

The human biocomputer has over *one hundred billion* cells, interconnected by multiple pathways. It is divided into two halves, or hemispheres, which have distinctly separate functions and both process problems in totally different ways.

THE LEFT BRAIN – YOUR DIGITAL COMPUTER

The left hemisphere of the brain is the focus of traditional education. It deals with numbers, logic, language, and factual analysis. The left side of the brain thinks in *words* and has a tremendous ability to solve problems in a verbal and mathematical manner, using symbolic and sequential logic.

THE RIGHT BRAIN – YOUR ANALOG COMPUTER

The right side of the brain, in contrast, thinks in *pictures and concepts*. It is this half of your biocomputer that activates when you recall a happy vacation scene, the face of a loved one, or a memorable place in the country you once drove through. Using the right side's creative faculty you can create a picture of the dream house, car or yacht you intend to acquire one day. The right side of the brain is the domain of artists, dreamers, visionaries *and* successful entrepreneurs. Traditional schooling, which stresses learning by rote and *no-nonsense logic*, is largely unaware of the right hemisphere and its *awesome* creative potential. Thinking in *pictures*, the right side does have formidable problem-solving capability; although not mathematical, it's far superior at drawing geometric figures. It synthesizes and solves its problems on a Gestalt, holistic and imagery basis, simply meaning that it can assimilate a vast amount of *visual* information, pull it all together and create something extremely meaningful out of it.

To generate **Eurekas! on Demand** and enjoy success, you must learn how to tap into the monumental power of your right brain, i.e. begin to think in *pictures* as much as you do in *words*.

CORPUS CALLOSUM – BROADBAND – THE BRAIN'S SUPERHIGHWAY

The Corpus Callosum is a broad band of nerve fiber joining the two cerebral hemispheres of your brain together, allowing *words* and *pictures* to inter-communicate. Interestingly, the Corpus Callosum tends to be more substantial in females, indicating perhaps that nature or nurture inclines women to more rounded thinking. Certainly in education, more boys tend to major in Science, Math and Law, more girls in Arts subjects. Irrespective of genetic debates, education policy is paramount; both girls and boys, from the earliest age, should be encouraged in the right brain activities of drawing, sports, painting, drama, singing, music and ballet. This should not be seen as mere playful diversion from *serious* language-based learning, or solely for theatre or art students. Rather, it should be recognized that developing right *and* left brain skills *in tandem* can dramatically improve an individual's chance of success.

Most Westerners live predominantly in their left brains, the language side. The Corpus Callosum is, if you like, the facility for broadband; but until you join up your left and right sides by deliberately using language *and* pictures, you're still operating on narrow band. No one who's graduated to broadband on the Internet would dream of returning to narrowband (dial-up) and this is true for your biocomputer – once you've learned to operate both sides of your biocomputer in tandem, you'll never go back! Broadband use of your Corpus Callosum really will make a dramatic difference in your life. But remember, you can *only* bring the Corpus Callosum into play by thinking in both words *and* pictures, so begin to think in terms of *joined-up thinking* and *whole-brain thinking*. People who are just working solely with words or solely with pictures can't possibly benefit from the magical biocomputer effect.

Hot Tip! The right and left sides of your biocomputer process information in totally different ways – one in words and the other in pictures. They also go about problem solving in totally different ways, the left going about its business using logic and mathematics, and the right using images and concepts. It therefore also stands to reason that the two sides of the biocomputer must be *programmed* in totally different ways. Controlling that programming – *input* – cannot be altogether simple, with one hemisphere placing its importance on words and the other hemisphere placing its importance on pictures.

WHY BIOCOMPUTER SOFTWARE IS VITAL

In Chapter One I talked about how – and why – software matters. Yet, as important as our biocomputer software is, most people are oblivious to the extent to which it affects their daily lives and determines whether they succeed or fail. Biocomputer software programs are physically manifested in the ganglia, which is the neuron chain – the individual cells or neurons that store the memories that we create when we learn a new skill: driving a car, baking a cake, stripping a V8 engine and rebuilding it, writing a book or business plan. Can you identify all the skills – the lines of code – that you have acquired since childhood? Don't take these skills for granted, there are many and some of them are quite complex. Even seemingly simple tasks like cooking will have entailed this hidden yet highly sophisticated activity within your biocomputer. If you can use a keyboard, put up a shelf or fix a car it is solely because at some point you inserted the relevant software program into your biocomputer. And if you *can't* ride a bicycle, play the guitar, ski, use an electric-arc-welder or tune a piano, it is only because you *haven't* inserted the appropriate software.

OUR SYSTEM SOFTWARE

Have you ever noticed how defensive Mac users are compared to PC users? Or is it the other way round? Don't laugh, because in a few moments you may find yourself getting defensive about a number of issues. The Mac guy swears by his user-friendly interface (courtesy of Steve Jobs and Apple who *acquired* it from Xerox) and the PC user swears by Windows (courtesy of Bill Gates and Microsoft who *acquired* it from Apple!) Many of us envy our colleagues' computers and think about upgrading our hardware.

When we buy a conventional PC or Mac it comes with system software pre-installed, and maybe this is where the distinction between software and hardware gets blurred – we equate the two because they arrive on our desk as one item, in the same box. Don't make this mistake with your biocomputer; remember, it's yours to *program* exactly the way you choose! Of course the human biocomputer does also initially arrive with system software pre-installed. In one part of the world over a billion biocomputers will be installed with Chinese language software, elsewhere another billion may have Spanish language programs. The same applies to faiths and cultures. And just like computer geeks get defensive about their particular equipment, we can get defensive about our language, faith and culture. Sociologists call this *ethnocentricity* and it's not necessarily a bad thing – all communities operate according to some kind of basic norms of behavior and outlook, *all singing from the same hymn sheet,* as they say. But even within a nation there can be a diverse range of software among the citizens' biocomputers. We have what we might call *large group* software – language, customs, culture, and national identity. We also have *small group* software – religion, county law, local attitudes and dialects. Then there is the *individual software* in our biocomputer – *input* by family, friends, teachers, the books we read and the TV shows we watch. Finally there is the software we write and *input* ourselves, where *we* decide the content. These programs are built on our goals, aspirations, desires and aptitudes. *This* is the human biocomputer software this codebook focuses on.

Protocol

If you want your mind to start performing like a billion-dollar computer (the one that will lead you, step-by-step, to realize your million-dollar idea) you have to start treating it like one. Protocol is the set of formal rules governing the exchange of information between operating entities. In IT-speak, protocol is a handshake between computers, in effect saying, "This is how we agree to communicate with each other" and this is the set of rules that governs the form in which data must be presented, for example, for transmission between computers – and indeed biocomputers. Those interested in extracting high performance *output* from their human biocomputers must realize that *nothing* can be done to program the mind for Eurekas! until we understand the mind's various protocols. What follows is the set of rules that will need to be adhered to, in order for your biocomputer to create and accept new programs.

Programming Language

Conventional computers only understand one language – 0s and 1s, known as machine or binary code. To write the number seventeen in machine code you would write 00010001; twenty would be 00010100. Since writing whole programs out this way takes a long time, shorthand software languages were developed (e.g. C$_{++}$, Python, Java, Perl, Pascal, Cobol) enabling programmers to work much faster. However, these programming languages must still be transmuted *back* into those machine code 0s and 1s for the computer to understand them.

Biocomputer Programming Language

Your biocomputer works in a similar way. You have to write your program in a programming language and then translate it into machine code for your biocomputer to understand. So where do you start? What is the biocomputer's programming language, and what is its machine code? I thought you'd never ask!

INTRODUCING BASIC WORD – AN IMPORTANT 5%

My First Futile Attempts to Program My Mind

I began to understand the software I now call **BASIC WORD** over thirty years ago when I got heavily involved in success and personal development. I read all the usual suspects of that era – *Think and Grow Rich, The Lazy Man's Way to Riches* and *Success Through a Positive Mental Attitude*. And I've continued to read those types of books – I now have an incredible, ever-expanding library of thousands of books and audio programs on success, self-help, business, sales, motivation, meditation, hypnosis, thinking, alternative health, magic, NLP, PMA, TQM, cybernetics, psycho-cybernetics, spirituality, computer programming, computer science, mysticism, scientific brain research, altered states, drugs, management, business opportunities, eastern philosophy and psychology. I had an innate, burning desire to succeed and be wealthy. I was also very tenacious. When I picked up Napoleon Hill's *Think and Grow Rich* I didn't really understand it and had no way of knowing what was right or wrong in the book. I felt the same with other theories and recommendations for success, but being persistent I did read Hill's book (and others) over a hundred times and frequently put their suggestions into practice, to the best of my ability.

I made a list of goals in **BASIC WORD** and religiously read them aloud every night and morning, as instructed. I read, "I will become a millionaire. I will drive a Rolls Royce. I will have a five-bedroom house with a pool." I did try to *see* myself in possession of the money, the car and the house – as Napoleon Hill suggested – but I didn't have much success in creating those images.

I Made My Lists of Goals in the Present Tense

Common sense told me that if I followed instructions like *write a list of goals,* it had to be better than going through life without a plan at all. It also seemed sensible to make those goals big, and for them to be broadly the things that I wanted. It didn't dawn on me then, as it has in recent years, how the biocomputer demands *precise* goals and faultless programming instructions – without which it will falter, or not perform at all. You may find, like I did as a young man, that success comes intuitively – even without using the programming methods we're talking about in this chapter. But without articulating your goal – and many potential routes to achieving that goal – in as much detail as possible, you won't be able to generate results every day of your life, in *everything* that you're trying to accomplish.

Clueless about where the real answers lay, at the time I thought that maybe I wasn't going far enough with my list of goals. Instead of saying, "I will be" or "I will own" I began writing out my goals in the present tense by simply changing the phrases to, "I have" or "I own" as if the goal were *already* accomplished. Yet I continued to find it very difficult to accomplish my goals – though every now and then there was glimmer of hope, I was making small breakthroughs and sometimes gained a little ground. But the majority of the time, it was sheer disappointment and frustration. Most of my goal-achieving efforts were based on pure faith, sometimes on desperation. Yet I persisted, completely unaware of the fact that what I was really doing was trying to program my mind to deliver Eurekas! that would allow me to accomplish my goals.

I Tried to Up the Ante by Making My Own Audio Tapes

Once I get the bit between my teeth on a project, (especially when I think I'm onto something) I tend to give it one hundred percent, to see it through to success. Not willing to give up my goal-achieving efforts, I tried something new; I conscientiously made a series of detailed audiotapes with all my goals articulated in great detail. I confess I listened to those tapes for literally hundreds, if not thousands of hours, on many occasions leaving the cassette player (no Walkman or iPods in those days!) on a continuous loop to play through the night while I slept. In retrospect, those hours of programming may have had some small bearing on my success, but nowhere near the demonstrable results that I expect *and* obtain from the methods I diligently apply today - powerful methods I'm revealing in this codebook!

I Had Already Achieved Success - But It Was Intuitive

Now let's go back over thirty years and look at what was happening in my life *prior* to reading mountains of self-help material. I was in my early twenties. I had finished my apprenticeship as a carpenter and my passion was motorcycles. I opened my first motorcycle shop the day I finished my apprenticeship, and expanded exponentially after that. I was winning races. I was minted. I already owned a collection of fast cars, including a seven and a half liter Pontiac Trans-Am, complete with Firebird decal on the hood, especially imported from the States. Life was great – moving happily along at well in excess of 800mph. I was getting loads of business ideas, everything I touched turned to gold. I didn't indulge in over-eating, excessive drinking or any kind of extreme behavior – other than fast motorbikes and cars of course! I did not have an abundance of business acumen, but intuitively I did spend a lot of time daydreaming and visualizing the things I wanted to accomplish in my own way. For instance, I had the *notion* that I'd like to own an Aston Martin, and within a few weeks I had acquired a powder blue DB6 – one up on James Bond's DB5, even without the machine guns or ejector seat!

That's the potted history, but I hope enough to illustrate my point that this early period in my career, the time when I was flying, was *before* I had ever opened a self-help book. I was *already* receiving *Colossus Output* and enjoying *magnificent* success – although I didn't realize or appreciate it at the time. A lot of people who are successful *intuitively* don't realize that they are indeed already successful – they're just doing what comes naturally! It never dawned on me, not once, that to acquire *sustained* success I should have kept doing *more* of the same! But I *assumed* there had to be something *more* or something *else*. I was already in the zone, getting Eurekas! on a daily basis - albeit not **Eurekas! on Demand.** I was going with the flow, being guided by my intuition and receiving a prodigious volume of quality *output* from my biocomputer. In those days I didn't call it a biocomputer, but I was aware of ideas welling up from my subconscious mind when I was relaxed. In an unsophisticated way, I did have a reasonable *vision* of where I was trying to arrive.

What Exactly Did I Do to Create Intuitive Success?

During my early years of success, before going to bed, I would relax in an armchair, not reading, thinking, meditating, watching TV or doing anything specific, for at least an hour. During this *quiet period*, my mind would *talk* to me and give an upsurge of fabulous ideas from my subconscious mind, hereinafter referred to as the biocomputer. When I slipped out of gear, because *I didn't even know I'd been in gear*, I found it unbelievably difficult to get back into gear - now there's an enigma!

Why BASIC WORD Is Only the First Stage

If you're anything like I was, you began to yearn for success early on – for money and to manage your own business. They're things you want for you and yours, and rightly so! These goals are often unique and individual, and many people, rightly or wrongly split them into three separate categories: short, medium and long term goals. Yet before you can reach your goals, you must translate them into **BASIC WORD**. You must write out descriptions of your *successful self* in as much detail as you can. Be specific in your descriptions: the number of bedrooms in your dream house, the figures on the checks you are hoping to receive, the interior design of your mansion, the color and make of the car, motorcycle or yacht you desire. These written goal descriptions in **BASIC WORD** are your programming language. Many success seekers get this far, diligently repeating their goals morning, noon and night in the form of verbal affirmations, yet end up bitterly disappointed with the results, or lack thereof. That's because **BASIC WORD** – a vital component, is only the first stage, it's only five percent of what has to be done in order to program your biocomputer to deliver *Colossus Output.*

In my *wilderness years* I got hung up on reciting **BASIC WORD** goals parrot fashion, worrying whether I was reciting them in the present tense or not, concerning myself whether I had said them for thirty-two days in an unbroken sequence as prescribed in at least one well-known self-help book – all that and much more. But I never really knew *why* I was doing it or *what* the outcome might be. Strange as it may seem now, I didn't equate affirmations and visualizations to producing *output.* I just accepted that I must carry out this practice as a matter of faith – not with any full understanding or having correct knowledge.

I can recall reciting my goals, early in the morning, and then again late at night by my bedside. My partner, not realizing how ambitious I was and how seriously I was taking all that self-help stuff, thought I was loopy! I also recited my goals, aloud and full of emotion, while in my car. I recall a particularly hot summer's day driving downtown, screaming my head off, then noticed all the traffic had stopped and I had come to a halt alongside a bus stop. My windows were rolled down and everyone in the line was peering into the car to get a glimpse of this man who had, they thought, completely lost his mind.

BASIC WORD programming is writing out your goals, saying, "I want to be a millionaire," "I want to own a Rolls Royce," "I own a five-bedroom house with a swimming pool" – all the words. Self-help books have been saying for years that you've got to have this kind of Basic Word programming – and that's true. But until you link those words to pictures – until you link **BASIC WORD** to **Basic Visual** – nothing really happens. You can have as many goals as you want written down, but that's just wishful thinking. It's just the title of the software (e.g. the title of the, *I want to be a millionaire* software).

You're not really going to accomplish your goal – becoming a millionaire, for example – until you coax the biocomputer into coming up with solutions of how you actually will do it. So if your goal is to be a millionaire, you have to start visualizing a million dollars in your bank account, so that the words in the **BASIC WORD** software program begin to match the pictures in your right brain, which leads me to…

INTRODUCING Basic Visual ANOTHER IMPORTANT 5%

Of course, in everyday life we have to use our language side of the brain and think in a word-dominated way. But for our purposes of goal accomplishment, problem solving, creating wealth and success (often out of nothing), connecting the unconnectable and solving the unsolvable, the biocomputer must be used in a precise manner – as much in *pictures* as in *words*.

You must now translate the **BASIC WORD** objective descriptions of your goals into subjective pictures. The *starting* point for this is **Basic Visual.** Most self-help books do advocate some form of visualization, but those methods I read about seemed to deliver little or no measurable results. Even here, **Basic Visual** is not the end-all – it's just another necessary but insufficient 5% of what we need to do to start generating *Colossus Output* on a regular basis.

Soon after my experiments with **BASIC WORD** I started trying to employ **Basic Visual** visualization, again with only very limited success – probably because of a lack of precise instructions. (I always struggled with self-help because the instructions were never articulate enough). I'll illustrate how my initial experiments with **Basic Visual** failed to materialize my goals using the common goal of, *I want to be a millionaire.* Let's analyze my mistakes:

By 1ˢᵗ January 20** I will have over $1,000,000 in the bank. I hereby sign this irrevocable contract with myself.

This particular goal is set by many in good faith, but they very quickly start to struggle to *see* themselves as millionaires, i.e. with that amount of cash in the bank.

Try as I might, I could never accept that *visualizing* a $1,000,000 bank statement would get me a *real* million dollars, although out of desperation and not knowing what else to really do, I practiced the routine for a number of years. I even went to the length of cutting, pasting and photocopying a bank statement to make it look as though I really had a million dollars in my account. After much practice, I did manage to create the *image* of that $1,000,000 bank statement in my own mind. I thought I was really onto something, but still no actual money materialized. Certainly not a $1,000,000!

In fairness to Napoleon Hill (*Think and Grow Rich*) – whose instructions I was trying to follow – I'm sure he also said, "See yourself giving an equal amount of merchandise for the money" but because I didn't fully comprehend the purpose of the exercise I wasn't nearly as diligent as I could or should have been. I tried other visualizations – seeing myself actually being a millionaire in a smart suit. But what does a millionaire look like? Many of today's young Internet entrepreneurs have long hair, T-shirts, baggy shorts and carry skateboards under their arms.

I know hundreds of self-help pupils who, in trying to *imagine* that they are millionaires, invoke all sorts of dream-building techniques: visiting expensive homes, staying at luxury hotels, dining at five-star restaurants, staring in jewelers' windows, buying lavish lifestyle magazines. All of this is part of **Basic Visual** programming, and make no mistake, it's all good stuff. But it still only accounts for 5% of the work required to really program your biocomputer *correctly* – and that's the only thing that will *guarantee* creative juices flow and solutions arrive on a daily basis. Let's analyze another typical goal:

By 1st January 20** I will earn $100,000 annually as a result of performing to my best ability as salesperson/architect/lawyer/ entrepreneur (insert your profession or business). I hereby sign this irrevocable contract with myself.

As a young entrepreneur I really struggled with this one because every time I tried to visualize selling the required number of motorcycles to meet my financial target, the mental shutters came down; I knew I couldn't afford to buy that many bikes in the first place, let alone create a cost-effective marketing campaign that would sell them all.

Exactly how does a salesman go, say, from earning a $50,000 commission each year to double or triple that? To sell twice the amount of vehicles from a car sales lot usually requires twice the amount of stock and twice the number of punters kicking the tires. Then you have to grab hold of those prospects, quickly establish a rapport with them, and actually close the business. Visualizing these and similar scenarios for your business, in a haphazard, half-hearted way will *not* produce the miraculous results you want. Perhaps the salesman can *see* in his imagination that he is working two or three times as hard, servicing more clients, driving more quickly between appointments, executing more calls?

Such visualizations can help - they're the important 5% **Basic Visual** programming. But, alas, they're definitely not sufficient to create the kind of long-term, sustainable, everyday Eurekas! you want.

Here's another example of how *not* to do it:

By 1ˢᵗ January 20** I will own an eight-bedroom mansion in Beverley Hills or Long Island or Hampstead Heath (name your dream location). My mansion has an outdoor pool and barbecue area. I hereby sign this irrevocable contract with myself.

If you get really creative, you can enhance this mental image by subjectively visualizing and putting yourself in the picture. You can even *hear* the gravel kick up as you accelerate your imaginary Porsche up the drive, *see* red roses on a trellis around the front door and actually *smell* lemons on the tree in the garden and freshly baked bread in the designer kitchen. You can *feel* the cool water as you take an imaginary dip in the swimming pool. *Listen* to congratulations from friends at your house-warming party. *See* the view from your Malibu Beach home overlooking the deep blue and white surf of the Pacific or an imposing loft in Manhattan overlooking the majestic New York skyline and Central Park or a country retreat set among rolling hills in leafy Connecticut.

Here we have a classic example of many people's dream, and I have met and spoke with numerous people who have *visualized* it all, yet materialized none of it. Don't get me wrong, a few of them did attain their goals, but the majority I spoke to ended up bitterly disappointed. Some experienced astoundingly clear visions of the dream home they desired – but *still* nothing materialized! It's evidence that, again, **Basic Visual** is just a *starting point* for translating words into pictures. It's only 5% of what's really needed to attain sustained success – you'll soon understand all the reasons why.

I recall the fruitless times when I'd drive over to St. Georges Hill in Weybridge, before it became a gated community. It's an exclusive nine-hundred acre estate in the heart of the Surrey countryside, regarded as the most prestigious private estate in Britain. I'd often sit outside these homes with my tongue hanging out, for an hour or more. Apart from being lucky that I wasn't arrested, my behavior was what I now call *looking* without *seeing*. You may want to try to work out the *powerful distinction* before we come to it!

After drooling over the beautiful homes I wished I lived in, I'd drive two miles down the road to the Brooklands Motor Museum and the partially banked circuit, where I'd dream of breaking speed records of my own. How I would realize that dream I didn't really know. Like the dream houses and dream cars, I just *believed* I would. I really did *believe* that *belief* could make things happen – how wrong I was!

If you look at a conventional computer it doesn't have to *believe* anything - and nor does a human biocomputer! With adequate software installed it will perform efficiently day in, day out. A human biocomputer also performs incredible feats day after day. Look at any pilot, electrician, or brain surgeon. Belief doesn't come into their work – once they installed the program (*Fly a 747, Wire a home entertainment system, Remove a brain tumor*) they just get on with the task. And that's true for any of us – any task – any goal – once we have the program!

The 747 pilot doesn't need belief before he takes off or lands. He knows he can fly the plane because he's had simulator training and practical experience, i.e. the program has been installed. Likewise, when you get in your car, you drive; no belief is necessary, you just do it. In fact, you do it without even thinking about it. You literally run on autopilot on the, *I can drive a car* program.

Let me indulge one more example of how **BASIC WORD** and **Basic Visual** alone won't give you the kind of sustainable, usable *Colossus Output* that will allow you to achieve your goals, large and small, every day:

By 1ˢᵗ January 20** I will own a brand new Rolls Royce / Porsche / Cadillac. It is metallic blue, fully loaded, with Bose sound system and has magnesium wheels. (Use your imagination here – I'm just giving you clues!) I hereby sign this irrevocable contract with myself.

On many occasions in the mid seventies I'd glide around the corner to the local dealer and stare lovingly and longingly at the stunning Rolls Royce Silver Shadows, and the equally graceful Bentley Corniches. I could be there drooling for an hour or more. I'd often go in, kick tires and pick up glossy brochures, press my nose against the Connolly hide and caress the polished walnut-veneered dashboard and eventually, I'd even go for test drives, but still practicing the art of *looking* without *seeing*.

You won't be surprised to know I've met many people like me who have stared wide-eyed into showrooms and taken test drives in luxury cars while imbibing the smell of real leather. I have known people to carry out this activity for years without ever owning the object of their dreams. Their visualizations are very strong; they tell me at my seminars how they can *see* themselves driving the car along *and* parking it at their own front door, but still no real car materialized for them in the real world. All of this got me thinking, because I *knew* visualization worked and I wanted to get to the bottom of why it works for some and not others, and why not all the time. The answer: visualization – **Basic Visual** – alone is not sufficient. That's where *Basic Visual InAdvance* comes in.

In my own life, I have to say that the majority of my dreams have come true, but only years later than they should have done, simply because I didn't know enough about carefully and diligently programming my biocomputer for specific results. Otherwise I could have dramatically *shortened* the distance between the peaks and troughs of my life and accomplished my goals a whole lot quicker and certainly with less heartache and frustration. **Basic Visual** is only a starting point and lacks the real biocomputing muscle that is crucial for anyone who is really serious about goal accomplishment – and that means you!

I now feel we have a good grounding in what doesn't work, and I hope you can relate to what we've been talking about. To reiterate, **BASIC WORD** is 5% of what you need to do to get on the right track for success, and **Basic Visual** is another 5% of what you need to do. Having laid the tedious but necessary groundwork, we're ready for a quantum leap!

INTRODUCING *BasicVisual InAdvance* THE VITAL KEY TO SUCCESS THAT WILL TRANSFORM A REGULAR BRAIN INTO A BILLION-DOLLAR SUPER-BIOCOMPUTER

BasicVisual InAdvance is the only biocomputer software that will produce brilliant, dynamic, earth-shattering **Eurekas! on Demand** – solutions to problems and an abundance of creative ideas, day-in and day-out. Comparing **Basic Visual** to *BasicVisual InAdvance* is like comparing early computer games such as Pacman to the latest console games: Pacman and programs like it took relatively few lines of code; console games take up many, many times more. The same dramatic leap occurs between **Basic Visual** and *BasicVisual InAdvance.*

Like **Basic Visual**, *BasicVisual InAdvance* is all about visualization. Only it's *immeasurably* more powerful. *BasicVisual InAdvance* represents the difference between people who *only* visualize their goals in **Basic Visual** and people who actually accomplish them. With *BasicVisual InAdvance*, instead of just visualizing a Rolls Royce, you start visualizing how you actually got it - you visualize bucket loads of ideas about where it came from and how you paid for it, whether or not they appear practical, relevant or even feasible. That's just the *kick start* the biocomputer *demands!*

You visualize hundreds of possible routes to achieving your dream - borrowing money, getting a job, raising capital, finding a business partner, re-locating, selling some furniture, whatever it is - helping the biocomputer along as much as you can with as much *input* as you can. Once you've used ***Basic Visual InAdvance*** to input the ideas about how you might get your Rolls Royce, then the biocomputer will start working ever so quickly to generate the Eurekas! and the action steps that you will have to take in order to acquire your Rolls Royce in the most expedient way and quickest time frame! Though the *Colossus Output* that leads you to the actions that allow you to get your Rolls Royce may not look anything like the ideas that you *inputted* in ***Basic Visual InAdvance*** – but that's the beauty of the biocomputer!

Basic Visual InAdvance involves intentionally visualizing multi-dimensionally, using all the senses. So in addition to pictures, you will be adding sounds, colors, emotions, tactile sensations and even smells to your inner scenarios. Your visualizations must be *supercharged* with such ferocity and intensity, (way beyond anything you have ever managed with **Basic Visual**) so as to burn the images of the goals you seek onto the neurons in your biocomputer. You will soon be moving beyond visualization to a process of dramatic – projection, beaming yourself up Star Trek-like to completely inhabit your imagined future world. Unless you're very lucky, this skill won't come at the first attempt but with practice you'll get there, and quickly find yourself looking forward to those special times you set aside for ***Basic Visual InAdvance***. In fact, by the time we've finished this codebook, you'll be thinking four-dimensionally – and aspiring towards the achievements of three legendary multi-dimensional thinkers, Alan Turing, Stephen Hawking and indeed Noble prize winning scientist Albert Einstein who frequently complained that creative thinking was stifled by rote learning. I will now give you specific examples of ***Basic Visual InAdvance,*** from which you can create your own multi-dimensional, multi-sensory scenarios relevant to your personal goals and circumstances…

How I Used *Basic Visual InAdvance* Intuitively

Over forty years ago I was in the habit of trying to attract things to myself and stumbled onto a crude form of **Basic Visual InAdvance.** I was a lowly-paid apprentice carpenter and chanced on a hardware store with a beautifully engineered wood turning lathe, all dressed up in the window. I hadn't yet discovered girls; instead I fell in love with the lathe – I knew I just had to have it! Every night on the way home from work I parked my motorcycle and gazed at that wonderful tool that was way out of my price range. Dreaming of all the things I could do with the lathe, I eventually saved up a small deposit and asked the storekeeper to put my name on the wonderful machine. He agreed and I started slowly paying off the installments each week. As my desire for the lathe grew, so did the pictures in my head of what it would be like to own it. I cleared a space in my workshop at home and prepared myself to accept the beautiful equipment into my life. I continued racking my brain as to multiple creative ways of raising cash to secure the beloved tool. I must confess that most of the things I thought of to raise money were totally impractical.

One day, while putting the magic eye on the shining steel implement, a minor Eureka! *popped* into my head, "Ask the shopkeeper if I could take the lathe now, and I could start turning out magnificent wooden bowls of mahogany, teak and birds-eye maple." (Plenty of off-cuts in my trade!) To my amazement, the shopkeeper agreed – he even delivered the lathe to my home. On reflection, I think that was his way of making sure he knew where to come and repossess it, if I had defaulted on the payments! I was soon churning out beautiful bowls, cheese boards and other trinkets that I sold via the shop – like hot cakes – to quickly pay off the outstanding balance on the lathe. By that time, though, I was already bored with wood turning, for I had now discovered girls, and was also getting heavily into motorcycles and speed. The shopkeeper was quite disappointed when I stopped supplying the beautifully polished hardwood bowls.

Important Footnote: When this little Eureka! *popped* into my head it was just an idea that I happened to follow through. I definitely gave it no credence at the time, nor understood the full significance of it or how important *output* is; but in essence that is *all* there is – and *output* can and must be deliberately *invoked* and *improved* upon.

SCIENTIFIC KEYS

"There are billions of neurons in our brains, but what are neurons? Just cells. The brain has no knowledge until connections are made between neurons. All that we know, all that we are, comes from the way our neurons are connected."

Tim Berners-Lee, founder and inventor of the Internet

How I Closed an Un-Doable Deal

Fast-forward ten years in my life, and now I desperately wanted to acquire a specific motorcycle shop in Sunbury near Hampton Court called Jones Motors. I knew several of my competitors had made offers to the owner of the shop, a larger than life character by the name of Bill Jones, who'd told them in no uncertain terms that the shop was not for sale, although the word on the street said it was. Maybe they didn't offer enough money, or even think to ask what he wanted out of the deal. Perhaps they simply never established a rapport with Bill. Truth to tell, I wasn't a particularly sophisticated deal-maker in those days; all I knew was that I had to get my hands on that shop, which would hold a strategic place in my rapidly expanding motorcycle empire.

Every night for a number of weeks I'd drive over to Jones's shop, park my yellow truck around the corner and stare into the window. But this time, I wasn't just *looking* at the shop – I was actually *seeing* myself inside the shop carrying out various tasks. *Insight, not eyesight – right!* One day I'd be sweeping out the shop with a broom, another I'd be shifting boxes of spares around. The next I'd *see* myself in the shop, serving customers. I couldn't afford to buy the shop, so I started playing games in my *imagination,* mentally toying around with hundreds of various possible sources of money. I'd *visualize* selling my car collection, asking the bank manager for a loan, approaching investors, running *hundreds* of different film sequences deep inside my cranium, mentally playing out all the *options* for finance I could think of. Then I'd return to the *vision* of being inside the shop, being the owner, talking to people, selling motorcycles and spares, making myself at home in the place. I then *saw* myself changing the signboard outside from Jones Motors to Aladdin's Cave, which I thought was a much more marketable name.

One night, while going through my mental machinations of owning *and* paying for the business, I really did have a major Eureka! – I suddenly knew not only where to secure the money, but how to consummate the deal with the current owner who had so stubbornly refused other offers. My mind told me in great detail about ten specific sources of cash, from each of which I collected a portion of the required funds. Eureka! In a flash I also knew how to make the purchase, and when the time came, it happened exactly as had been revealed in my Eureka! – and you'll see how that was played out shortly. All the ideas came in one brilliant burst. I have heard that composers like Beethoven and Brahms composed complete concertos in one fell swoop. I can't write a note of music, (no program) but I'm convinced the *process* was the same for me – as it can be for you. I've experienced these Eurekas! – flashes of sudden knowledge and enablement many times since. Many times!

Anyway, getting back to motorbikes, I walked into Bill's shop and made my proposition. Bill told me the business was not for sale but I was ready for this, having had my Eureka! and retorted, "OK, maybe you don't want to sell the shop as a going concern, but would you consider selling me loads of stock, for cash, at wholesale prices?" His response, "Sure, why not?" and my plan swung into action. Immediately I said, "I'll buy that engine, those four wheels, those six gearboxes, ten of those tires, six gas tanks, four of those frames, ten mudguards, six noggins, twenty seven widgets" and so forth. I deliberately pulled out a wedge of cash sufficient to choke a bull, paid for everything and loaded it onto my pickup truck. The next week I came back for more, "Seven wheels, ten engines, six gearboxes..." Same routine: got out the hip-pocket roll, paid, loaded up and drove off. The third week I arrived and started my spiel, which, to both Bill's and my amusement was becoming a little routine, "I'll buy five wheels, six frames, seven noggins, four pogelers, nine engines…" but before I could finish, Jones quipped, "The way you're going, it would make a bunch more sense if you bought the whole shop."

The rest is history. We struck a deal and I took over the shop. Within days the sign writer had changed the name to *Aladdin's Cave* and I *really* was in the shop, sweeping with a *real* broom, lugging *real* boxes of stock around and serving *real* customers. The *real* cash flowed in – it was boom time and motorcycle heyday!

Extremely Important Footnote: Those of you who are looking for the secrets of success will have picked up some vitally important clues. When I was staring into Bill's shop every evening, I really could *imagine* I was in there as the owner, ***InAdvance*** of it happening in the real world. But even more importantly, I gave my mind something to work with in terms of actually being able to purchase, with cash, the entire business. I fed into my mind hundreds of crazy ways that I could have got the money ***InAdvance*** of it really happening. In effect, I was assisting my biocomputer, programming it so that it could come up with an infallible plan of action for getting me into the shop and paying for it – and it did. Never forget a Eureka! is simply a load of jumbled up pictures, concepts and words that already exist in your biocomputer, as a result of your programming, but *computerized labor* assists them to come out in the right order! When you get *your* Eureka! you'll know *exactly* what to do – believe me!

People who use only the inferior **Basic Visual** software may clearly visualize themselves in a dream home or business but fail to *kick start* their biocomputer with at least some basic information of how they may actually accomplish that objective. And until your biocomputer gets that *kick start*, your dreams will remain only dreams.

How to Build a Path to $1,000,000 with *Basic Visual InAdvance*

Seeing a bank statement with $1,000,000 on it or a dream house is relatively easy (**Basic Visual**). As we all know, materializing either in the real world is much harder. But it can be done. Let's *see* that bank statement again, with $1,000,000 printed on it with your name on top and ask yourself some questions. Was that one deposit of $1,000,000, or was it hundreds of smaller transactions paid in over many months? Before you paid the money into your bank, where did it come from? What type of business generated that money for you? Did you sell one product with $1,000,000 profit (maybe a yacht, airplane or a commercial property) or ten items with $100,000 profit each (maybe some houses, diamonds, a database, industrial equipment or plant or some bespoke software packages?) Perhaps you sold a million items with $1 profit in each (some business information marketed over the Internet or some noggin or widget that you imported from China, or made cheaply and re-packaged creatively and sold via mail order). The money must have come from *somewhere* – it didn't just materialize; that only happens in self-help books, not in the real world!

Many people I've interviewed did accumulate a real million – some of them many millions, often way beyond their original target. In *every single case* their money came as a *result* of good business being conducted – products or services being sold at a profit, putting cash in the bank, and ultimately showing up on a bank statement. That sounds like a statement of the obvious, but it's amazing how many people *do* need reminding of the obvious.

The most important instruction here is to drive your vision back even further. Once you can *see* an established business or businesses, start using your creative imagination to visualize *how* you got it up and running (without capital, if you have none) and ultimately produced a good cashflow and profits that result in your $1,000,000 bank statement. Once you have created a path from the starting point (where the money comes from) to the finishing point (the bank statement with $1,000,000 on it) all in your imagination, your biocomputer will relentlessly start churning out ideas and solutions, all the way until your dream turns into reality. The biocomputer will only stop delivering *output* if you stop the daily *inputting* process – which is you *seeing*, in your visualization the *complete* outcome you are seeking to attain.

How I Lost Millions Because of Incomplete
Basic Visual InAdvance **Programming**

In 1979 I decided to leave the UK. I had set my sights on America, and my vision was to take the largest market in the world by storm. People in the United States have always been interested in personal development, and after the success I'd enjoyed with *Debt Free with Financial Kung Fu,* I figured my latest offering, *Talk & Grow Rich,* would sell like hot cakes from L.A. to New York. In Britain, it was the start of the Thatcher era, when a lot of get-setters, creative people (and ex-motorcycle dealers!) became fired up with the general feeling that if you had ambition, the world was your oyster – you could dip in and scoop up a bucketful of success wherever you fancied. Many of us felt the States was where it was all at, and I too saw a bright green light beckoning from across the pond. My particular street sign was pointing to the Big Apple, publishing capital of the world, New York, New York.

Now, here's a confession. In 1979, not only had I never been to America, but also I had never flown before. So boarding a plane was itself a big deal for me, let alone getting a publishing deal in the city that never sleeps. So I set about programming my mind. I would drive out to Heathrow every night, and imagine myself jetting off to the States, arriving in New York and getting the offer of a major deal. The vision I held was always the same; I was taking the elevator to the 69th floor of a skyscraper in New York City, then I was being ushered into a sumptuous office overlooking Central Park where the chief executive made me a fabulous offer for my book. I saw this happen over and over again in my imagination. I was inputting biocomputer programs intuitively – and naively.

Before long I had bought my Freddie Laker Sky Train ticket and, with an exchange rate of two dollars to the pound, I felt I couldn't put a foot wrong. I landed in New York and quickly found my way to the publisher. I was literally living the dream. I took the elevator to the 69th floor and – just as he had in my visualization, the chief executive put money on the table. He offered me $125,000 on signing a contract, a $200,000 promotional budget, a four-week author tour and a whole list of other perks. An incredibly good deal for 1979 - so what happened next?

Perhaps you've guessed: the deal never came off. Why? It was all me; I wouldn't sign the contract. Whether it just seemed too good to be true, whether I thought I was being ripped off and should hold out for more, I just don't know. Maybe it was the old Groucho Marx gag: I didn't want to join a club that would have someone like me as a member. Whatever the reason, I blew it that day, and it took a long time to recover both in financial and psychological terms. But, hokey as it sounds, that fateful day on the 69th floor was a unique and – ultimately – an extremely profitable learning experience. Here's why: telling my story on the lecture circuit in the United States made me a fortune. Americans loved my British accent and I was surprised how many people related to my story of self-destruction on the 69th floor.

The reason for my meltdown in the Manhattan publisher's office in 1979 if you haven't already guessed, was *incomplete* visualization. I only got as far as my biocomputer program would take me, and its source code not only had a missing link, it was missing a complete line! The one that *saw* me accepting the check! When my program reached that point, I came to a grinding halt. It was as though some tiny, unconscious fear had stopped me from programming that vital step. If my final program in **Basic Visual InAdvance** had been complete, I'd not only have *heard* the New York cabbies, *smelt* the plush carpet in the executive offices, and *felt* the welcoming grip of the chief executive's handshake – I would have also *seen* that check in my hand, *seen* myself depositing the check in my bank…*and* spending the money, perhaps even investing a little of it! The moral of the story? A biocomputer program is only as strong as its weakest code.

Hot Tip! When the words and the pictures are pulling in the opposite direction it is always the pictures that win – without exception. The corollary: when the words and the pictures are harmoniously pulling in the *same* direction – the *irresistible* force of *Colossus Output* will result. The biocomputer effect has started to manifest itself!

How I Now Invoke *Basic Visual InAdvance* Intentionally – and Fully!

There are some simple, practical things you can do to focus your visualizations. Here's one little trick I have found that *boots up* the mental engine. When writing a book, I always make a physical mock-up of the finished product, literally a dummy book. I take a book already in print, strip off the dust jacket and create one of my own – I may even make a dozen of these mock-ups and leave them lying around my home office, all printed with title, cover blurbs and of course, my name. I *hear* in my imagination my editor phoning up and saying, "Yes! I love the manuscript; in fact it's one of the best self-help books I've ever read. We've got a deal – when can you come in?" I then program the image of the physical book into my mind and *see* it displayed in bookstores. I *see* tens of thousands of copies rolling off the printing press and being packed into boxes. I carefully visualize booksellers seeing an advertisement for the book in the trade press then ordering it from the wholesaler, where I can *see* boxes of the books stacked high. I hear the workers in the warehouse laughing and joking as they go about their work, packing up large numbers of orders for my book and shipping them to bookstores across the country. I smell the freshly bound pages and printer's ink – the smell of success! More importantly, I actually *see* customers going into stores and buying copies of the book, ordering it over the Internet and through mail-order houses. I *see* in my imagination sales being made – lots of them. I *see* people talking to each other about the book and I *see* people e-mailing their friends to recommend the book. I *see* a whole viral campaign taking off! All this in great detail – in the code! I pay great attention to every aspect of how I am going to *create* my own success *InAdvance.* The devil is in the detail, ask any computer programmer. So is success!

Indeed, the supporting details are a vital part of the visualization process. I *see* myself traveling around the country, staying in hotels overnight, and getting up fresh and excited each morning to appear on radio and TV shows talking about my life's work. I *see* myself on Oprah and *hear* her saying, "I read the book and loved it," (as she does) and then continuing, "I do all that visualization stuff myself for the show. I *see* the guests; plan mentally what I am going to say, where they will sit and what we are going to run through with them. How I will create excitement and a viewable and memorable show. I already do all that. What I did learn from the book, though, is I ought to be doing that with every other aspect of my life – and that is quite exciting."

I *see* myself squeezing in a few extra bookstore visits not on my original itinerary and maybe dropping off a bottle of champagne for the friendly, helpful staff as I persuade them to make a special display of my books in the window. I *hear* imaginary conversations with the bookstore people **InAdvance** of the event and the pop of the champagne cork, the buzz of excited chatter, the first eager customers arriving through the door, the clamor and glamor of the press, the flash and click of dozens of cameras.

I do this kind of visualization on a daily basis, for every aspect of my business and my personal life – my books, seminars, my clients and even my beloved motorbikes and cars. But I must make one thing clear, I am not advocating that *you* visualize *hundreds* of goals and try to bring them all off simultaneously from the word go. Instead, start sensibly, visualize one small goal then work through the programming process until you actually accomplish that goal. You'll see that the *output* from your biocomputer is based on what you consciously and consistently *input;* then you'll know that you've grasped the technique. This will be a very uplifting moment – savor it; you'll have worked hard to get there! You should then rest for a while, recharge your batteries before taking your next confident steps towards achieving your bigger goals.

Note carefully: There is a big difference between what you *may* accomplish *intuitively* and what you *will* accomplish by *intentionally* invoking the incredibly powerful **Basic Visual InAdvance** software. When you deliberately use your biocomputer you exercise much more control as you insert specific software programs.

Stop *kidding* yourself and *start* dreaming! Start using **Basic Visual InAdvance** and really start accomplishing your goals. It's quicker and easier in the long run to do it properly rather than suffer years of frustration fooling yourself by taking short cuts. Use subjective images that pertain only to you – *your* house, *your* bank statement, *your* specific goals, *your* clients' goals, *your* business and *your* life. Go right back to the point where the success would have started to materialize so you can work out many *options* of how to create your success. Personalize your visualizations by putting yourself in every picture – all of them, and from every angle, in full color. Before I forget, injecting mammoth volumes of emotion into your visualizations is so important we'll cover it in great detail, at a more appropriate time.

What your biocomputer can't do is follow *imprecise or incomplete* instructions. It has the same need for *specific* source code as a conventional computer. There can be no ambiguity. In other words, your biocomputer can be told that you want to be a *millionaire tycoon / real estate entrepreneur / stock market wizard* – or whatever, but it can do no computing with such vague single statements. The same is true of words like *dream house* or *yacht* or *chairman of the board.* You might think these are *specific* goals, but your biocomputer simply will *not* recognize them. It's like a travel agent trying to arrange a vacation without any details of destination, time, flights, hotel or itinerary. To go from an idea to a real event you must define it and *input* many *precise* details and numerous road maps that could lead you to your goal, only then will your biocomputer *kick in.*

Let us briefly summarize the *dramatic and distinctive* differences between the three major biocomputer software programs:

- ❑ **BASIC WORD**
  The left-brain is extremely useful, analytical, and certainly powerful enough to get you through life, help you hold a steady job for the next twenty years, pay the mortgage every month, take a vacation once a year – if that's what you want? **BASIC WORD** is an extremely good tool for writing to-do lists, goals and verbal affirmations but because it is only the *title* of the software program, not the code of the program itself, therefore it lacks any *real* computing power until it is paired with…

❏ **Basic Visual**

This is your machine language, the only one compatible with your biocomputer, and is the start of whole-brain thinking. A great number of people confuse *looking* at dream homes and exotic cars with visualization – they're completely different; it's the difference between *looking* and *seeing*. By thinking in pictures, actually creating powerful images in our neurons, we embark on the process of linking the left and the right sides of our biocomputers together via the Corpus Callosum. Pictures are inordinately powerful and just by invoking this **Basic Visual** programming we enable our biocomputer to *start* coming up with a *trickle* of ideas and solutions. However, supercomputing power – a steady and reliable stream of daily Eurekas! – only comes when you deliberately invoke. . .

❏ *Basic Visual InAdvance*

If you're one of those people – and I suspect you are – who wants everything out of life, this is the only program to use because it supercharges your creativity. It ensures real connectivity between the two sides of your biocomputer and ensures a continuous outpouring of ideas, solutions and **Eurekas! on Demand.** The *whole-brain* power only kicks in when you *deliberately* start thinking through every aspect of your life, deals and business, *InAdvance* of it happening – *including* visualizing both practical *and* creative ways of how you will actually attain the goals you seek. A *major* key is to **INTERNALIZE** those images so they're actually burnt into your neurons, thereby creating extraordinarily powerful biocomputer programs. *Basic Visual InAdvance* harnesses the art of *seeing*, not merely *looking*.

Let's throw further light on the subject by paraphrasing what Confucius was credited with saying over two and a half thousand years ago: "A picture in *Basic Visual InAdvance* is worth a *million* **BASIC WORDS!**"

Hot Tip! For more detail on the power of the three biocomputer software programs and to compare them to each other, consider these words that are synonymous with each software program:

BASIC WORD: Bored, steam-driven, enigma, survival, employee, no comprehension, tired, unfulfilled, jobsworth, hand-to-mouth, looking, eyesight, inferiority complex, going around in circles, hard work, miniscule output, survival mode, in debt, living beyond your means, logic, lack of understanding, scarcity, going backwards, everything's an effort, little or no ambition, timid, spectator, excuse me for living, I can't do that.

Basic Visual: Glimmers of hope, occasional dribbles of output, many goals, ambitious, nearly closed the deal, self-employed but struggling, occasionally gain a little ground, edges of creativity, coal-powered, frustration, mediocrity, wannabe, so near yet so far, occasional ideas, a little comprehension, start/stop, intermittent successes.

BasicVisual InAdvance: Eureka!, ultra-creative, fun, indomitable, sustained success, genius, bliss, driven, invincible, ease, fearless, leader, solutions, confident, biz-wiz, abundance, self-reliance, *seeing, insight,* business leader, voice of God, quantum leaps, job satisfaction, participant, high–achiever, *Colossus Output,* astronomical amount of code, master of own destiny, goal oriented, problem solver, *small still voice,* take on the world, effortless, vast amount of daily *Output* sufficient to take you to any goal, self actualizing, nuclear-powered, **Eurekas! on Demand.**

In Chapter One I talked about how, in order to unlock your biocomputer – in order to decode your *Enigma Output* into *Colossus Output* – you'll need to find your own unique *keys,* or combinations of *keys.* Now that we have an understanding of how your biocomputer works and the three software programs you'll need to start with, you'll be able to look for the *keys* that will turn your biocomputer **ON.** Here's the first of many:

KEY – WHEN YOU'RE WITHOUT – PRACTICE WITHIN!

The *reason* why visualization works so well, and implants *Basic Visual InAdvance* into the biocomputer at a cellular level, is as simple as it is profound. The human biocomputer cannot tell difference between a real experience and a vividly-imagined experience. Once the mechanisms of the biocomputer are engaged, they don't know where the impetus came from; this means you can activate your biocomputer by carrying out a function in the real world *or* by *visualizing* it inside your head. This means that you can take planned advantage of *visualization* to make all sorts of exciting things happen in your life, such as:

o **You can come up with a never-ending supply of staggering ideas, elegant solutions and Eurekas!** This is the crux of this codebook. Insert a program via visualization of all the goals you wish to accomplish *and* also insert into your biocomputer as many ways as you can conceivably think of how to attain that specific goal, whether or not you consider those ideas are practical or workable. Your biocomputer will take all of those ideas, assimilate them and then add its own creative mix, mobilizing literally billions upon billions of neurons, taking other *words* and other *images* and mixing these with the ones you have painstakingly inserted and then sending these *combined* messages down trillions upon trillions of synapses, seeking out and *creating* potential matches and solutions. The biocomputer then completes its computerized labor and fills in *all* the missing gaps and out pops a Eureka!

There really is an enormous amount of biocomputing done subconsciously once you've done the hard *inputting* work. The next five chapters elaborate on how to make this happen with unfailing regularity – the wonderful mystery is revealed!

o **You can improve your memory and recall:** By linking people's names and events (*words*) to actual *pictures* in the biocomputer you can increase your recall by a staggering amount. This works particularly well if you make the image that you link to the name really funny or farcical. I often astound people with my recall ability – but it's only because I've linked Mr. Merryweather to a vision of him being extremely merry, jumping up and down with balloons pinned to his outrageous checkered jacket and laughing his head off in a howling thunderstorm.

o **You can work things out *InAdvance*:** If you were to plan a 3,000 mile road trip across the Australian outback from Perth to Sydney, then Sydney is where the program should begin. Using ***BasicVisual InAdvance*** you could deal with the logistics of transport, supplies, communications, spares, fuel, snake-bite kits, flares and hundreds of other details, working all the way back to the Perth, raising funds for the trip, buying tickets and getting to Perth Airport. You control reality simulation in the comfort of your own living room and in doing so ensure your trip runs without hitches, because you thought it all through *InAdvance*. Human beings are the only living creatures with this ability – unfortunately most of them don't use it. Of course, I know as well as anyone that things don't always go according to plan; nevertheless, it's important to see the complete path to your goal in as much detail as possible, even if you find rocks in the path later.

o **You can improve your game – dramatically:** Sports heroes such as Tiger Woods, Dawn Harper, Andre Agassi, Kelly Holmes, Lewis Hamilton and many others have proven time and time again that by imagining that you are engaging in some activity you'll get better and better at it. You do this by iteration. Within your own head, you hit a golf ball or a tennis ball or complete a downhill ski run and measure your performance in your biocomputer. You then mentally rehearse again and again and again so that when it comes to the real event, you're a winner! These days, many sports champions spend nearly as much time mentally rehearsing as they do in live practice. Astronauts have carried out similar routines for decades. First-man-on-the-moon Neil Armstrong, renowned for saying, "A giant step for mankind" said in his next breath, "Just like it was in practice" – referring, of course, to the thousands of hours spent rehearsing on the ground, both mentally and physically – putting the program into the neurons - before ever landing on the moon.

o **You can enhance your health and well-being:** You can take advantage of visualization to improve your health and well-being. It's sad to say, but the scientific and medical communities lag well behind in this area; I think it's probably because of the obscene amount of money made by pharmaceutical companies across the globe – they may want to suppress any information about complementary and alternative therapies, especially those to do with mind power.

In 1979, Norman Cousins debuted with his groundbreaking *Anatomy of an Illness* about a life-threatening illness he suffered in 1964. Later, Deepak Chopra wrote *Perfect Health* and *The New Physics of Healing*; many others have followed. I concur with them that your mind can have an overwhelming influence over your mental and physical health. Case in point: in 1998 I was hit with a devastating mystery bug that chronically affected my respiratory system. Yet I absolutely refused to spend time in hospital. I did, however, book myself into a private clinic for a few hours and got an MRI heart scan and blood tests – all of which proved inconclusive. I suffered three months of absolute agony but by visualizing myself well; by visualizing my internal organs healing themselves; by sending white light to the affected areas; and by engaging in numerous mental exercises that mobilized billions of neurons, I pulled through – and I guarantee these won't be my famous last words!

Interesting footnote: During that same year, five of my peers, in the U.S. and the UK got hit with a mystery bug too. Whether it was exactly the same one that affected me we'll never know, but they all allowed themselves to hospitalized and pumped up with drugs and modern medicines. Sadly, not one of them survived.

TEN PROFOUND LESSONS I LEARNED THE HARD WAY BUT YOU CAN LEARN IN THIS CODEBOOK

1) I did not really understand the difference between affirmations (the title of the software – e.g. *I am a millionaire* or *I own a Rolls Royce*) and *visualizations* and how they create powerful biocomputer code in our neurons, (the actual software). It didn't dawn on me that if I got the process right – especially the *visualizations* – I would receive powerfully augmented *Colossus Output* in the way of solutions to every single problem I had. I didn't realize that *everything* I should have been doing was to program my mind properly in order to receive *Colossus Output*.

2) I spent inordinate periods of time *looking with my eyes* but not *seeing inside my brain*. I would *look* at dream houses, exotic autos and my dream book that was overflowing with goodies I wanted to acquire. It wasn't until I started *seeing* them – **INTERNALIZING** them in my imagination, deep inside my biocomputer – that exciting things really started to actualize for me in the real world. *Insight not eyesight – remember!*

3) I didn't *input* detailed enough or sufficient enough code to get me to the goal and enable me to *keep* the goal once I realized it. I had numerous houses and cars repossessed because I failed to insert the program of how to pay for them once I had acquired them.

4) I concentrated on static images – even when I put myself in the vision. I set goals without programming in hundreds of different ways in which I could accomplish them, whether those ways were practical or not; in other words, I wasn't giving my biocomputer any *kick-start* programs to work with.

5) I didn't act enough on the small ideas and hunches. Little did I realize that if I had acted upon those, bigger and better ideas would have started to flow.

6) I set far too many big goals before I had even proved to myself that my biocomputer really worked, producing **Eurekas! on Demand,** allowing me to attain my smaller goals. I didn't work out a methodology of the specific *keys* that actually worked for me – so I could then replicate that success formula repeatedly at will.

7) I spent an inordinate number of hours reading self-help books, listening to audio tapes and attending seminars – all left hemisphere *input* – rather than actually *practicing* thinking in pictures within the right side of my brain.

8) I got stuck on one success philosophy. For a long time I was hung up on Napoleon Hill's *Think and Grow Rich* and was reluctant to read anything else on the subject of self-help. When I did finally branch out – picking up Joe Karbo's *Lazy Man's Way to Riches*, that book had a profound effect on my life, almost immediately. I learned a valuable lesson about looking in different places for the various *keys* that would unlock my biocomputer.

9) In my very early days I already had a biocomputer that was functioning perfectly. I was intuitively successful and my biocomputer was already delivering prodigious *Colossus Output.* Yet I was trying desperately hard to find something else or something more, so I drastically and unwittingly changed my own success formula (and as a result, I went backwards – big time). All I should have kept doing was more of the same. Remember, though, that if you're *inputting* intuitively, you won't get the kind of sustainable, regular *Colossus Output* for everything you do, that you'll get if you *input* your goals deliberately through *Basic Visual InAdvance.*

10) The biggest mistake I made was not practicing complete success principles. It was very easy to read out a list of goals parrot fashion. But being dedicated enough to do daily meditations *and* visualizations was much more difficult. It was much easier to skip those *mental* exercises and just pay lip service. I now

realize it takes concentration, effort and discipline – all of which I do now - and reap bountiful rewards.

!!! Even when you know exactly what to do, and how to do it, *and why* you are doing it…you still have to actually do it!

Very, Very Hot Tip! Don't lose what you already have! In other words your biocomputer may *already* be operating at optimum – and you don't even realize it. If you already get a profusion of usable *Colossus Output* and *act* on it, you are probably already doing ninety percent of the stuff in this codebook, either intuitively or intentionally. There really isn't a lot more, other than perhaps a little tweak or two; so it's imperative you don't lose what you already have. If this does apply to you, maybe it's a *key* and all you have to do is think a little bigger - perhaps?

CRACK THE CODE!

❖ Success philosophies are easy to talk about, harder to write about, and even more difficult to implement.

❖ Your hardware already works brilliantly – concentrate all your efforts into understanding and installing software programs and making them work.

❖ Your left computer, the one that thinks in words, is already functioning optimally. You need to activate the right side of the brain, the hemisphere that thinks in pictures.

❖ Do you know what your goals *really* are? Define them now and write programs for them. Convert goals from **BASIC WORD** to **Basic Visual** and then to *Basic Visual InAdvance*.

❖ Your biocomputer has a broadband facility in the Corpus Callosum. Merge words and pictures when installing your success programs and **INTERNALIZE** them for truly joined-up whole-brain thinking.

❖ For your biocomputer to work like a computer you must program it like a computer.

❖ The most productive and creative thinking happens when you are not- thinking!

❖ Success is an idea away. Sustained success is multiple ideas – and actions – away!

❖ Repetition of mental images *of the future* of *every single goal* you are trying to accomplish is the only language of the biocomputer.

THE THIRD KEY

BESPOKE INPUT

Any human task is accomplished simply, *once* you have correctly installed *appropriate* software.

– Ron G Holland

Enigma: No reasonable person would expect to receive usable output from a conventional computer if it did not have the correct software for the job installed. But every day of the week, people try to accomplish their goals and tasks with totally inadequate or inappropriate biocomputer software and in some instances, I'm sure – no software at all!

Eureka! Carefully installing the correct biocomputer software for every single task and goal you set guarantees that you will receive powerfully augmented *Colossus Output* that you can use to propel yourself forward in a meaningful and effective way.

KEY – SET SOME GOALS, EVEN IF THEY AREN'T PERFECT:

To generate *Colossus Output*, you have to create *Bespoke Input* for your biocomputer to run. So set some goals that are both specific and tailor made to suit you, today, even if they're not perfect! You can alter them later!

Let me introduce Ian. Like many people, Ian had experienced varying degrees of success in his life, but for the past twelve years, life had been difficult for him. As we talked, it became clear to me that Ian's problems were rooted in basic indecision: should he try all out to become a millionaire, train as a life-coach, get into mail order or become an author? These options were the mere tip of his iceberg of vacillation. I knew Ian was highly competent in many areas of his life, but he just couldn't get his biocomputer to deliver sustained success.

I gave him the following advice, "First think about a computer. Before it can function, it must have software installed in it, but it doesn't care *what* software. If you insert the *Paint* program, you can paint. If you want to write, you pop in the word processing package and you write. The computer is a machine; it has no preferences and will operate as instructed."

I continued, "Ian, though you are a human being, your biocomputer will also operate as instructed. But until instructed to do *something*, it will do *nothing*. This is a crucial *key*. Until you decide whether you want to be a millionaire playboy, famous author, mail order whizkid, film star or successful entrepreneur, you will be doomed to inertia, frustration and poverty. Fear of inputting the wrong software means your biocomputer remains idle. If you really cannot select an overall goal, set a few interim objectives and program your biocomputer to achieve them. Your interim objective could be as simple as starting some small service business and aiming to save $5,000 in six months, writing an outline for a novel or taking acting classes. Whatever the objective is, your biocomputer will heave an almighty sigh of relief and thank you for giving it some work to do. Your mood will lift and ideas, inspiration and even Eurekas! will start flashing up in your mind. Before long, I guarantee your overall goal will become clear, and it may be something you hadn't even considered before. You'll not only achieve the sought after rewards of money, happiness, self fulfillment and new life skills, but you'll have *booted up* your biocomputer – the most valuable achievement of all!"

!!! All it takes is some *basic* goal-setting software to get your bearings. A biocomputer without software is like a ship without a rudder.

KEY –VISUALIZE, EVEN WHEN YOU CAN'T VISUALIZE:

Many of the self-help books I've read talk about visualization as if it's second nature. One book suggested that *98 percent* of the adult population can visualize with ease. In truth, only a small percentage of people find visualization to be easy (certainly not me).

Visualization is difficult for many people because their right brains have been atrophied by formal education, which emphasizes the three Rs – reading, 'riting and 'rithmetic – almost to the exclusion of everything else.

Yet as difficult as it can be, visualization is extremely important. By practicing visualization you can expand your biocomputer use from 10 percent or less (not nearly enough to generate *Colossus Output*) to 100 percent. But it's not like hitting a barn door with a Magnum; for most of us it takes concentrated effort!

So who are those who can visualize effortlessly? Very probably: Leonardo da Vinci, Thomas Edison, Margaret Thatcher, Mary Kay Ash, Albert Einstein, Coco Chanel, Bill Gates, Olive Anne Beech and Tony Sale of the Colossus project, to mention a few. And Ron Holland? No, I definitely can't; I really have to *persevere* with my *visualizations;* but in doing so I have created fabulous success for myself, and by showing them what to do, many of my clients and my readers as well.

SCIENTIFIC KEYS

It is crucial to carry on your attempts at visualization, even if all you *see* at first is a foggy mess. There is an abundance of scientific evidence to suggest that even *going through the motions* – for want of a better description – is beneficial because *mental images* are generated by building them up, part-by-part, layer-by-layer over a period of time.

The late professor Roger Sperry said, "Neurons acquire individual identification tags, molecular in nature." Meaning that neurons can recognize other neurons that have similar knowledge in them, although this information may come into the biocomputer at different times.

KEY – INTERNALIZE:

Internalization is a way to take possession of a concept and *be possessed by it.* Don't worry; we're not getting into the occult here, though the effects may seem magical. I have taught myself to **INTERNALIZE** raw data to produce usable information. A large amount of *research material* – gleaned from newspapers, web sites or conversations at a mastermind group – needs to be assimilated by your biocomputer in order to be useful – and that takes time. Your biocomputer must *process* your *Bespoke Input* before you profit from it. To *input* material from a magazine, business plan, wish list, book or any other place on earth it must be **INTERNALIZED** *inside* the neurons, mixed up with the electricity generated from the elements of sodium and potassium; otherwise the biocomputer can't and won't use it. In other words, you must take data from the outside world, wherever it is at the time, and then impregnate *that* data *into* your neurons. This needs to be done *before Colossus Output* arrives, in order for it to arrive at all.

Hot Tip! The biocomputer will only process information that is **INTERNALIZED**. Once that's done – once the biocomputer has completed its computerized labor on your **INTERNALIZED**

information – you'll start receiving lots of Eurekas! and solutions to your problems.

KEY – INTERNALIZE YOUR DREAM BOOK:

Collect photographs and cuttings of all the things you are going to accomplish in your life. Some people buy up-market lifestyle magazines such as *Fortune, Classic Car, Architectural Digest, The Robb Report, Country Life, Wallpaper* and *Hello,* hoping the good life will rub off on them. If you've tried this and failed, by now, you probably know why. *Looking* at pictures, even with your tongue hanging out, doesn't work until you start **INTERNALIZING** those images and deliberately implanting them in your biocomputer's neurons. Pasting pictures of exotic Italian cars, dream homes and fabulous six-berth yachts into a book may seem frivolous but it provides a powerful focus for your *imagined* goals. In other words, *intentionally* implant a program in your mind – **INTERNALIZE** it and voila! *Colossus Output*.

!!! Your Dream Book is no mere scrap album; it is an essential dossier for success. But it only works when it's INTERNALIZED!

Hot Tip! Have you noticed how some paragraphs stimulate and appeal to you and others don't? Good – maybe, just maybe, the ones that grab you are *your keys*; highlight them and revisit them frequently. From my perspective, it's a formidable task to write a codebook for six billion biocomputers that are all wired up differently – and are all at different stages of their own personal development.

KEY – GO WHERE YOU HAVEN'T BEEN BEFORE:

Let's assume you've taken on board all of the *keys* we've talked about so far. Now it's time to visualize some goals you have set yourself. Say you need to do more marketing for your business, to dramatically increase sales. The usual advice would be, "*See* advertisements in magazines and PR stories in the newspaper. *Visualize* rolling out your whole marketing campaign, in as much realistic detail as you can."

Yet the usual advice, in my experience, is nowhere near enough. You need to employ your imagination to get into the thick of things. Go where you haven't been before and don't limit yourself or add restrictions – despite the fact that you may not have a budget, resources or sufficient people to carry out the marketing function. In your mind's eye *see* complete TV ads for your company and its products. *See* press coverage like you have never had before. *See* yourself interviewing, all in your imagination, maybe as many as ten different PR, marketing and advertising agencies. *See* yourself employing a full-time sales and marketing professional. *See* yourself recruiting a heavyweight-marketing professional as a non-executive director or consultant. Go the extra mile! *See* yourself looking at five or ten different brochures or posters you have had designed to promote your products. Study, in your imagination, ten different designs of new packaging and read copy from five different copywriters.

The secret is to keep *seeing* the imaginary marketing campaign until you've burned those images onto the neurons within the biocomputer and given it enough source code to work with. Start giving your imagination (the right side of your biocomputer) lots of work to do; don't run by rote all the things you have already done in the past – push the envelope. Don't *you* decide which marketing methodology to use or not, simply because you don't have the budget for it. The whole idea is to give your biocomputer mega *Bespoke Input* – loads of ideas about how you could possibly go about achieving your goal. Forget the puny volume of *input,* if any, you have given it in the past!

Once you have *really* impregnated the neurons with your *imaginary* marketing campaign you should expect a flood of creative ideas and solutions of how to proceed – including detailed descriptions of where the necessary resources can and will come from. Put an Olympian effort into getting the right side of your biocomputer working furiously to produce *Colossus Output.*

Alan Turing arrived at solutions by looking at non-solutions - millions of them! Indeed, your biocomputer needs lots of *Bespoke Input* of potential solutions *and* non-solutions to come up with creative ideas (Eurekas!) that you'd have never thought of consciously in a million years. Turing was fond of saying, "From contradiction you can deduce everything."

KEY – INPUT NON-SOLUTIONS, TOO:

One self-help book that had a profound effect on my life was Joe Karbo's *The Lazy Man's Way to Riches* with its incredible Dyna/Psyc program. Karbo touched on the idea of using the mind as a subconscious computer, something that was of immediate practical use to me because I had an engineering problem that had been bugging me for months. One of my racing motorcycles had tiny roller bearings in the supercharger drive chain that were tending to seize and absorb power. I tried running a deeper oil bath, different makes of chain, larger sprockets to reduce the speed of the chain, all to no avail.

Karbo's approach to problem solving was to list all *potential* solutions, then cross each one out, stating aloud the reason for its rejection. You should then let go and leave the problem to the subconscious computer to solve. Perhaps you see some resemblance here to Alan Turing's methodology of eliminating millions of non-solutions? I tried this with my supercharger drive chain problem and was delighted when, a few days later, the *real* solution popped into my head, "Use a chain that's much wider than the sprocket, which will allow it to fully float." It is of paramount importance to realize that this particular solution from my biocomputer was not one of the many *potential solutions* I had inserted as a *Bespoke Input;* it was a combination of things that my biocomputer, in its infinite wisdom and computerized labor had come up with – Eureka! I won my next race at record speed. More importantly, I had hard evidence that the biocomputer worked – and I have used it ever since to solve my own and clients' problems. Even more importantly, that experience motivated me to investigate more deeply the awesome power of the biocomputer; you could even say that Karbo was highly instrumental in *booting up* my own biocomputer. God bless him!

KEY – CONSIDER THE GOOD, THE BAD *AND* THE UGLY:

When inputting for success it pays to consider all aspects of your life – the good, the bad *and* the ugly! Sometimes you can make Midas-like profits and quantum leaps based on your failures and life's reverse gear. I did!

As a young entrepreneur I had extremely worrying financial problems. Fortuitously for me, I met an astute old Irishman called Seamus O'Rourke who helped me turn those financial challenges – and my flagging motorcycle shops – into a triumphant success. In the process I picked up the wiles and ruses of a successful business consultant. That experience, needless to say – is now literally a cornerstone for everything I do.

The experience led me to my first book, *Debt Free with Financial Kung Fu* which sold like hot cakes with the simple classified advertisement; *CashFlow Problems? Creditors Putting on Pressure?* That led me into business consultancy, helping others turn *their* failing businesses around.

As a somewhat older (and only somewhat wiser!) entrepreneur, I struggled to raise money for my new business ventures. I worked hard to discover all the insider secrets and short-cuts to funding a business – and I've put that experience to work in my consultancy business, raising equity funding for others. Indeed, most of the great business moves I've ever made were driven by my own tough experiences.

Have you had a negative or tough experience that you can (with proper programming) turn to your own advantage? Maybe you have had business or personal problems that you have solved and can now offer solutions to others, who will willingly pay you for your sage advice! Perhaps you had a problem buying a piece of real estate and can now offer assistance to those needing help and advice in the same area. Perhaps you have overcome an illness and can pass on tips and hints that worked for you to alleviate a lot of pain, suffering or embarrassment.

I'm sure that you can think of hundreds of things in your life that don't work, annoy you, or are pet hates. Can you bend your mind to developing useful content for a mobile phone service, a better pepper grinder, a novel way of meeting new partners or friends, a way to buy or sell books, electrical spares, pet food, fuel or groceries without going to a store, or design a new kind of bicycle that can be more easily folded up and carried on the bus or subway? With *correct* programming you really can make piles of money capitalizing on life's experiences – even (or especially) those experiences that have proved in some way difficult for you in the past.

KEY – YOU CAN START A BUSINESS FOR UNDER $10:

Do you want to change your life for the better? One sure-fire way of accomplishing that is to start your own successful business. Many wealthy entrepreneurs have done this, starting from scratch, with *little* or *no* resources. To stimulate your imagination I have written a useful booklet entitled *100 Businesses You Can Start for Under $10* – it's available on the Internet for free: www.eureka-enigma.com. What I suggest you do is download it and study the contents. Try to *visualize* each business in turn, with you actually running it. Then *visualize* a creative mixture of business, marketing and promotional methods described in the booklet. Finally try to *visualize* the businesses mixed up with marketing and business ideas of *your own*. Then let it all percolate between the two halves of your biocomputer. As the percolation process clears, a vision will emerge. The *clearer* your vision, the *louder* will be the resultant *sound* of ker-ching!

Hot Tip! The Internet is the cheapest *global* market place where anyone can set up a stall and sell anything to anyone. That really is a Eureka!

KEY – FLOOD YOUR BRAIN WITH CREATIVE OPTIONS THROUGH RESEARCH:

I regularly use business libraries, the Internet, industry-specific magazines and governmental and scientific white papers (among other resources) for my research. But be aware that you can easily get sidetracked when researching, especially if you have an omnivorous mind, and the Internet can be a notorious time-waster. On the other hand it can sometimes be serendipitous to flip through books at random. I've had some marvelous Eurekas! in libraries (but not aloud!), finding ideas for projects quite unconnected with what I came in for. When starting *The

Eureka! Enigma project I searched Google and other search engines for entries on mind power, right, left and whole-brain thinking, altered states, the reticular activating system, neurons, mastermind groups, lateral thinking, biocomputer, permutations, psychology, visualization, education, creativity, thinking and hundreds of other related topics to get me up to speed with current debate. Over a 4-year period I used over 40 reams of paper (20,000 A4 sheets) and a ton of ink! I sped read *and* **INTERNALIZED** every single page. And "Yes" I do feel sorry for the trees, but I find it very difficult to read on the screen!

Eureka! – A Big Noise Heard Over the Silence!

I want to expand my thoughts about **INTERNALIZING,** because I often see students studying research papers, then putting them down and moving to the next one. Many students can intellectually consume information, *but* they don't **INTERNALIZE** it. They understand the words, but the *meaning* isn't *absorbed* and *assimilated* into the neurons. I want to scream out and say to them, "Excuse me, but I don't see you closing your eyes and entering the *inner world* of that research, creating detailed, colorful pictures and actually impregnating that information onto the neurons." Two dimensions may be appropriate for the groves of academia – but it's *multi-dimensional* and *multi-sensory* **INTERNALIZED** thinking that leads to success – via *Colossus Output*.

KEY – DO YOUR HOMEWORK:

In any consultative relationship your clients always have a head start – because, hopefully, they know their business and you don't. How can you get to know a client's business sufficiently well to solve their problems? I first access Google and then perhaps a dozen other search engines, collating industry background, trends and current issues. I usually find that within 24 hours I am up to speed on my client's particular field and in fact I often surprise them with the latest news on say, health farms, wine growing, wing nuts, tea marketing, hair products, leisure travel, sportsware, property or whatever, over our first business breakfast. Serving a range of client's means I can also transfer knowledge from one industry to another. Many times I encounter companies stuck in industry-specific patterns. Drawing on the technology or culture of an entirely different type of business often enables me to break open a problematic mindset. The client really does think outside his own box at last and I can accelerate his company to a much higher gear – faster!

Extending your range of personal contacts is both sensible and valuable. From my research and networking, at both industry-specific functions and at broad based business-focused groups like BNI, I retain names and contact details of industry leaders, journalists, consultants and advisers and many of whom love to share their expertise and opinions. When you get to know or hear of such people, don't pester them endlessly, but don't stand on ceremony either. When you want to know something, phone them and politely pick their brains.

"Just how realistic is this approach?" you ask. A classic story has it that the U.S. military once paid IBM $2 million to ascertain the most effective way of finding an answer to any given question. Apparently IBM's research took five years and the result was this: make five phone calls, the first to someone you *think* may be able to help you. He will suggest someone else who is a little more knowledgeable on the subject and he in turn passes you to his colleague who is an expert in the matter; it is he who gives you Mr. Green's telephone number who is not only an expert in the subject but is actively involved in a similar project and talks the language. Mr. Green recommends you call Ms. Brown, who is the world leader in the topic and answers your question. I don't know if this particular story is true or not, but I *do know* this simple stepping-stone method of research works regularly for me. Often I find a usable answer or contact before I've even got to a Ms. Brown.

Billionaire Rich DeVoss of the famous and incredible Amway Corporation always bounced his ideas off at least three people in the course of each working day – not only his professional advisers, but also janitors, mechanics, the pizza guy, people that live in the *real* world.

Rich never underestimated the grounded and intuitive wisdom of the layman.

Once I've done my research – libraries, Internet, phone calls, bouncing ideas off people and mastermind group *input,* I'm ready to program my mind. I *visualize* the problem and its desired outcome, incorporating as many potential solutions as I can think of; *input* the raw data of my research; and then relax while my biocomputer does its work. The resultant *Colossus Output* shows me *precisely* how to help my client.

KEY – IMMERSE ALL YOUR SENSES TO PROGRAM FOR SUCCESS:

Let's take a major program: *learning Chinese.* It seems like an insurmountable challenge, but there are over a billion people who speak, write and read Chinese, not only fluently, but also effortlessly. How? From birth, Chinese is all they hear, see and do – their senses are totally *immersed* in this major biocomputer program; there is no other option!

I am a millionaire is also a major program, and therefore you must totally *immerse* all your senses in it. Study the language, actions and thought processes of millionaires if you really wish to become one. Read about rich people, mingle with the wealthy, be seen at places where they hang out, rub shoulders with them. Use ***Basic Visual InAdvance*** to *imagine* you are a millionaire!

Yet when you use your imagination it's not always as easy as you think. You have to *apply* yourself. Where do millionaires hang out? How are you going to meet them and make their acquaintance? Start by looking deep inside your own mind to recall various golf clubs, yacht clubs, country clubs, or big city clubs that you may know of. Maybe you can bring to mind the most influential person you can think of and get him to introduce you to some high flyers – what we in London call the *Movers and Sheikers* - maybe at a social occasion such as a river cruise, movie premier or opening of a new building, art gallery or restaurant. Maybe you can encourage a lawyer, an accountant or PR friend to introduce you – it happens all the time in the real world, but it can happen *quicker* if you program it in your biocomputer first! Maybe you can use advertisements to attract millionaires into your life. Hey, I'm just using *my* imagination, now it's time to use yours!

Hot Tip! One of the most closely guarded *secrets* of millionaires, multi-millionaires and billionaires is that *invariably* they have worked very *hard* at building a positive self-image by visualizing and role playing; watching endless hours of DVDs of their peers selling, closing deals or performing; and bridging the gaps of any particular weaknesses they may have. They *mentally* practice over and over again in areas that they feel particularly weak in. Through *repetition* they create powerful programs in their biocomputers and mobilize literally billions upon billions of neurons to do their bidding for them – automatically. They do not even *attempt* to go out into the real world with incorrect, inappropriate or inadequate software!

KEY – PULL, DON'T PUSH:

Despondent and depressed people unintentionally use their biocomputers to repel the things they really desire. How many times have you seen a guy approach the prettiest girl on the dance floor, all set to get in the groove, then chicken out at the last moment? His *imagination* got the better of him – he was so afraid of rejection from her and humiliation from his friends that was all he could imagine. So instead, he goes for a much less desirable – but in *his* mind, softer – target. He doesn't know it, but his chances of getting a dance with the prettiest girl are as good as getting a dance with the plainer Jane. Many people, sadly, go through their entire lives – and I do mean entire – actually *repelling* cars, money, dream houses and all the other accoutrements of success, because they *know*, or *think* they know, that they just can't attain them.

What the young lad on the dance floor should have done, in the weeks prior to the dance, was *see* himself acting out the scene as he wanted it to happen (closing the deal, if you like). You need to *employ* your imagination in the exact same fashion to elicit *Colossus Output* for money, planes, boats, sports cars, helicopters and executive jets – or V8 motorcycles, if that is your desire.

Spend more time drawing to the *front* of your mind the things you really desire and much less time conjuring up negative images because you *think* you can't accomplish your goals. Lamborghinis, Sun Seeker Yachts, Executive Lear Jets and nitromethane-guzzling supercharged motorcycles were built for the likes of you and me. So were mind-blowing *experiences* like taking a helicopter ride through the Grand Canyon, swimming with dolphins in New Zealand, taking a trip into outer space, or the thrill of a lifetime hitting 7Gs in a Russian built MIG-15. Ask yourself, "If not me, who? If not now, when?" Then start programming, *InAdvance* – right!

KEY – PROJECT OUT, NOT IN:

Although you must **INTERNALIZE** everything, sometimes the image of what you are trying to accomplish works better if it is projected *outside* of the biocomputer. For example, as I'm running images *inside* my head of detailed scenarios that I'm working hard to bring about, I know that one of the best methodologies that works for me is projecting those scenarios somewhere between twenty and fifty yards *outside* of my head.

I try to bring into focus, as best I can, (and remember I really struggle with visualization) images playing on the lawn or street or wherever the projection ends up. I play around with those images and projections and *concentrate* on them for as long as I can – often only twenty or thirty seconds, but occasionally as long as ten or fifteen minutes. I know from experience that even *small* periods of time projecting mental images can bring *stupendous* results into my life and therefore I deliberately bring these projections into play as frequently as I possibly can. Foggy images tend to get clearer and clearer with each performance and I often find that by the time the image is brilliantly clear, I am then looking at the real world manifestation of whatever it was – money, cars, closing deals, vacations, race results or relationships – that I was working so hard to mentally picture.

KEY – IF YOU HAVE A MENTAL SCREEN, USE IT. IF NOT, DON'T FRET!

All too often life-coaches, trainers, NLP practitioners and other professionals advise *seeing* an image projected on the screen of your inner mind. They tell you convincingly to create a large image on your mental screen of the things you don't want to happen in your life, all the time playing a smaller image of the things you do want to happen, in the bottom right hand corner on another much smaller imaginary screen. And then, *swish* you're supposed to very quickly swap the larger negative image for the smaller positive image.

Now tell me, *what* screen? I don't have one, and I have talked to hundreds of others across the globe who don't have one either. Maybe one person in a hundred can bring up that small screen. Usually, the younger the person you talk to, the more likely they *will* be able to create vivid images on their internal, imaginary screen – they have an innate ability to do so, at least until the heavy moving equipment of formal education has completely eradicated it.

I'm not negating the other man's philosophy – far from it! All I am doing is pointing out if one *brilliant* strategy doesn't work for you, don't think it's because your biocomputer isn't working. All it means is that you are not wired up that way; you simply need to try other *keys*. One thing is for sure, if you are not getting *Colossus Output* that is moving you forward at a nice steady pace, you have to keep tinkering with your *Bespoke Input* until your biocomputer does *boot up*.

Hot Tip! The *swish* screen method is just *one* key. I am pretty confident you will need *multiple* keys to turn your biocomputer **ON** - to full capacity.

KEY – KEEP TINKERING:

Getting a stubborn biocomputer to *boot up* is a little like tinkering with your desktop PC. Your screen freezes, it crashes, you can't open the last chapter of your latest book or business plan, you have a nasty bug and it frightens the pants off you. You give up! You're either going to throw the blooming thing out of the window (it's happened before!) or buy a new one (it happens frequently!) Then your best buddy visits, delves into a few windows you didn't even know existed, deletes some old programs, installs some new ones, in general ferrets around at lightning speed, your eyes pop out of your head and you feel a nervous twitch in your left eye. You think to yourself "I'll never get the hang of these computers as long as I live." Your helpful friend then shuts down, reboots and presto, not only has the glitch taken a hike, but in the process you have learned at least ten brilliant short cuts, found new applications and discovered other astounding things that you can do with your computer.

Now you have to apply the same type of computer science to your neck-top computer. Click, probe, open windows of your biocomputer you didn't even know existed, delve deeper than you have ever dared to go before, look into hidden files, and play *mental* games, even though you fear you may be out of your depth, until the glitches finally disappear and you do start receiving *Colossus Output.*

Hot Tip! Success will often come through the back door – providing you leave it open!

!!! The never ending, up-swelling, churning out of creative ideas, magnificent hunches, promptings and **Eurekas!** on **Demand** is the *only* thing that is going to turn your corner store, part-time mail order business, or one-man engineering works into the next Wal-Mart, Hammacher Schlemmer or General Motors.

KEY – KNOWING, AS OPPOSED TO KNOWING ABOUT:

When I was a child at school we had a lesson on dinosaurs. Our teacher, Mrs. Talbot, brought the subject to life in a remarkable way. I'm showing my age here, but this was in the days long before *any* type of visual aids had arrived – I suppose I'm going back fifty years. Instead of just spouting the long names of these defunct beasts, she encouraged us to close our eyes and *visualize* a gigantic Brontosaurus as she vividly described it. Meanwhile, she played a soundtrack on a large, clunky tape player of raging storms, gigantic trees crashing down, wolves howling in the background and the simulated roaring of dinosaurs. This brilliant teacher went further than showing us illustrations in a book. Using *imaginative* techniques, she'd engaged our right brains to give us the *total* dinosaur experience. I wish there were more educators like her. After that lesson we didn't just know *about* dinosaurs, we *knew* dinosaurs – and boy were they scary! Mrs. Talbot's favorite expression was, "Children, I'm teaching you in *words*, but you need to *think* in *pictures*" – not bad for the nineteen-fifties, eh?

KEY – THINK LATERALLY ABOUT LATERAL THINKING:

I have asked numerous teachers of lateral thinking to explain this popular concept to me. They talk of non-linear thinking, not taking "No" for an answer and contrarian strategies. And so many of them love to *think outside the box*. But as author of *The Tipping Point*, Malcolm Gladwell has suggested, perhaps this means they'd be better to just change the box. You can think laterally about anything – even lateral thinking! I firmly believe lateral thinking is only a tiny percentage of the *complete success philosophy* equation – perhaps an important 1%, but nevertheless still only 1%. Edward de Bono believes our thinking would be 400 years further on if it hadn't got stuck in the groove of Socrates, Plato and Aristotle. I believe we must not remain over-reverent about the ideas of Jung, Grinder, Bandler, de Bono, Hill, Karbo, Gladwell, Buzan, Ron Holland or the current educational system, for that matter. In a changing world we must continue to push the envelope, remaining open to new ways of thinking about both whole-brain thinking *and* non-thinking.

KEY – FIND A FRIENDLY RUBBER DUCK TO TALK TO:

Bruce Snyder is not only my business partner of almost 20 years but he's also a multi-millionaire, entrepreneur, super-consultant, physicist, mathematician, scientist, good friend and all-round *clever-clogs*. He's a big advocate of the *rubber duck* principle – he uses a colleague as a sounding board (even if what he's saying is way over that persons head) without expecting any response, in effect as though he were talking to a rubber duck.

I have had the privilege of being Bruce's rubber duck and listening to his mathematical ruminations for hours on end. (It's not really as bad as it sounds). Bruce can solve problems this way by hearing his own voice and saying to himself, "That's ridiculous, it just doesn't sound right, there must be another way." He continues talking through the problem until a solution emerges. I'm sure being a rubber duck has also helped me – I just haven't worked out how yet! Many therapists still use the *talking cure* to help patients help themselves. Maybe this is the *talking solution* for problem solvers, which you could try with a friend – but take turns at being the rubber duck. It is a *key* for Bruce and it *may* turn out to be a *key* for you, too!

KEY – TURN ON *AUTO* SUGGESTION:

When I was a young man, I decided to build a garage by the side of our house. I had just completed the first wall when my father came by. When he realized what I was doing, he began to laugh heartily – he'd never owned a car in his life. He was amused because he didn't think I had the financial resources at that time to buy a car – and he was right. I couldn't have bought a new car, or even a second-hand one – not even an old jalopy was within my means – *not right then*. And this is the operative phrase – *not right then*.

Though I was building the garage before I knew how I was going to obtain a car, this seemed perfectly logical. I wanted a car, and so I'd need a garage, and to demur about it would negate my intentions. I had to *assume* ownership and *see* my dream car proudly installed in the garage before my biocomputer would figure out a way for me to get the car I wanted. Indeed, just a few weeks after the last wall of the garage went up, I had a brand new, elm green Volkswagen Beetle delivered courtesy of ***Basic Visual InAdvance*** or, you could say, *auto* suggestion!

At my biocomputer seminars I often meet people trying to attract new *significant others*. If there's still evidence of a former husband/wife/boyfriend/girlfriend in the home, I tell them to clear out the wardrobe and make plenty of space for the new partner's clothes. I tell them to lay out the breakfast table for their new partner in anticipation of his or her arrival. "But," some ask in response, "Isn't this jumping the gun a bit? Isn't it a bit sad, creepy even?" On the contrary, jumping the gun is exactly the way to get what you want – once you're sure what that is. (And if you are seriously wanting a partner, then sad is where you're already at). Create an attitude *and* an environment conducive to a new partner and, very soon, one will appear – trust me.

KEY – LISTEN TO THE SOUND OF MUSIC:

I have always known that music has a calming, magical effect. When my wife Elisabeth was pregnant we would play classical music to our baby in the womb. Brain scans show that 4 to 6 year olds who are given music lessons generate more sophisticated responses to all sorts of questions than those who aren't given lessons. The kids' brain-processing systems worked faster and general memory capacity increased.

Indeed, music and musical training can have a beneficial effect on how the brain gets wired for general cognitive functioning related to memory and attention. Children who have been exposed to music benefited from greater general skills in areas such as literacy, mathematics and IQ. Researchers have also measured changes in brain responses to sounds using magneto encephalography, a non-invasive brain scanning technology. They found that children had better responses to tones and their brains worked faster at processing sounds than children of a similar age.

I still ensure that my daughter Kay has sufficient stimulation in every conceivable area, *including* music – to create as many possible synaptic connections in her brain that will allow the *words* and *pictures* to flow, amalgamate, create and ultimately turn into Eurekas! – so she can glide merrily through life with a fully-functioning biocomputer. I delight every time I see the look on her face when *The Sorcerer's Apprentice* or *Peter and the Wolf* are played – she steps out of herself and I know new neuron chains are being created; these pathways vigorously strengthen the links between the auditory and visual centers. I can already appreciate from her prodigious *output* that her biocomputer is working magnificently!

It's not too late for anyone to develop a passion for music and *open up* more neuronal pathways – in effect *unblocking* anything that has come between you and your dreams and accomplishments (usually a little code, or lack of it).

SCIENTIFIC KEYS

Nobel laureate David Hubel, a famous neuroscientist, was asked whether he had any interests other than his specialty – research into the visual brain. He replied, "Actually, I seem to spend an inordinate amount of my life at the piano." *All* brains come alive to the sound of music!

KEY – ASK A FRIEND FOR GUIDED VISUALIZATION:

If you have a trusted friend, business partner or confidante, describe to that person your dreams and aspirations in as much detail as you can. Then, totally relax and allow your friend to talk you through detailed steps towards accomplishing those dreams – while you devote all your energies to *visualizing* every detail they are describing. If this *key* works for you, employ the strategy on a regular, but I suggest, reciprocal basis.

KEY – LINK YOUR BIOCOMPUTER TO OTHERS IN A MASTERMIND GROUP:

I first came across the mastermind group principle in Napoleon Hill's classic *Think and Grow Rich,* over thirty years ago. Hill got the idea from the richest man in the world at the time of writing his book, which was first published in 1937 and has never been out of print. That man was Andrew Carnegie, a Scottish immigrant who owned and ran the United States Steel Corporation. (I have visited Carnegie's former home, Skibo Castle, in the Scottish Highlands many times).

In his book, Hill recounted how Carnegie explained to him that no man could create impressive wealth on his own, but only as part of a harmonious group of people generating and implementing ideas. I took this principle on board and acted upon it immediately. I had one motorcycle shop at the time and when I announced to my salesmen and mechanics that they would now form my mastermind group, they fell about the floor laughing hysterically. After the hooting, hollering and snickering subsided, we had some great brainstorming sessions – the group came up with all sorts of creative *and* practical thoughts on developing the business. The camaraderie was wonderful and the *output* and implementation quite remarkable. We quickly expanded to seven motorcycle shops and also diversified into two furniture outlets and a 40-bedroom hotel. (Not Fawlty Towers – but very nearly!) The employees who made up my first mastermind group all shared in the increased profits.

Thirty years since that first bike shop, I now have a mastermind group of around 20 individuals, clever guys and girls from all walks of life: millionaires, media moguls, tycoons, accountants, lawyers, property developers, marketing experts, stockbrokers, artists, Swiss bankers, fund managers, actors, actresses, corporate financiers, engineers, scientists, physicists, life coaches and mathematicians. I brainstorm with them on an ad-hoc basis over the phone and sometimes in a group, bouncing around problems and challenges that various clients of mine face – with a view to coming up with valuable feedback that can be **INTERNALIZED** and used in my biocomputer. One thing I want to point out, is that my mastermind group took 30 years to assemble and I still use many laymen as well.

When you link more than two human biocomputers together you increase the amount of mind power *exponentially*. Put a team of people together, working in harmony and motivated appropriately, and you'll accomplish your goals - and more! Business Networking Organization, BNI, attributes its success to its philosophy of 'Givers Gain', which ensures that all BNI members benefit from mutual, motivated support of others in the group.

I am truly a believer in building far reaching networks – in my opinion, these ought to mimic the neuronal networks that exist in the human biocomputer. The more links, passageways and connections you can create the easier it will be for you to source money, deals, products and create ideas and solve problems. I firmly believe the best networks come out of relaxed meetings, friendships and talking to people – my own personal network extends to every continent and continues to grow daily; I not only work on it, but also extend a warm invitation for you to join it, go to: www.eureka-enigma.com

KEY – BE OPEN TO NON-SOLUTIONS IN YOUR MASTERMIND GROUP:

In my early mastermind groups, I was frequently annoyed by totally off-the-wall contributions. But the more I unravel the mysteries surrounding the Eureka! Enigma the less dismissive I am of peripheral observations or suggestions; they're all potential non-solutions, which can lead to the ultimate solutions.

I made a big mistake with my first mastermind group. Big mistake – huge! Our weekly meetings were always electric, nurturing great team spirit with ideas crackling around the room. One day, a member of the group returned from vacation with a flagon of strong liquor to share among his fellow master-minders. In those days I was a heavy drinker, and lost no time getting stuck into the spirit of the thing – so to speak. The meeting degenerated into a jovial bun-fight concluding in no productive *output* for the business. In subsequent weeks, others brought booze along and our meetings went steadily downhill. The business lost that vital spark and we soon found ourselves going backwards, partying our way to oblivion – and patting each other on the back as we went over the precipice!

KEY – DOUBLE THE SEX & DOUBLE YOUR POWER:

Mastermind groups can get a big boost from members of the opposite sex. Women's problem-solving powers are deceptively simple. Traditionally women were brought up solely as home-makers and mothers, encouraged in cookery, sewing, cleaning, flower arranging, dress-making, music – all right-brain activities that established complex neuronal connections. Left-brain learning and the academic side of things was the boys' domain, grooming them for the role of breadwinner. When a man thinks, he switches on neurons in very specific areas of his brain, like a single searchlight. When a women thinks, her brain cells light up like an aerial shot of Las Vegas at night.

So putting women and men together in a mastermind group is like combined right-brain and left-brain thinking – doubly powerful!

KEY – DRAW SPAGHETTI, OCTOPUS AND MIND MAPS:

At the start of your mastermind sessions write a core objective in big letters in the center of your flip chart and invite the group to add boxes, links and suggestions; these can be used as *keys* and to articulate the map's design as it expands and emerges. These visual mind maps can serve as prototypes for your business's success programs. You can draw these maps on your own, too, of course. Writing your thoughts down clarifies them. Once you *see* what you say, you'll *know* what you think. If you are part of a mind mapping session, you realize, of course, that you will get 90% more out of the session if you **INTERNALIZE** everything on the map, not just *look* at it; because once you have **INTERNALIZED** the map, then the real work begins – the biocomputer starts its own computerized labor!

KEY – EMPLOY *VISUAL* BRAINSTORMING:

This is a powerhouse descendent of the good old-fashioned suggestion box and the movie version of the round robin. Group members are given, say, an hour, to create mock-ups, prototypes, cartoons, simple illustrations, adverts, press items and general ideas. The results are pooled for discussion and pasted on a flip chart, while the members' biocomputers **INTERNALIZE** it all. When the process is repeated a few days later, once everyone's biocomputer has had time to assimilate and *process* all the *Bespoke Input,* the leap forward in creative output can be astonishing. Put egos aside and focus on the goal as a shared achievement. Such sessions can be extremely enjoyable and highly productive.

KEY – THINK *INSIDE* THE BOX:

I have heard the expression, "Think outside the box!" shouted out at board meetings and brainstorming sessions more times than I can count. One day I got to thinking about it and coined the expression, "Think *inside* the box!" which I have to say is eminently more powerful than thinking *outside the box*. But whatever method of thinking you use, until you **INTERNALIZE** it *inside* your very own brain box, your mind will not start operating as a biocomputer and delivering *Colossus Output*.

KEY – COMBINE IDEAS TO CREATE YOUR OWN WINNING COMBINATION:

When writing *The Eureka! Enigma* I needed to focus throughout on the brain/computer analogy. But how should I connect my twin themes? Anyone who's played poker or been to Las Vegas has seen the Riffle Shuffle: you cut the deck then closely place the two halves together, give a deft flip and *riffle* the cards so each deck interweaves a single card at a time. If you're a Vegas dealer, that is – those guys in the casino pits are real pros! Most of us end up with clumps from each deck and a few cards on the floor!

The image of interwoven cards was perfect for the text of this codebook; I could cross-relate brains and computers throughout and provide a structured analogy for the reader. So I cut the mental deck with my *Eureka! Enigma* manuscript on one side and the likes of *Apple Bible*, *JAVA* and *Programming for Dummies* on the other. It's not a perfect Riffle (that would make for a boring book) but *The Eureka! Enigma* is your winning deck! Can you riffle a number of business ideas *combined* with creative marketing methods and create your own winning combination?

KEY – GIVE YOUR BIOCOMPUTER A SPECIFIC PROJECT:

"The mass of men lead lives of quiet desperation," claimed Henry David Thoreau. I meet desperate, angry, unhappy, unfulfilled, frustrated men and women at my seminars and workshops almost every week. No, it's not because they're disappointed with me; rather they're disappointed with *themselves*. They want something to happen in their lives - but they don't know what, and they don't know how.

Let's look at it from a scientific perspective. When my partner Bruce (a scientist) was invited to get involved with the *Exocet* missile project, he huddled in a room with a group of other scientists, mathematicians, engineers and related specialists, and they *worked the project up*. They didn't set the goal of say, building a new type of missile and expect it to just happen. They *dwelled* in the subject - lived it, ate it, played it and slept on it, sharing their thoughts, ideas, experiences and dreams about how the project *could* take shape. One of the *key* elements was a continuous supply of tea, coffee and donuts – together with card games and easy chairs. The working day was a creative pot roast of serious debate, electronics, computer sciences, number crunching, metallurgy, jokes, games, refreshments and resolve. Frequently they would work all through the night, on many occasions having sleeping bags on the job.

At some point one of the team had a Eureka! – usually a brilliantly clear holistic understanding of how the project *could* be realized. This vision was often adopted as the prevailing consensual idea, then further brainstorming would take place, filling in detail, fleshing out practicalities, logistical and financial issues. Interestingly, Bruce says the Eurekas! never happen when a project manager is around. It seems overt leadership can sometimes inhibit the flow of the team's creative juices. Or maybe just the flow of the coffee pot…

You don't have to be a top-flight scientist to get a taste of Bruce's experience. You don't necessarily have to work in a team. But you do need a goal. Being a millionaire, like building an *Exocet* missile is a big goal that requires big thinking. If you are one of Thoreau's *mass of desperate men* (or women) you can do something about it. Start work on a project, something, *anything,* even if you hate it, deliberately force your biocomputer to kick in. When you generate *some* cashflow you'll feel so much better. You will have written and *inputted* your first successful program, then many more will follow as you begin to verify your own results – and continue with your *bespoke programming!*

Humorous Titbit: During one of Bruce's most intense sessions working on the *Exocet* project, one absent-minded scientist came in early one morning and complained to his colleagues that his apartment smelled extremely musty and all his house plants had mysteriously shriveled up. Bruce quipped, "Well, I'm not surprised; you hadn't been home for three months!"

KEY – USE MENTAL ENERGY TO MAKE IT HAPPEN:

A few years ago I heard some beautifully inspiring tapes by Dr. Wayne Dyer called *The Secrets of Manifesting Your Destiny.* Wayne – who I've met on a number of occasions – tells how an Indian guru, Sri Guruji Pillai, entered his life and taught him how to manifest his goals. My first thought was, "Why doesn't a guru like this come into my life? I could really learn something from such a master." My second thought was to subtly emanate the notion that I would someday meet this guru. I gently fed this out to the ether and then let go.

About a year later, staying at my friend Gisella's house in Belgium while on business, there was a phone call for me. It was a mutual friend, Frederick. He said, "Ron, I have a house guest here who's seen all your books and tapes stacked high on my coffee table. He's fascinated and would very much like to meet you." I asked who the guest was. "Have you listened to Wayne Dyer's tapes *Manifest Your Destiny*?" replied Frederick, "Well he's the guru, Sri Guruji Pillai, and he's staying over at my place. Are you up for a meeting?"

Within an hour I had driven into downtown Brussels and we sat around Frederick's coffee table. On the way, I'd thought eagerly of a hundred and one questions for my favorite guru, but was now tongue-tied. Guruji looked at and me and said, "Have you read *Think and Grow Rich* by Napoleon Hill?" "Of course, that book inspired me to write *Talk and Grow Rich*," I replied as I pointed to my book on the coffee table. Guruji continued, "There are many people out there who want to materialize things and they try to achieve cars, houses, money, accoutrements. They get very frustrated when they fail to materialize. What they need to do is come back to Hill's famous success formula, 'Whatever the mind of man can *conceive* and *believe* he can *achieve*.' What do I mean by *conceive*?" Before I could answer he continued, "Conceive – creating *mental images* over and over again in your mind's eye of the things you want to materialize. Once you can clearly *see* what you are trying to make happen, you *will* be able to believe it. The *achievement* of your goal will happen shortly after that, almost *automatically*. What you have to do Ron, is get out there and tell people to start at the right end of the formula. Tell them to stop trying to *achieve* and instead put serious *mental* energy into *conceiving*. Tell people to *see things in advance of them happening*."

Guruji continued his revelations for nearly three hours. I never asked a single question, yet he spoke about everything that was in my mind. It was as though he had a sixth sense, an invisible connection right into the inner depths of my mind. When Guruji had finished, he rose, clasped his hands together, bowed his head and left the room. I haven't seen him since – talk about meetings with remarkable men.

KEY – PRAYER AND PROTOCOL:

I have used prayer successfully on many occasions, though sometimes feeling guilty about what I prayed for. Others tell me that prayer is more hit and miss for them. But if you **INTERNALIZE** your request with emotion, your prayers are more likely to be answered! Let me lay it on the line for you. If you say a prayer as in, "Please God, give me $10,000 - cash, a girlfriend or boyfriend, an accountant to help me run my company or a new car," it is highly likely your prayer will have been in vain – you can probably verify this with your own experience. However, if you say the same prayer *combined* with *emotion* and at the same time *visualize* in great detail whatever it is that you are asking for, as though it has already happened, it is *highly* likely that your prayer will be answered – *especially* if you add many options in the prayer of ways it *could* be achieved.

Everything about biocomputers, software and programming is about protocols, i.e. how to get the two sides of your biocomputer, the right and left sides of your brain, the *words* and *pictures,* communicating with each other in the most effective way. As it says in the bible, "When ye pray, use not vain repetitions, do not heap up phrases (**BASIC WORD**) as the heathen do, for they think they shall be heard for their much speaking. Do not be like them, for your Father knows what you need before you ask Him" and "Through lack of vision my people perish."

The prayer is the *title* of the software program – the words describing what you want to achieve. The *vision* of it already happening, not in the real world but in your *mind's eye,* is the *actual program,* **Basic Visual InAdvance.**

KEY – BECOME A *MARTINI* PROGRAMMER:

There's an old advertizing slogan for the aperitif Martini, "Anytime, Anyplace, Anywhere." If you can visualize and program your biocomputer in any situation, it gives competitive advantage. I prefer the absolute quiet of my bedroom or favorite easy chair on my patio, but if I have to, I'll attend to my inner software, impervious to distraction, on a train full of stressed executives inanely yelling their ETAs into their mobiles phones *and* my ear! Actors learn concentration by reciting a speech as their colleagues interrupt or whistle *The Star Spangled Banner* with Eminem playing at top decibels. If you can manage the latter, you're probably a natural, able to switch off the outside world at will and give total attention to your biocomputer. If so, you may find a still, quiet environment as distracting as others find noise.

A few years ago I was invited to a London hospital to beta-test some experimental equipment, courtesy of an Israeli manufacturer who was due to IPO. The company was launching a device to address irritable bowel syndrome, and the product worked like a biofeedback machine, helping the user to relax naturally without drugs. During the trials, the technicians were amazed that I could take my mind to the slow Alpha rate in unfamiliar surroundings within seconds *without* the use of their biofeedback equipment. But it had taken me a lot of practice to achieve that ability to switch off anytime, anyplace, anywhere. Biofeedback is a great resource to teach you how to accomplish Alpha state and buying a small handheld biofeedback device may turn out to be a great investment – and a *key!*

KEY – SUBPROGRAMS SUPPORT MAJOR PROGRAMS:

As I grew to know, like and respect Tony Sale at Bletchley Park, we had many stimulating conversations about computers and biocomputers. Tony had worked on some major IT projects – not just the 12-year

Colossus computer rebuild. Tony has an interesting background: he worked with MI5, including a period as technical assistant to Peter Wright (of *Spycatcher* fame) who, at the time, was catching various Russian spies in London. Tony once said to me, (jokingly, I think) – "If I tell you much more about Colossus and Enigma, I'll have to kill you!"

When Tony was faced with the often daunting task of rebuilding the Colossus computer, it was entirely from scratch with neither working models nor original drawings – nothing but a few fading photographs of the wartime machine. Tony's approach was, in effect, to program his mind, thinking three dimensionally about what Colossus would have looked like and how it would have worked. He has had the ability, from childhood, to form clear mental images at will and is completely untutored in this respect – he admits it was probably a great advantage that he never had a formal higher education. Tony spent hour after hour visualizing every component of Colossus, all standard post office equipment of that era, and how each part and valve (vacuum tube) were inter-related. Furthermore, he visualized and empathized with the mindset of the men of the 1940s era – Tommy Flowers, Max Newman, John Tiltman and Bill Tutt – and *saw* clearly, in his imagination, what resources and technologies were or were not available to them at that time.

Step-by-step, Tony's mind delivered the successful rebuild of the world's first semi-programmable and production line computer. When I pressed Tony about his number one Eureka! for the Colossus rebuild project he insisted there was no *one* Big Idea, but literally *millions* of them – solutions, ideas and hunches – all contributing to the accomplishment of his mammoth challenge.

Tony Sale's *continuous* stream of creative solutions for Colossus came to him as a result of his subprograms – smaller programs that augmented his larger, *Rebuild the Colossus Computer* program. Even if you have only one major goal – one major program – in life, you will still require many biocomputer subprograms. Subprograms can supplement your main program in two ways:

1. They can serve as preconceived aids to your overall goal, e.g. learning marketing at night school to boost the success of your daytime business; taking a weekend job to fund an expansion of some kind; plus all the separate activities that are part of your overall goal (opening six retail outlets would need six subprograms).

2. They can be contingency options for the unexpected, e.g. building an indoor sports center as a wet-weather adjunct to your golf driving range; developing a consultancy business in case your industry or sales career falters; (not to infer that all consultants are failed businessmen, except perhaps for the best ones!) Subprograms are also good to have on hand when you know the main program or road ahead may fork, but you need to delay your choice of direction for some reason.

You will certainly need many subprograms of the first kind – they are the small streams and tributaries flowing into the larger river of your overall program. The second type of subprogram might be compared to ramps on the highway, emergency routes for when the main route you'd planned to take is obstructed for some reason. Conventional programmers refer to this as *branching*. You will need to visualize all the stages of your subprograms, using **Basic Visual** and *Basic Visual InAdvance.*

KEY – TURN FAILURE TO YOUR ADVANTAGE:

Since I set out as a young entrepreneur I have had my fair share of failures. Not that failure is something to be proud of, but it's nothing to be ashamed of either. As an author, I have always been an open book – I talk as openly about my failures as I do about my successes. I have had cars and homes repossessed, companies go down the gurgler, run out of funds on numerous occasions and been dragged through various courts – but always managed to come out the other side smelling of roses! A few profound lessons spring to mind:

*   Most people striving for success don't fail nearly enough; that's because they never try anything – instead they go through life

in a cocoon. They *desire* success, *talk* about success, *wish* for success and buy a lottery ticket – but they never really dive in at the deep end, put in their all, set goals, even small ones, and deliberately start programming for them.

- Most of my big successes have morphed directly out of my big failures. I wrote *Debt Free With Financial Kung Fu* after my first major failure over thirty years ago. But my biggest struggle was the battle with my own mind, trying to get my biocomputer working effectively – that has caused me more pain, embarrassment, frustration, suffering and heartache than all the business failures put together; but again I have turned this *major* failure into monetary success *and* global recognition. I don't say that every failure can be or should be turned around just by writing a book, but failure can definitely be the greatest and most *powerful* contributor of knowledge into a person's biocomputer.

I wrote this *key* to *motivate* you to make many more attempts at success, no matter how many times you've failed; to *embolden* you not to be frightened about pushing the envelope; to *encourage* you to recognize that when one has few or no resources you have to take *more* and *bigger* risks – not fewer and smaller ones! When you have everything to gain and nothing to lose, do it now! Where to start? Set some goals and start programming – of course!

RON G HOLLAND

TOP TIPS FOR
SUSTAINED SUCCESS

This is what I did – what will you do?

To *reboot my* own personal biocomputer I did *many* things including:

- Visualized using ***Basic Visual InAdvance*** everyday – even when the images were not clear I kept persisting with this.

- Started taking long county walks – alone.

- Set many new goals, including many small ones. Then developed *Bespoke Input* for every single one of them.

- Got a new wife.

- Meditated every single day.

- Sprung into action whether I felt like it or not. I forced myself to work on manuscripts, client's projects and my motorbikes.

- Stopped drinking alcohol.

- Acted immediately on any *output* that I received – no matter how small the idea.

CRACK THE CODE!

❖ *Bespoke Programming* in ***Basic Visual InAdvance*** requires concentrated effort.

❖ When *looking* at dream homes and $1,000,000 bank statements, step backward to the starting point, to *see* exactly *how* you arrived at the destination.

❖ Set up your own mastermind group – connect your biocomputer to other biocomputers.

❖ Input vast numbers of *potential* solutions as well as the end goals, in pictures, words, colors, feelings, sounds and smells all in great detail – give your biocomputer some programs to work with.

❖ The art is to *visualize* everything you want to accomplish, ***InAdvance***, every single day – for the rest of your life!

❖ Think *inside* the box, *inside* your own head, in pictures, ***InAdvance***.

❖ Having a specific goal that is **INTERNALIZED** in *pictures, InAdvance* is the *only* basis of deliberately inserted *Bespoke Input*.

❖ *Only* information that has been **INTERNALIZED** can and will be used by the biocomputer.

❖ **INTERNALIZED** Visual Input = Extraordinary Colossus Output.

THE FOURTH KEY

GESTATION & COMPUTATION

There is nothing more futile or frustrating, than waiting impatiently for *Colossus Output* - when the dues haven't been fully paid.

— *Ron G Holland*

Enigma: An opossum has a gestation period of 13 days; a ferret takes 42 days; a mink 50; a pig 113; a reindeer 245; an orangutan 275; a giraffe 425 and the African elephant takes an impressive 640 days to grow from conception to birth. The human baby arrives at around 270 days, closest to the orangutan, reflecting Darwinian theories about our closest relatives in the animal kingdom. There seems to be a vague correlation between the size of a species and the length of its pre-natal period, but what is remarkable is the fixed nature of these time frames. Ideas, in contrast, don't have a specific gestation period. Eurekas! come and ideas go, but for the uninitiated, the process usually takes as long as it takes. For the initiated – those who *have* found their unique *keys* to generating *Colossus Output* – ideas can be conjured up at will, **Eurekas! on Demand**.

Eureka! It took me years of reflection to fully understand what is behind the saying that successful people *work hard and play hard*. Analysis has shown me that many successful people achieve their success intuitively; nevertheless, when their *habits* are studied, distinct patterns emerge. Successful people tend to drive themselves and others, pushing projects forward, gathering and assimilating *extensive* quantities of information pertaining to their tasks in hand. This is their intuitive *inputting*. Then, without fail they let go; relax, play, swim, go on vacation or do whatever it is that takes them completely out of themselves and puts an end to their internal dialogue. It is in this *Gestation & Computation* period – this relaxing and letting go – that phenomenal *computations* are done - and where real breakthroughs are made, problems solved and ideas generated, often by the bucket-load. Maybe the actual time span for creating a Eureka! can't be written into a scientific formula, but there is undeniable truth in the expressions, "The harder I work, the luckier I get" *and* "The more I relax, the more creative I become."

This chapter will give you detailed instructions for *Gestation & Computation* techniques – how to allow your biocomputer to perform its computerized labor with maximum efficiency. The *key* to *Gestation & Computation* is relaxation, letting go, the stilling of conscious thought on any given problem. When most people think of relaxation, they often see themselves chilling out in front of the television with a six-pack and a big bag of nuts. However, this is the route to *couch potato*, not the road to genius, wealthy entrepreneur or success in any endeavor. The type of relaxation that'll *kick-start* the biocomputer is wholly different and usually involves *playing hard* and other techniques – which is what this chapter is all about.

KEY– UNDERSTANDING GESTATION:

Gestation for ideas: conception and development in the mind – what could be simpler? Nothing really, except when you begin to ask, "Well how long should I wait for an idea to emerge? What is the shortest time and what is the longest time for an idea to be conceived? What can I do to speed up the process? What if I'm in a real hurry – I need a solution right now? What if I've never had any ideas in 30 or 40 years – why should they come to me now?" These are all pertinent questions that I have come across before. You may find the answers a little surprising but in the following *keys* I hope to answer all your questions – and a few more besides. The good news is that if these *are* your concerns you're asking all the right questions – and delving deeper into the success process than you have dared go before and because of that you will be well rewarded!

KEY - UNDERSTANDING COMPUTATION:

When we talk in terms of our PCs we are used to the fact that they appear to churn out work and solutions immediately. In actual fact we are lulled into a false sense of their efficiency. True, these days computers are relatively fast and the small amount of work we give them to do, they usually handle very quickly. However, there are simple tasks that are way beyond the capability of an average PC. This is where the supercomputer comes in. With a starting price of over $1,000,000 and that is with just one processing rack. Apparently they can take up to 64 racks, each costing a further $1,000,000 each. Total price $64,000,000 - so I don't suppose they sell too many of them. (I wonder what the commission is?) These supercomputers can perform 70 trillion calculations per second and for big operations they run constantly and effortlessly at this speed for hours, sometimes days, even weeks on end. Some scientists estimate the human biocomputer has 20 times the capacity of a supercomputer! 20 times $64,000,000 is $1.28billion – now you know why I keep referring to your brain as a billion-dollar biocomputer! Scientist Ray Kurzweil estimates the brain can do 20 million billion calculations per second (based on 100 billion neurons with only 1,000 connections per neuron, times 200 calculations per second, per neuronal connection). And many neurons have over 10,000 connections – wow! Your job is to harness this super power – my job is to show you how! The biocomputer revolution hasn't happened – yet! Believe me!

KEY – SUCCESS IS A STATE OF MIND:

We need to become aware of the many altered states the mind can present to us – the more you become aware of how your mind operates, the better you can utilize more of its awesome processing power. By getting to know four important altered states, maybe you'll come to realize that one or more of them maybe a *key* to help you generate *Colossus Output!*

For the most part people are oblivious to the fact that daydreaming, sleeping, dreaming and meditation are altered states, which if harnessed, can maximize our potential as human beings. Your biocomputer, being a sophisticated piece of electrical hardware, generates as much as ten watts of electrical power, and if ten brains were wired up together, they could probably light an electric bulb. The brain's electrical activity manifests itself in waves. These can be observed, for example, on a lie detector graph, where an increase in brain wave oscillation betrays tension in response to certain questions.

Different brain wave rates have been dubbed Alpha, Beta, Delta and Theta. These different states have a profound bearing on the relative effectiveness of our biocomputer's *Bespoke Input, Gestation & Computation* and *Colossus Output.* Left to its own devices, the brain will gravitate to whatever wave rate our own mood or external stimulus dictates. But with practice, we can take control of the process. It was Marvin Minsky who quipped, "there's something queer about describing consciousness. Whatever people mean to say, they just can't seem to make it clear" I'm pretty sure I can, so let's look at four brain wave frequencies and see how each of them affects biocomputer performance.

KEY – GET TO KNOW BETA STATE:

Beta is the necessary state for day-to-day functioning, running our lives and businesses. The frequency of Beta waves runs from 15 to 40 cycles per second, (cps) and is the operative state while working hard mentally, e.g. making a speech or teaching. Beta is the dynamic state of mind I run on while performing on stage at one of my seminars. It is essentially an active, questing, striving mode.

KEY – GET TO KNOW ALPHA STATE:

A lot of controversy surrounds the Alpha state – the *Alpha industry* still booms with people making small fortunes from meditation courses,

Alpha conditioning parlors, biofeedback machines and other devices. The scientific community is divided as to the benefits of tapping into the Alpha state.

Fortunately, we don't have to rely on either the *Alpha industry* or the scientific community - my experience with altered states is highly practical. It comes from 30 years of observation, my time spent as a professional hypnotherapist, through discussions with literally hundreds of people at my seminars, and as a result of my own mind programming experiments. In those 30 years, I've noted how various states of consciousness actually work in the *real* world of business *and* in the great game of life.

In contrast to Beta, Alpha is a highly relaxed state of mind, with a brain wave frequency from 9 to 14 cps, although the precise meaning of Alpha rhythm continues to be debated among brain researchers.

This deckchair level of consciousness is one of the best states in which to receive *Colossus Output,* with Eurekas! and ideas flowing unbidden from the biocomputer. Alpha occurs at the very gateway to sleep – which explains why we often get many of our best ideas just before nodding off or upon awaking. For this reason, I always keep a pen and paper at the side of my bed in order to capture any Eurekas! before they evaporate in the daylight or vanish in the fog of slumber.

Alpha is also very amenable to *Bespoke Input* and, in my opinion, highly necessary for the correct installation of programs – if you can take yourself into Alpha state before you start to *visualize* your goals using **Basic Visual InAdvance** you'll bypass the intellect and any resistance to those suggestions very quickly. It's Alpha state that the clinical or stage hypnotist takes you into before making any hypnotic suggestions. We'll expand on this major *key* later.

Certainly there are some places that are more conducive to slipping into Alpha state than others – lying on the beach on a warm sunny day with the gentle sound of the waves that you hear, for example. But since you can't always be on the beach, it's necessary to learn how we can slip into Alpha at will. There are various ways of doing so – marijuana isn't one I'd recommend. Some people use alcohol, but again its better if you can master your biocomputer without the aid of chemical props. Meditation in Alpha state is at the very top of my list – so relax and grow rich!

Hot Tip! Relax when you *input* – relax to get *Colossus Output!*

Penultimate Word: The late Milton Erickson, the world's most renowned clinical hypnotherapist (NLP was modeled after his methods), said that as long as he could take his patients into *any* relaxed state he would start his therapy, implanting new programs for permanent change. He stated that good hypnotherapy could be carried out regardless of the *exact* relaxed state his client was in, and he proved time over that he could hypnotize anyone.

Final Word: While we are talking about Milton Erickson I want to explain in a little more detail what his actual magic really was. Like all good teachers, Milton used stories, anecdotes and metaphors when talking to patients who were under hypnosis. His magic was to get them *thinking in pictures* by creating graphic images using verbal stories they could *relate* to (even though many times Milton's stories had absolutely no obvious connection to his patient's condition). Erickson was a consummate master of getting the right side and the left side of the brain, the words and the pictures, the conscious and the subconscious to communicate with each other.

KEY – GET TO KNOW THETA STATE:

Imagine that you have no cashflow, more credit card bills on your mat than there is junk mail, creditors hounding on the phone and your partner is on the verge of walking out the back door as money flies out the front. More than one *day in court* looks imminent for you. To make your misery complete, *booming bass* from the neighbor's hi-fi and your own internal dialogue is driving you to distraction. Outside the weather is teeth-rattlingly cold, freezing rain and the car won't start; one last drive before it is repossessed would have been nice, but hey, this is hell on earth, so pull up a chair and make yourself at home. If you think this is an exaggerated scenario, let me assure you that it's based on direct personal experience. Believe me, you don't become a *success guru* by dealing only in theory – I live in the real world, same as you!

At times like these, how can you possibly think of pleasure? On the contrary, I say, how can you *not* think of it? In such drastic circumstances, when whatever decision you make seems painful, and life is totally bereft of anything approximating pleasure, it is precisely pleasure that you should be seeking. Go for a sauna, wander around an expensive department store, take tea at the Waldorf or breakfast at Tiffany's, make love or watch a movie in the middle of the afternoon. Walk through a fancy part of town, mingle with beautiful people and study menus in restaurant windows. If you really can't afford to eat out, decide exactly what you'll order, Chateaubriand or Lobster Bisque or both, in a few months time, when everything's sorted. Put on some music or just go jogging and let endorphins flood your system.

All of these activities represent Theta mode for the brain – the pleasure principle. A little Theta-level pleasure boosts your inner strength in times of crisis. It's like a warm bath for your body and soul, after which you can return refreshed to your problems, see them in perspective, and with the help of a fully recharged biocomputer – solve them!

With so much pain going on in your personal world, you need to rebalance the psychological scales and remind yourself that life is still worth living. You must put *real life* – those bills, creditors, the complaining partner – on hold for a few hours; it can't get any worse, so just enjoy yourself for a while. Worry wears you out yet doesn't solve anything. So what if you spend a little more money you don't have? It's not going to make much difference in the long run. Just because your income's dropped to the level of a monk, it doesn't mean you have to wear the hair shirt as well. So give your biocomputer a rest and give yourself a break. Treating your senses and your imagination is a way of reminding yourself there's a world out there, a very different one from the hell-hole you temporarily inhabit. This is not escapism – it's actually *planning* your escape, sampling the sweet taste of freedom until you're able to enjoy it full-time again.

KEY – GET TO KNOW DELTA STATE:

Deep sleep occurs at Delta level. You may think there is no *Colossus Output* to be had from your biocomputer while sleeping deeply, but nothing could be further from the truth. World leaders, millionaires, artists, inventors and many creative people know the magical power of sleep. They have unequivocally found that their working output rises dramatically when they have the optimum amount of sleep. Equally, too much sleep has an adverse effect; as I can testify. When I have been depressed, (there was a three-year period in my life when I suffered severe depression) I would often sleep ten to fifteen hours a day. Perhaps this was the search for oblivion; perhaps it was just extreme lethargy, symptomatic of a lack of motivation and inspiration. Whatever the cause, excessive hours of sleep were dulling my brain and blanking out the desire to do anything but seek further solace in unconsciousness as soon as possible. It was a real downward spiral of inertia – that through *sheer persistence* on my behalf I finally snapped myself out of.

The optimum level of sleep varies from one person to another, and the traditional healthy average of eight hours is not necessarily appropriate for everyone. Many find they need less sleep, as they get older. The summer months, with warmer days and brighter mornings also predispose most of us to be up and about earlier. Personally, I tend to be a seven-hour man, but get a heightened alertness and creativity when I slightly starve myself down to five or six hours. If I occasionally drop to four hours sleep, then the mental capacity can accelerate still higher. This can be deliberate if I have a deadline for some work, or happens spontaneously when I'm engulfed in a flood of Eurekas! At such times you can produce brilliant work, riding the waves of *Colossus Output* and oblivious to the hands on the clock. You *go with the flow,* writing, thinking, forging ideas in a white heat of creative fervor until the biocomputer tells you the *Colossus Output* is complete and it's time to rest. Such intense bouts of productivity should be followed by a very pleasant catch-up period. Your *sleep-bank* is repaid at a modest and fair rate of interest and you return to the routine seven hours of sweet dreams; peacefully celebrating your achievements.

Whenever I receive a business proposal that catches my eye, I always like to sleep on it before making any decisions. As I turn in, I ask myself, "What's missing? Whose advice can I seek? What should I look out for? Is this a good deal?" This is deliberate inputting – a request to the biocomputer for guidance, for **Eurekas! on Demand.** The amount of *Computation* that this can produce is often amazing. Often the *Colossus Output* starts to appear way before the dawn, not just once, but successively through the night. I frequently wake and have to scribble furiously as Eurekas! arrive. I love it!

KEY – BANISH THE BOREDOM STATE:

Much of today's juvenile crime, delinquency and anti-social behavior is brought about by the state of mind known as *boredom*. It really doesn't matter how many new police initiatives are launched, until this core problem of boredom is addressed, crime, joy-riding, petty theft, vandalism, graffiti and violence will continue.

All human beings have a built-in need to alter their state of consciousness from time to time. Bored kids need to have a myriad of different, healthy, safe and legal ways to achieve that altered state. Get them off booze and drugs, which provide an easy but damaging high and instead encourage boxing, skateboarding, rollerblading, snowboarding, BMXing, white-water rafting, rappelling, rock climbing, grueling cross country runs, motorcycle racing, mini-motos, extreme sports and sports that haven't even been devised yet. And curb the nanny state health and safety culture a bit – kids love to take risks – and so do I!

These pursuits could be held in *respect zones* where kids would find all sorts of exciting and creative challenges 24/7, and where *their right* to get into altered states would be accepted and, indeed, *respected*. Altering states is a global multi-billion dollar industry – ask any alcohol or tobacco manufacturer. We need to use that knowledge to provide equally exciting but positive, harm-free outlets for youthful energy, experimentation and natural highs. Perhaps you can carve yourself a niche in this industry – do some good and make a fortune at the same time – time to get programming, perhaps? Another *key* – perhaps? Well what are you waiting for!?

!!! You wanna start taking this thing seriously!

KEY - UNDERSTAND TIME FRAMES:

When it comes to goals and biocomputers most people don't understand time frames. The most important thing is to avoid fixed assumptions; for example, believing that accomplishing X goal will take Y amount of time. Setting a rigid time frame for your goal might lead you to miss out on fantastic opportunities – and never forget that a properly programmed biocomputer can operate at lightning speed!

To explore this concept, let's return to a common goal, that of becoming a millionaire. Many readers may set what they consider to be a realistic time frame of, say, five to ten years to achieve this goal. But why and how do they arrive at this period? If you set yourself a specific task, say, building up a chain of stores, it's logical to estimate a specific number of years to complete it. In this case, you begin to understand a time frame for example, by preparing a comprehensive feasibility study having researched the logistics of planning permission, contractors, finance and cashflow. But does the biocomputer need five or ten years to create a foolproof, deliverable plan for achieving your goal of becoming a millionaire? Absolutely not! As soon as you begin clear, consistent programming in ***Basic Visual InAdvance*** the biocomputer will start to produce regular *Colossus Output.*

While top-down programming requires a clear end result, the code leading to that end must be written with plenty of branching opportunities. You won't necessarily know, until the program's actually running, what all your options and possibilities are. You may find that these are more varied and *accessible* than you had first thought possible.

Let's look at a couple of scenarios. Say you've come up with a brilliant idea for a book, but maybe you're not primarily a writer, or you are too busy earning a living to produce the book quickly. Either way, it will take you a long time to put in the required work to create what you hope will be a blockbuster. You therefore err on the side of caution and set a time frame of say, five years to compile the book.

However there is another option you may not have considered, an option that would produce your book in much less time and enable you to enjoy the profits, credibility and prestige much sooner. You could do this by using a ghostwriter who would talk to you in depth about your proposal, then go away and turn your idea into a book within a few short months. The ghostwriter would perform this service either for a flat fee or a percentage of the royalties from the publication. Your name would be on the front cover and the majority of the profits would be yours – as would be the fame and glory! And you would be free to pursue other goals and ideas while your book was being taken care of. Maybe you could use the time to think up other titles, perhaps a series of publications you could commission from your ghostwriter. With an agent and publisher on board you could be on your way to making millions, extremely quickly. Multi-millionaire and best-selling author Jeffery Archer (*Kane and Abel, First Among Equals* and *Not a Penny More, Not a Penny Less)* has used this exact formula for years! Archer produces his books very quickly – and because he uses a ghostwriter, he can publish a bestseller every five months, not every five years! He even churned one out while he was in prison – how's that for turning a difficult situation to your advantage!

The second scenario is if you were building a chain of retail outlets. Rather than follow the arduous path of finding sites, obtaining planning consent, contracting shop-fitters, staff hire and other logistics, there's a realistic short cut to creating your retail empire. Maybe you can dramatically shorten the required time frame by going on the acquisition trail. Any business can be grown more quickly through acquisition than organic growth. If you think such an approach is only for the Phillip Greens and Bill Gates of this world, you may be undervaluing your abilities. There is no mystique about company takeovers or consolidating fragmented cottage industries. Do your research, invest in a few books, make lots of phone calls, get yourself into a business library, talk to experts and *input* various information about these wealth-creating strategies – and *Colossus Output* will result!

The bottom line here is this: don't assume that *Big Ideas* must take a proportionally large amount of time to implement. It's *what* you actually do that counts, not how long you take doing it. Most millionaires I know look for the fast track and the path of least resistance. Why make things slower or more difficult than they need be, especially when you have a dramatically under-utilized, billion-dollar, super-duper biocomputer at your disposal?

KEY – PROGRAMMING FOR OUTPUT BEGINS WITH DECISION:

Let's say you are reading this codebook in a park or in your own living room and waiting patiently for *output,* as you do at the beginning of a *Gestation & Computation* period. Maybe you want things to happen more quickly in your life – a career change perhaps? Possibly you are a lawyer working in a large firm and want to break out on your own, so you can *eat what you kill.* Perhaps a new relationship is in the cards or you are desperate to start an exciting new business or relocate to another city or country. You have to start making conscious decisions to speed up the whole process. In other words, once you *start* taking command of your life you can then show your biocomputer what it is that you are trying to make happen on a conscious level.

KEY – RECHARGE YOUR BATTERIES:

Don't feel you have to wait until you're tired or in a crisis before you take a break. Rest and Recreation – R & R to anyone with a military background – should be a planned part of your routine. If you work for a company, you expect regular breaks throughout the day for coffee, lunch and tea. This is not only a lawful requirement, but corporations know a happy and regularly refreshed workforce is, in the long run, a more productive one. Your employer probably offers paid vacations and, of course, there are the weekends.

Why then, if you work for yourself, should you expect anything less in terms of time off? We all know that running your own business is likely to involve longer and more irregular hours than being on someone else's payroll. But don't let longer, irregular hours drive you to the point of exhaustion. The heroic 70-hour week might be sustainable while we're starting up or during a busy period, but to work at such a pace all the time means either you are a masochist or there's *something wrong* with the business. If we feel we're not making enough money to take vacations, maybe a few weeks' wages should be factored into what we're charging our customers. This will ensure we can get away occasionally while keeping our annual profits stable.

R & R doesn't necessarily mean sandalwood bath oil and foaming unguents, unless like Dr. Frasier Crane, this is your idea of ultimate luxury. If it is, fill the tub and enjoy! Discover what makes you feel like royalty and do it. You won't actually need a king's ransom – just enough for that occasional bottle of red wine you particularly love, a visit to your favorite restaurant and a taxi home, some hand-made shirts from London's Jermyn Street, an expensive and very discreet after-shave or a box at the opera. Maybe just a day off doing absolutely nothing, enjoying the luxury of sheer idleness in silk or Egyptian cotton sheets is all it takes. I do all of the above – regularly – but replacing the red wine with Red Bull!

KEY - POWER NAPPING:

Older generations called them daytime dozes, catnaps or having forty winks. In hot countries, an afternoon sleep is a siesta, a cultural custom dictated by early morning fishing and farming, then sheltering from the sun's hottest hours. Only in recent years have we heard the term *power nap* for taking a short sleep during the day. Joe Karbo called them *silent treatments* and they're something I have been practicing for years. Supervisors in some big corporations are now instituting the power nap as official policy among management and staff, convinced of the impact on alertness and general performance in personnel. As far as the power nap is concerned, it could well be time for a wake-up call!

You can adopt my favorite methods of curling up like a cat in a comfy chair or pulling the duvet over your head in bed. But remember not to sleep longer than 20 minutes. You can *take a problem to bed with you* or just enjoy the rest. Either way, your biocomputer is likely to do some silent *computation* and problem solving while you're out for the count. If I do enter my power nap with a specific aim in mind, I spend a maximum of thirty seconds *inputting* the problem, before hitting the sack.

KEY – DOWN TIME:

We've talked about the *keys* of power napping and recharging your batteries. Down time is a more serious and structured application of these combined *keys*. I recently read a fascinating piece about New York property tycoon Donald Trump. The article discussed his views on beautiful women, architecture, skyscrapers, raising hundreds of millions of dollars for projects and making money. But the paragraph that grabbed my attention was about down time. Trump needs four hours a day, on his own, with absolutely no company, female or male. Phone calls, visitors or interruptions of any kind are prohibited. During this period of solitude, the tycoon goes *inside his head* and *sees* his businesses, preparing and thinking through his strategies.

After this four-hour isolation, the public Donald Trump re-emerges to face the world. For 50 percent of the average working day he *appears* to do absolutely nothing. But, as this kind of down time shows, appearances can be deceptive; Trump is highly productive – apparently he makes and receives over 1,000 phone calls a week. Each lasts an average of 20 to 30 seconds, providing concise, accurate and effective management of his vast billion-dollar business empire.

Over the years my motorcycle racing and engine-tuning pursuits have become ever more important to me. I find the time I spend hack-sawing, argon-arc welding, metal-bashing and generally working my hands in steel is a tremendously beneficial distraction for the left side of my brain. I spend lots of quality time at my workbench, blue-printing and tuning engines, then further hours testing them on a dynamometer to see precisely how I can squeeze out that elusive extra brake-horse power – or two. People often ask me how I manage to spend so much time on my hobby. The truth is that I make time because I know it's fundamental to my sanity, creativity and overall well being. I fit the hours in early morning, late evening and weekends, in among all the other activities of family, social and business life – like you do and like you have to!

!!! Alan Turing often wrote about the times he spent in solitude, particularly at Grantchester Meadows, a stone's throw from Cambridge, eating strawberries with cream and watching daisies grow and kingfishers dive. It was in times like these that he came up with his *world-changing ideas* and undertook the labor of seeing them through, constructing and writing his brilliant thesis.

KEY – NINE TO FIVE TREADMILL OR FIVE TO NINE WINDMILL:

For years I've been working five to nine and it pays dividends. This is what I do: I rise at 5 a.m. every day including weekends, when everything is quiet and I practice my Silence, Stillness and Solitude. W. Clement Stone used to call this time Study, Thinking and Planning time. I gaze out of my patio window, create plans at a subconscious level by inserting *Bespoke Input,* listen to my mind, meditate, visualize, slip into Alpha state and let it *happen.* At this time of the morning I am at my most creative and can also get *staggering* swathes of work done. Then at 9 a.m. the phones start to go crazy and there's no peace for the wicked. However, the day unfolds according to that early morning *Bespoke Input* – which puts me, Top Biz Guru, firmly in control.

Noise Kills Genius!

KEY – ENJOY A WALK IN THE PARK:

Come wind, rain or snow, give the biocomputer time to compose itself and *compute* its Eurekas! Go feed the ducks, stroll through the park for 20 minutes or better still, 3 or 4 hours. Don't take your worries with you, but at the same time don't try to force the problem out of your mind. As Eastern philosophy observes: *If you try not to think about the monkey, you won't be able to think about anything else but the monkey.* You may want to replace the word monkey with *money!*

If you find it too difficult to avoid thinking about the goal you're trying to achieve, maybe you're waiting impatiently for *output* that's not yet due. To find out if that's the problem, ask yourself two questions:

- Am I programming correctly?

- If not, why not?

The first question can be answered easily. Have you set absolutely specific goals, just out of reach but not out of sight? Are they what you really want and are you applying ***Basic Visual InAdvance*** intently, subjectively, with yourself in every picture? Are you also programming in as many ways as you can consciously think of, as to how you will actually achieve these goals?

I have never said any of this is *easy*. To create code within a biocomputer – where the *computing* faculty may have lain dormant for 10, 20 or even 30 years is *not* easy. It takes courage, concentration and a willingness to continue despite seemingly slow progress and insubstantial images.

The second question is harder to answer; but no less important. Turn back the pages and read again; think about how seriously you want success and face up to the not-inconsequential amount of *mind power work* that *must be done* in order to achieve it. This codebook negates every single excuse and alibi for not doing the required *mind power work*. You are already finding time to study the principles – now you must make time to *act on them* and work hard to discover your own *keys*. Only when you've programmed correctly according to the principles in this codebook can you expect – indeed, demand – *Colossus Output* from your biocomputer.

KEY – ASK FOR OUTPUT:

In your *Gestation & Computation* period, especially when in transition from solely left-brained thinking into creative right-brain endeavors, you will begin asking, probably a little impatiently, "Well, just where is the *Colossus Output?*" This isn't a bad thing; it actually means you've taken on board the fact that having deliberately *programmed* for specific outcomes, you can expect *Colossus Output* to assist in accomplishing your goals. When you've got to the stage of asking where the *output* is, it's just a matter of time, tweaking your own *Bespoke Input* and using as *many* keys as it takes, before the unlocking process begins and the creative ideas, solutions to problems and Eurekas! start to flow.

KEY – AN ANTIDOTE FOR FRUSTRATION:

Over the years I have had my fair share of depressed walks in the forests, parks and beaches of the world. Many times I've sat alone, frustrated with failing businesses and my lack of resources and wondering why the world and his brother seemed to be conspiring against me. But in these situations it was *never* the world that was to blame, or his brother for that matter; it was *me* not controlling my own mind, *me* not diligently setting goals, even small ones, *me* not tirelessly and relentlessly inserting programs in **Basic Visual InAdvance.** Every single time I got to grips with *myself,* my *own* mind, circumstances in my life – in the real world – started to turn around astonishingly quickly. The starting point is invariably the same: you too will need to get to grips with your own biocomputer by setting goals, even *tiny* ones to begin with, and *visualizing* successful outcomes for them. There isn't a more powerful antidote for frustration! In actual fact there is no alternative! None!

Dwell on the fact that if you are frustrated with life it is probably *highly* likely that you haven't installed the *correct* biocomputer software for the tasks and goals you have set yourself. In actual fact you are probably trying to accomplish goals on *totally inappropriate* software. It's no good trying to become a millionaire or film star or best-selling author on the: *I can ride a bicycle, drive a car, sew, polish windows, count to 1,000, speak English, repeat the alphabet, I'm an accountant, I've graduated or I have an MBA,* or any of the thousands of other programs you already have inserted in your biocomputer for other tasks. I am suggesting that when you set *specific goals*, whatever they are, large or small, you will need absolutely *specific programs* for them too – if you are going to accomplish them in the real world.

!!! Once you have discovered your *key* or *keys* - you really will begin to the live the dream – your dream!

KEY – LOCK UP THE LEFT SIDE OF YOUR BRAIN:

I am hoping, by now, you are getting a good feel for your biocomputer. By that I mean I hope you are getting attuned to it and becoming more aware of the internal dialogue, *Gestation & Computation, Colossus Output* and the *small still voice,* in all its varying guises. I yearn for you to start using the vocabulary of these concepts, for in doing so you will grow continually more attuned to what is going on in your billion-dollar neck-top computer.

Take pains to develop an understanding of the dynamite potential you are unleashing with the aid of intelligent programming in ***Basic Visual InAdvance.*** Experiment with what locks up the intrusive left side of the brain when need be. It might be loud pop music, classical music, jogging, making love, swimming, horse riding, chanting, hard physical labor, driving fast, walking briskly through countryside. For everyone it is different, but the end result is the same; the more you can silence the incessant left-brain chatter (*Enigma Output*) at will, the more likely the right side of your brain will come through loud and clear. Stop the internal dialogue and hear the Eurekas!

KEY - EXCITING THINGS WILL HAPPEN - NOT!

Over 30 years ago I read in a self-help book that *something exciting is about to happen.* Hooray! I thought, what great news, I could hardly contain myself – seriously! 30 years on I can reliably inform you that absolutely *nothing* exciting is going to happen *until* you get to grips with your biocomputer and start programming it for success. Maybe, this is the point where you start to overcome apathy, and therefore precisely this moment in time – look at your watch – constitutes the most important tool relating directly to your success and happiness. Maybe only now the time has come for you to stop being *oblivious* to your biocomputer, stop pretending it doesn't exist, stop ignoring it and stop abusing it – and start using it!

Maybe this is the turning point, when you truly realize this really is the first day of the rest of your life, and how different it is going to be from here on in. Maybe this is the place where you start giving serious attention to your biocomputer, affording it the time, devotion, respect and *detailed bespoke programming* it deserves. Maybe this paragraph is *illumination* for you – maybe it is *one* of *your* keys! If so, now is the time to *turn* it.

Hot Tip! Make something happen – program your biocomputer, NOW!

KEY – DECODE YOUR INNER VOICE:

By studying this codebook you will start to get ideas on how to move forward in life. You can't do this without change, and you'll need to listen to just *what* your *small still voice* is urging you to change.

A few months ago, a client came to me for help; she had spent the past year miserably failing to get her Internet-based business off the ground. She'd spent much of the time staring blankly at her computer screen, wondering how to attract website hits and customers. As her efforts yielded precisely nothing, she began trying to *decode* her inner voice; she asked me to help her figure out what it was saying.

When I asked her to describe her feelings and thoughts I was amazed because she articulated everything so well. How did she not know what to do? It was because she wasn't decoding her inner voice properly, and therefore failing to act on its instructions. Sara told me she was getting the *feeling* she wasn't cut out for sitting in an office all day long, staring at a computer screen, wondering incessantly whether business was coming or not. In actual fact she hated it! She felt the potential for creating a big success with an Internet-based business was incredibly exciting, and could see the big vision, but *virtual business* just wasn't her. Sara was a *people person* who enjoyed talking to folk on the phone or meeting them face-to-face. During the isolation of remote working, every sinew in her body and every cell in her cranium screamed at her to get out and interact with walking, talking, living customers. Clicking a mouse to make money, however much, was for her a claustrophobic, depressing way to pass the days.

Once we had figured that out – decoded her inner voice, it was simply a matter of Sara deciding exactly *what* to sell and getting out there and selling it. Having escaped from her four walls, within 8 weeks she had earned more money than in the previous 52. Her depression lifted, her creativity clicked in and her biocomputer was now showing her numerous ways to generate even more leads, set up appointments and close sales. *Colossus Output* for Sara had arrived!

SCIENTIFIC KEYS

The most recent estimate of the brain's potential, in terms of numbers of connections or *thoughts* it can set up is: 1,000,000,000,000,000,000,000,000,000,000,0 00,000,000,000,000,000,000,000...

Now continue this line of 0s for another 9.8 *miles*, give or take a googol or two. I'm not talking about Stephen Hawking, Albert Einstein, Alan Turing or Ron Holland – this is you; and again I reiterate the only way you can take advantage of your brain's immense power is to utilize it like a computer. I would like to suggest that ideas or thoughts that have significant meaning (Eurekas!) are words and pictures coming out in the right sequence, i.e. *Colossus Output*. With these astronomical numbers involved, the only way *Colossus Output* is ever likely to happen, is if that arrangement is generated by subconscious computerized labor. The brain boggles the mind – or is it the other way round!

KEY – RESTORE YOUR BIOCOMPUTER
TO A PREVIOUS DATE:

If you are having trouble unlocking your biocomputer to translate *Enigma Output* into *Colossus Output*, try going back to a point in your life, or *number* of points where you were having success or *feeling* successful and try to replicate exactly what you were doing with your life and mind to enable it to produce *Colossus Output,* even on a small scale.

When doing an analysis of past successes you need to look at *every* aspect of your life – including things that may appear to be insignificant – and not just the handful listed here:

- Where were you living when you were successful?
- Did you have a partner, friend or colleague who you were having stimulating conversations with?
- Were you drinking more or less alcohol than you are currently?
- Did you have goals?
- Did you reach your goals and forget to set new ones?
- Did you have a better sex life?
- Has your diet changed considerably, or even a little?
- Were you taking any prescription or illegal drugs?
- Is your business thriving now; was it when you were successful?
- Has your bank manager changed?
- Has your business changed in any way?
- Have you had a career change?
- Were you more or less aggressive?
- Are you sleeping more or less?
- Are you watching more or less television?
- Were you carrying more or less weight?
- Were you listening to different music then or none at all?
- Was your environment quieter or noisier?
- Were you taking more or fewer vacations?
- Have you lost your vision, drive, chutzpah, independence, goal-setting ability, sense of humor, ability to take risks?

You need to complete a detailed analysis, over the period of a number of clear-thinking – dare I say – booze-free days. Leave no stone unturned and probe right to the bottom of what was *booting up* your biocomputer at the time of past successes – then replicate all the things needed to spring you back into success mode. Restore your biocomputer to a previous date!

CRACK THE CODE!

❖ *Gestation & Computation* periods vary. Don't expect your Eurekas! to fit pre-defined time frames.

❖ Don't fret while awaiting *Colossus Output* – relax or work on something else.

❖ Down time isn't a guilty pleasure - it's a creative and essential tool.

❖ Both relaxation and perspiration bring inspiration – work hard and play hard.

❖ Visualization and programming get easier *and* more effective with practice.

❖ Check that you've *inputted* properly. Reprogram with ***Basic Visual InAdvance.***

❖ Run a check-list to make sure that you really are due *Colossus Output*. Have you been programming based on the *keys* in this codebook? Are you allowing for sufficient *Gestation & Computation* time?

❖ Procrastination is the thief of time. Don't delay - start today.

❖ Don't get hooked on the promises and opinions of others. Enjoy independence of thought and action and enjoy your own mind.

❖ If you're having trouble generating *Colossus Output,* try restoring your biocomputer to a previous date when it *was* functioning effectively.

THE FIFTH KEY

COLOSSUS OUTPUT

A single good idea is as much use as a single brick.

- Ron G Holland

Enigma: For me, the steps along the yellow brick road to generating great ideas, solutions and Eurekas! have always been:

1) Input: research, brainstorming, visualization, exploratory work, mastery of the subject.

2) Gestation: relaxation, downtime, letting go, assimilation, computerized labor, switching to other projects, simmering, processing.

3) Illumination: at first glimpse this would appear to be a single major solution, but the truth is, when you delve deeply into *Colossus Output,* you discover that *Output* comes in many guises, some of which is so subtle, that it is often missed.

The Enigma is that most people know these three important steps - but still find it practically impossible to create big ideas, Eurekas! and meaningful results.

Eureka! This codebook concerns itself not with just creating a Big Idea, Killer App or Eureka!, but even more *importantly*, creating the thousands of ideas and solutions (or however many as it takes), that are necessary to bring a Big Idea into tangible reality. The goal is to create *Colossus Output*, which could include many small ideas, Ahas, hunches, epiphanies, solutions and, of course, Eurekas! *One* good idea is as much use as single brick – unless of course it is the *final* piece of the *jigsaw* puzzle; as when Edison had 10,000 ideas for his electric light bulb, but it was the 10,001st idea that solved the problem – now that was a good idea! As Sheila Johnson, A.J.Rowling, Thomas Edison, Ron Holland, Tony Sale and Alan Turing along with countless others have discovered, the secret is to keep the great ideas and solutions coming – until your mission is accomplished. Then set new goals!

Many people are oblivious to the fact that they even have *output;* let alone the fact that *output* can be dramatically enhanced – changed from *Enigma Output* to *Colossus Output* – through *bespoke programming.* Most people try to function with the *Enigma Output* they get; this codebook is about realizing that you can do a whole lot better.

In this chapter, we'll explore the different types of output – *Enigma Output, Colossus Output*, and everything in between. I'll also introduce a wide variety of different *keys* that could help you generate *Colossus Output* on a regular basis to solve your problems and get you to where you would like to be.

OTHER TYPES OF OUTPUT YOU CAN ATTAIN IN ADDITION TO EUREKAS!

Because of the importance of all types of *output,* in addition to Eurekas! let's examine some other types of *output* – including negative and positive thoughts, habits, dreams, internal dialogue and reactive output.

NEGATIVE THOUGHTS:

Over 30 years ago when my life was a chocolate mess, I had all sorts of negative thoughts welling up in my cranium, awake and asleep. I discovered a methodology for conquering those demons and I'll pass it on to you: I began to turn those negative thoughts into the most outrageous scenarios I could imagine – completely ridiculous yet also humorous.

Say, for instance I was worried about a particular creditor who was hounding me about some paint I hadn't paid for. I would visualize the worst possible thing he could do to me - standing me up against a wall and having me shot at dawn by a firing squad. But at the moment the guns opened fire, instead of bullets, paint would spurt from the barrels, spraying everyone, my creditor included, in a rainbow of colors. Alternatively, I'd see my creditor hurling me from the top of a 30-story building, but instead of smashing to my death I'd land on top of a policeman who'd chase me down the road until his trousers fell down around his ankles. If the creditor put me on a medieval torture rack I'd simply stretch so tall I'd be unable to enter his office to pay the debt. These surreal worst-case scenarios, full of riotous slapstick, soon banished my worries. By asking myself, "What's the worst that can happen?" I soon realized, "Not very much."

I'd then use the *same* creative process to build *positive* scenarios about negotiating with my creditor, keeping him as a friend and supplier and paying him off – albeit slowly. Making a negative situation farcical takes the pain out it and gives you back control of your thought processes. I employed this methodology for a short period of time to get me through a particularly bad patch.

Hot Tip! The more you use the principles in this codebook – meditation, visualization, inputting of all types, halting the internal dialogue, specific and detailed goal setting – the more you will notice a *dramatic* swing from negative to positive thoughts, and from *Enigma Output* to *Colossus Output*.

HABITS:

Habits form a major part of your *output* and although you may not recognize it as such, it is illuminating to realize that our habits stem from our *programmed input,* especially from the formative years of our youth. Habits like cleanliness, thrift and manners, for example, are the result of your parents repeating injunctions to you over and over again until they formed neuron chains in your biocomputer, ensuring that you carried out the habit automatically. A staggering 90 percent of what you do in a day is governed by habit – which in turn is governed by your biocomputer programs!

Tardiness / punctuality, carelessness / perfectionism, quitting / perseverance – any of these bad or good habits can be completely eradicated or dramatically improved. You can swap any bad habit by diligently *visualizing* yourself **InAdvance** performing the desired new habit over and over again until it's an integral part of your behavior. If you are persistently late for meetings you won't survive long in business; people will not rely on you. *See* yourself in your *imagination* arriving early for appointments, having a cappuccino, composing yourself and practicing your sales pitch, making sure all your necessary notes and papers are in the right order. I am often amazed by the number of people I see turn up at meetings unable to find a vital document at a crucial moment. They haven't developed the simple habit of preparation.

Learning how to create new good habits can be an awesome tool for self-development. Whether it's 14 days or 32 days or 69 days, according to whichever self-help book you read - it's not a long process to change the habits of a lifetime. For instance, you may want to *see yourself* completing all your mental exercises as matter of *habit*. This really is an exercise in creating code that creates code! You may wish to take the process one step further and, again via visualization, *see yourself* mentally practicing *all* the habits you'd like to acquire – becoming, in short, the precise person you desire to be. You can continue these mental exercises until the desired habits are part of who you are. It's possibly the greatest secret in the world – you become what you persistently and consistently *visualize!*

Many of my good business habits I learned in the real world from one of my mentors, the incredible Seamus O'Rourke. When we were business partners going to meet prospective clients, we would always arrive early and have a cup of tea and a sticky bun in a local coffee bar to brief ourselves beforehand. Often we'd travel up the night before, especially if the meeting was a long distance away. That habit of *prepping* is invaluable. From Seamus I also learned the habit of *a place for everything and everything in its place.* Then there were the habits of squarely facing up to creditors and other tough situations rather than letting things drift.

I learned about action, the habit of *buying* right as well as *selling* right and of giving more than you were paid for – going the extra mile.

Now, maybe you don't have a mentor like I had in Seamus, but the biocomputer doesn't demand it. As we've discussed, your biocomputer can't tell the difference between a real experience and a vividly imagined one. So when you examine the habits you'd like to instill in yourself, you may find it useful to ask, "What would Ron and Seamus have done?" and then vividly *imagine* that *we* are mentoring *you*!

Interesting Footnote: Start to analyze your habits and swap bad ones for good. *Recognize* that habits are a *major* part (albeit, an unnoticed part, for most people) of their general *output*. Understand that you have complete control, *through visualization,* over the process of creating the habits you desire. Remember, it's just as easy to form good habits as bad; and just as bad habits are part of your *Enigma Output*, good habits are part of *Colossus Output*.

POSITIVE THOUGHTS:

Years ago I wrote a book entitled *Escape From Where I Am*, and in it I stress that positive thinking *alone* is often not enough to help you achieve your goals. What do I mean by that? Well, I regularly meet people who say they are positive, are already thinking in pictures, yet still, frustratingly, cannot get ahead in life. Lots of people talk and even write about positive thinking but *don't really know* what it is or how to go about it! The secret is that any old positive thoughts won't work. You must create *exactly the right type* of positive thoughts and pictures – *specific* goals and objectives. These must be combined with as many of your own possible solutions for getting to your goal as you can imagine, plus a serious amount of research, *Bespoke Input* and brainstorming. The biocomputer needs all this *input* to complete its *computations* and deliver a permanent flow of usable ideas. A single idea won't deliver sustained success.

DREAMS:

Don't dismiss dreams too quickly. They can be an invaluable part of the *output* process. Scientist Friedrich August Kekule spent months trying to unravel the mystery of carbon compounds – in particular benzene, which is made up of six atoms of carbon and six atoms of hydrogen. The puzzle was to arrange the atoms so as not to violate the laws of chemical balance. Kekule spent months on this problem, inputting as much data as he could, until one night he had a dream about two serpents joined in a circle, biting each other's tails. His *correct interpretation* of the dream led to the arrangement of the carbon and hydrogen atoms, now known as the benzene ring.

In a similar fashion, molecular biologist James Watson and his partner Francis Crick asked the question, "What is the design of DNA, the chemical foundation of all life?" After years of investigation and *Bespoke Inputting,* Watson also dreamed of two snakes, in this case intertwined, and his *correct interpretation* of that dream as the double helix was accepted without the verification of a single experiment.

I personally haven't had much joy with dreams but I know others who most certainly have, including Paul McCartney who dreamed *Yesterday* – and had the wisdom to *write it down* before it was forgotten. Actually, I can remember a dream in which I ate the largest marshmallow in the world, and then woke to discover my pillow had disappeared – but that's only a joke! Just because dreams haven't played a big role in my personal success doesn't mean they won't work big time for you – they could be just the *key* you need for success.

INTERNAL DIALOGUE - OTHERWISE KNOWN AS INFERNAL DIALOGUE:

Internal dialogue is the roof brain chatter of continuous thoughts, often *Enigma Output,* which seems to be with us every waking moment. It is mostly *output* that cannot be utilized for success – so you have either to stem its debilitating flow or convert it to positive *Colossus Output.* You can stop internal dialogue by regularly practicing meditation – an art that has been revered in the East for thousands of years. In fact, Eastern philosophy has produced literally hundreds of books about this six thousand year old subject, teaching meditation and mantras and many related techniques as a way of stopping the internal dialogue. Not that it's easy; over the years I have received tens of thousands of letters from all over the world and this is the one subject people find the most difficult to master and want more advice on.

Zen is a powerful Eastern philosophy based upon non-thinking. The more you focus your mind on stopping your thoughts, the more likely you are to solve even the most intractable problems through achieving a *state of oneness* known as *Sartori* (literally no mind). *Sartori* is a brilliantly clear mental state in which minute details of every phenomenon and problem are revealed to you. I first talked about turning Zen into Yen in *Talk & Grow Rich* in 1981 and have developed the practice even further since then.

Personally, I find it impossible to *completely* stop the thoughts in my mind but I have *noticeably* decreased the frequency and intensity of those interrupting thoughts and continue to make progress in that direction. I can assure you, the more *non-thinking* I do, the more profound my thoughts become and the more success I attain. More periods of *non-thinking* proportionately equates to even more *Colossus Output,* which in turn leads to sustained success. You can *Think & Grow Rich* or you can *Non-Think & Grow Richer!*

I could leave this section on internal dialogue right here and move on – but I can't, because I am honor bound to tell you everything I know. We have now reached Crunch time, and that's Crunch with a Capital C. We have reached the part where I have to tell you that only *hard work* and *concentrated effort* will help you in your quest to stop your internal dialogue. Many times I concern myself with whether I should tell people how hard things are because I know that is not what they want to hear. But the truth is, I wish someone had articulated in my early days exactly what I had to do – tell me how tough the process was – then at least I could have got on with it.

Years ago, I got into desperate financial and relationship problems. I found one of the best forms of therapy was being alone, walking in the woods or by the river. When you start, the process of being alone and non-thinking it can be extremely uncomfortable – especially with no mobile phone or iPod! You may not enjoy your own company at first and find solitude unpalatable even for a mere five minutes, let alone an hour. A full day in the countryside enjoying nature and being away from it all may seem tortuous;

your internal dialogue may drive you mad. But over time you will come to appreciate that silence really is golden – like I did, despite myself.

This codebook is all about creating useable *output* from the mind, self-talk that takes us forward, not holds us back. I revealed a major secret regarding how to do this in 1981, when my international bestseller *Talk & Grow Rich* was first published. In the first chapter entitled *The Principle of Power* I disclosed the $$$ formula, Silence, Stillness and Solitude, and explain in great detail how to stop the internal dialogue. The secret begins with finding your own method of meditating. Meditation can happen either motionless or moving, and freeing the mind doesn't always mean stilling the body. So while some people meditate sitting cross-legged in front of a candle, others find swimming, jogging, cycling, gardening or even scraping off wallpaper does the trick. Mountains of scientific research have proven that *regular* meditation begins to synchronize the two halves of your dualistic biocomputer to create a perfect balance – allowing *computation* to take place and enabling you to access the stupendous biocomputer effect. You will feel less separate, feel more connected and anxiety will fall away. When you are in a meditative state, negative self-talk evaporates and the flow of mental energy is reversed. Through calm, healing thoughts, literally trillions of neuronal connections begin to establish themselves. Taking up regular meditation is sure-fire formula for attaining Alpha state!

There is no *one-size-fits-all* approach to meditation. You can always combine your methods, using the candle-flame one day, a physical activity the next, lying in a hot tub with Beethoven the next. English poet Samuel Coleridge, mused about *the hooks and eyes of the imagination* and you will actually feel them joining together when you take on board this success philosophy – not just in words, but also in spirit and *particularly* in action. Whatever works for you, go with it, but the *key* is to meditate on a *regular* basis. Stop the internal dialogue and you can hear the Eurekas! Go to www.eureka-enigma.com and download your *free* copy of *The Principle of Power* and the amazing $$$ formula.

!!! Ideas and solutions come when you are not thinking!

REACTIVE OUTPUT:

Most business people and entrepreneurs, especially those involved in start-ups as opposed to mature businesses, constantly find themselves under enormous pressure. This can result from trying to raise funding; trying to instigate a marketing campaign that actually works and returns a profit instead of gobbling up money; trying to engineer a prototype product that functions properly and ticks all the boxes – or any number of stressors in the life of every start-up entrepreneur. This is real business at the coalface and many times the financial horizon is literally only months, sometimes weeks, even days away. Fifty percent of businesses *don't* solve their problems quickly enough and fail within five years of opening their doors. This is *the* acid test of ingenuity and creativity that exists on a day-to-day basis, in real time.

Reactive entrepreneurs are driven by circumstance and have to react daily to employees, banks, creditors, customers and engage in regular firefighting – crisis management – all of which has a devastating impact on their thinking. With such short time frames to work within, the necessity of focusing on sales and the myriad of other decisions an entrepreneur has to make, reactive entrepreneurs can't possibly have time to allow the biocomputer to assimilate properly – and that means that they never get ahead, never have time for generating the *Colossus Output* that is necessary to propel their business to the next level. They start each day as if the previous one never happened – doing everything they can just to keep the business afloat.

All of this *reactive* thinking leads to non-profitable, struggling companies that are unwittingly using their entire *cashflow* just to survive. Treading on molasses everyday is not exactly the best way to ensure that the biocomputer functions effectively.

Tip! Entrepreneurs who do make their businesses work are usually the rare breed that can step outside themselves and get ultra-imaginative; they have learned how to unlock their creative genius. They apply this creativity to fundraising, marketing, and every other aspect of their work – coming up with literally hundreds of ideas and solutions every day; and all the *keys* for doing *just that* are in this codebook!

COLOSSUS OUTPUT, INCLUDING EUREKAS!

EUREKAS!

How big does an idea have to be before it's classed as a Eureka!? Most people think in terms of the Big Idea, the one that will make them a million; but the truth is that when big ideas come, it is often the small, supporting ideas that go on to facilitate real world success. Those supporting ideas might include solutions for raising seed money, paying for patents, finding a warehouse, locating a cheap office or manufacturing unit or even producing the prototype of an invention. That's why this codebook is focused on creating an abundance of smaller usable solutions that will allow you to keep driving projects forward - supporting your Big Ideas.

OUTPUT TRIGGERED BY A PRECIPITATE EVENT:

This is the classical Archimedes type of Eureka! and I begin with it first not because it is the most popular or regular method of receiving output, far from it, but because it is so classic. Archimedes wrestled with the problem of how to measure irregularly shaped objects but when his bath water overflowed as he lowered himself into it, he not only came up with a solution to his problem, but probably started the whole Eureka! industry. Gutenberg spotted a press at his local wine festival and went on to develop the printing press and Darwin read a totally unrelated book that perchance contained the *key* to his puzzle that allowed him to formulate his theory of evolution.

I have had a small number of these events transform my life's work on various occasions, but the trouble is with genuine *precipitate* events is that they can take weeks, months or even years to appear, if at all. This type of Eureka! tends to be world-changing, often a major breakthrough and is usually the culmination of an inordinate amount of work, deliberation and research and tends to be very rare. Most people are extremely lucky to get one of these in a lifetime, after all, you never heard of Archimedes', Gutenberg's or Darwin's *second* Eureka! and I am sure that if they actually had one, the history books would have captured it.

EVOLUTIONARY OUTPUT:

"If I have seen further, it is by standing on the shoulders of giants."
— *Isaac Newton*

In the course of progress, people make other people's inventions, business ideas and products better and better. Like one of history's most influential physicists, Isaac Newton, most inventors and entrepreneurs *stand on the shoulders* of inventors and entrepreneurs who have come before them.

Evolutionary output is the *output* you get as you see things in the real world and get ideas for improving on them. It's exactly how the Internet has evolved so quickly – everybody jumped on the bandwagon and just started making it better, faster and more fun. It's like *compounding output,* every time you see something, you get an idea and implement it, which gives someone else an idea - and it just takes off.

If you examine early bicycles, airplanes and cars you will discover many iterations of each, to see where they are now. Can you use your imagination, ***Basic Visual InAdvance,*** to see where they will be in say ten, twenty or fifty years – I can assure you that there are ordinary people and entrepreneurs as well as inventors and innovators working on all these exciting projects, developing the *future,* as we speak. The next generation of products and the generation after that will be awesome! Last week I had the privilege of testing the latest generation of bicycle and due to an incredible transmission system that offers in excess of 200 percent more power - or conversely 50 percent less effort – to the wheel, it can propel you along at twice the speed or using only half the energy! Evolution can be slow or rapid, depending on how hard you drive it. You can use your creativity by taking an existing product or industry and transform, modernize or revolutionize it. Many times you can take ideas from existing products in a given industry, then add your own ideas, creativity and then combine other ideas from a totally different industry. Mix it up, let the biocomputer complete its computerized labor and see what evolves – maybe a revolutionary toaster, a self-cleaning oven that actually works, an eco-friendly transporter, an anti-flood device or an electric motorcycle – God forbid!

PROACTIVE OUTPUT:

For those who undertake creative development work, such as writing a book, you can see that by diligently working on a project you can attract various types of *Colossus Output*. For instance, in the writing of this codebook, by *regularly* visualizing, brainstorming and using as many *Bespoke Inputting* methods as appropriate, I generated a *mountainous* volume of ideas, hunches, promptings and occasional Eurekas! I find this methodology *extremely* reliable. If you study proactive artists and writers and others who are involved in creative development work you will often see that they have all the time in the world – they're not driven by making money or any other goal other than producing the best possible end result – be it a brilliant painting, symphony, novel, opera or scientific treatise. They make sure their circumstances are conducive to the flowing of ideas. Rich or poor, intentionally or accidentally, the artist or author has placed himself *and* his biocomputer in such a position that he can go about in his work, completely in control, *proactively* extracting the most from his *output*.

EMERGENCY OUTPUT:

Some *Colossus Output* happens immediately with absolutely no time for conscious thought. Racing drivers, downhill skiers, and people finding themselves in an emergency situation with only split seconds to act recognize this phenomenon. Racing drivers who are used to driving fast have usually served an apprenticeship, learning their craft, honing their skills on Go-Kart tracks before they try NASCAR or Formula One; downhill skiers start on *easy beginners slopes* long before they become fully-fledged professionals.

Once a racing driver or downhill skier has honed his craft, and sufficient neuronal passageways have been created, the biocomputer can operate with remarkable speed when called upon, and deliver *output* in fractions of a split second. If Lewis Hamilton or the latest NASCAR whiz is taking a corner at 180 mph and witnesses and incident in front, what happens? In the driver's perception the events are slowed down, (in actuality, the brain speeds up) allowing him more time to see his way clearly through the obstacles and get his vehicle safely back on course. There is a sense for these highly skilled individuals of *being in the zone*. They have, through long experience, *inputted* their biocomputers to cope with the contingencies inherent in driving at break-neck speeds in a competitive situation.

Lindsey Vonn, the U.S. born World Cup champion skier, hurtling over the piste at 80 mph is also *in the zone,* running on a *ski-racing* program that she's inserted over many years. To be in the zone means lightning-fast brain-to-body responses, with no conscious thought in the middle. Any attempt to *think about* what to do would mean the loss of a millisecond, and maybe loss of life.

NASCAR drivers and champion skiers are gifted experts in their field, and their ability to see events happen in slow motion actually enables them to respond more quickly. But this ability is not confined to specialists; have you noticed how people involved in accidents – freak storms, tornadoes or fires say – often recount their survival in terms of events occurring in slow motion, "The wall of water coming towards me seemed to take forever, though I'm told it was only a few seconds." The biocomputer speeds up, switches to auto-program – inputting, processing and delivering instant output for survival in the blink of an eye – sometimes even quicker!

In emergency situations, many ordinary citizens find they can act correctly, literally without thinking or even having time to think, as the emergency unfolds before their very eyes, and they often emerge as heroes. Certainly in my lifetime I have had a couple of nasty, close-to-death experiences, concerning fires and walls crashing down, whereby instantaneously I knew what to do and luckily saved lives. On *numerous* occasions, in very high-speed car and motorcycle incidents I have certainly had everything appear in slow motion – that allowed me to steer unscathed around the possibility of untimely death.

Ron Holland's Output:

The salient point of all my Eureka! experiences is this: most of my ideas are small, but by bundling them together you have, in my case, a complete book, a successful fundraising or an ongoing PR campaign – or all three working in synergy. Ideas can come at any time and won't necessarily be related to the project you are working on. The more you *use* the *output,* the more likely you are to connect the un-connectable. If I am getting *insufficient* output for a book, fundraising or successful conclusion to any project, I take it as a wake-up call that I am not devoting sufficient quality time to detailed *Bespoke Input* in **Basic Visual In Advance** for that particular project – it just means I have to focus more! And I do!

Hot Tip! Some of the *purest*, often life saving, *Colossus Output* comes in emergency situations when the biocomputer has absolutely *no time* whatsoever to be contaminated by conscious thought.

RON HOLLAND'S PERSONAL EXPERIENCE

- I can't express to you how *bad* it was during the *wilderness years* when my mind wasn't functioning like a computer and I received little or no *output*. I wanted to hide under a rock! I suffered depression, frustration, desperation, anger, poverty, hardship and humiliation – perhaps things that you are experiencing right now.

- I can't adequately describe to you how *hard* it is to discover and apply sufficient *keys* to actually turn **OFF** the *Enigma Output* and turn **ON** the *Colossus Output*. It does require effort, diligence, patience and persistence. Talk about jumping through hoops of fire! But I did it – and so can you!

- I can't describe to you how blissful the feeling is, to have a biocomputer that is functioning efficiently – I relish everything that goes with it; joie de vivre, abundance, laughter, success, wealth, health, happiness and a stress-free existence. I want to shout Eureka! from the rooftops – and I do! Eureka!

MORE KEYS!

Now that we understand the different types of *output,* we can look at different *keys* for generating the kind of *Colossus Output* that will help you achieve your goals. Remember, not every *key* will work for you, but you have to try them all to see!

KEY – DIFFERENTIATE BETWEEN IDEAS AND SOLUTIONS:

What exactly is the difference between ideas and solutions? Does it really matter? After delving into the core of what I consider to be a very serious conundrum, and thinking about it for extremely long periods of time I have begun to realize that not all thoughts are the same and not all ideas are useful. I have also come to realize the immense difference between ideas and solutions. The difference is chalk and cheese!

The majority of us have this never-ending stream of internal dialogue – our stream of consciousness. Out of that stream, we may get one or two good ideas. A few of us get so many ideas that none of them actually get implemented in the real world and converted into cash or other tangible results or assets.

The difficulty in differentiating between ideas and solutions is that they both stream out of the same biocomputer, sometimes at an unabated rate, so fast in fact that we often don't have time to really analyze what is going on. Let's take a closer look at the difference…

An idea could be a concept or image, an indefinite or vague impression or opinion. An idea could be a million-dollar Eureka! or a plain bad idea. Ideas can be unformulated and often come about by just daydreaming or casually letting the mind freewheel – with no specific goal in mind. Some ideas can also be so big and unwieldy that no person alive could ever bring them to fruition. Ideas come and go by the dozen, sometimes without us making any request for them whatsoever!

A solution is an answer to a problem or mystery. Solutions are totally different from plain ideas because they come as a *direct response* to specific problems. I suggest that for every Big Idea, you will probably need thousands of practical *solutions* to turn it into tangible reality. This really is a *key* and it will pay dividends to think about your own stream of consciousness as it arrives - and carefully separate the stream into ideas and solutions!

There is no such thing as a successful Big Idea that isn't followed by literally thousands of solutions. Many people I meet tell me they have many ideas yet nothing happens in their lives. Occasionally I meet others who do manage to turn their ideas into reality. I speak from personal experience when I say have turned many of my ideas into reality and have become acutely aware, over the years, of my own stream of consciousness, particularly pertaining to how I have been able to create success for myself and others.

When I get an idea I do everything conceivably possible to turn it into tangible reality in the real world. For a business idea I may immediately register a domain or corporation name and get letterheads printed. If I get an idea for a book I will instantly create a file in my filing cabinet and on my computer to place all the research and *Colossus Output*.

To create solutions to specific problems and for certain projects I diligently start to visualize, using **Basic Visual InAdvance**, every single aspect of the problem I am trying to solve or the project I am trying to actualize. If it's a business venture, I *see* in my imagination how I will create the funding, products and marketing. If I am trying to generate solutions for a book project I will deliberately go about programming my biocomputer with generous portions of *Bespoke Input* pertaining to the subject in question.

Very Hot Tip! I receive *many* usable solutions – Eurekas! on Demand – because I *visualize InAdvance* with laser-beam focus, on *specific* projects and *specific* problems.

KEY – COLOSSUS OUTPUT COMES WHEN YOU LEAST EXPECT IT:

When you go out on the town, don't assume *Colossus Output* is out of the question. The buzz of a restaurant, concert, disco, gallery or evening at the theatre can cause files in your biocomputer to merge and cross-refer, sometimes with startling effects. Simply being among different people, décor, music, sights, sounds and aromas can set your mind racing at an entirely new tempo. The biocomputer makes literally trillions upon trillions of involuntary connections; you see things from new angles.

A classic example of this is the true World War II story of the Bouncing Bomb, immortalized in the movie *The Dam Busters*. Richard Todd's RAF character has been racking his brains over how to deliver the bombs right against the walls of the Ruhr and Oder dams, in order to smash Nazi industrial productivity. He travels to London and during an evening at the theatre, becomes transfixed by the movement of two spotlights focusing on the Bluebell girls. When the spotlights merge into a single pool of light on stage, his fascination transforms into a brilliant idea: that bringing two powerful search lights positioned one at each end of the aircraft would in the same way enable the bomber crews to pinpoint their targets with a deadly accuracy – it would allow the plane to fly, by means of triangulation, at exactly at the precise height, for dropping the bombs.

The way this scene is portrayed says everything about how *Bespoke Input* and *Gestation & Computation* generate *Colossus Output* at the most unexpected moments. Todd has been involved on all the research and development work with Barnes Wallis, the inventor of the bomb, grappled with the problem of delivery, and now taken his *Gestation & Computation* time. And in typical biocomputer flair, it is the computerized labor – *trillions of computations* – that provides *Colossus Output*. Todd knows there's *something* vital about the way the spotlights interact, but the *significance* comes in a flash – a split second of mental revelation. So if you're going for a night out, be receptive to *Colossus Output*.

KEY – HAVE A PROJECT OR SUFFER THE CONSEQUENCES:

Actively working on a project is fundamental to creating breakthrough thinking, mind-blowing Eurekas! and solutions to major problems. Back in the fifteenth century Johannes Gutenberg, a German metal worker, decided to mass-produce books, in particular the bible. His big problem, one he really struggled with over a long period of time, was how to create a plate with type on it and then how to create enough pressure on that plate to imprint repeatedly.

The fact that Gutenberg was diligently working on the project allowed him, though a process of trial and error, to create a plate with movable type on it – an idea he transferred from stamps and seals that were in use in that era. But the big problem of getting enough pressure onto the plate to allow for quick repeated printing still eluded him.

One day, to take a break from his toils, Gutenberg decided to attend the wine festival in a nearby town. Among all the intoxicated revelers tasting a great selection of wines, bread, nuts, olives and other foods and a cacophony of excited conversations, Gutenberg spotted a wine press squeezing the juice from grapes – immediately a Eureka! struck him like a bolt of lightning; he could use a similar process to imprint his pages!

Hot Tip! The type of Eureka! that is triggered by a precipitate event can be the hardest to generate because you never know what experience can fire the trigger. What we do know is these Eurekas! only come to those working on projects. Of all the thousands of people attending the wine festival over 500 years ago, no other revelers suddenly came up with the idea that a wine press could be used as a printing press. Gutenberg was working on the project, so Gutenberg got the idea!

KEY - PROACTIVELY CREATE YOUR OWN PRECIPITATE EVENT:

The kind of precipitate event that gave Gutenberg the solution he needed to build his printing press doesn't come along very often. If you rely on those kinds of events, your Eureka! moments will be few and far between. But you can proactively create an environment in which you generate *Colossus Output* on a regular basis. Create your own precipitate event by busily getting into action.

I spend lots of time tinkering with extremely fast motorcycles. These motorcycles are not necessarily fast to begin with but the whole idea in my sport, sprinting, is to make them as fast as you can – particularly the acceleration from a standing start. In creating these machines, practically every single part of the engine, gearbox, fuel system, ignition and all the rolling chassis parts have to be modified or entirely re-made for optimum performance – in most cases these modifications really can be quite radical.

I start by carefully *visualizing* the component I'm trying to modify or manufacture and then maybe even reduce that *vision* to something on the drawing board. Then I start to cut, machine and weld and maybe even fix the newly made noggin to the machine or engine. I step back, and I can often see it's not quite right – maybe it's not aesthetically pleasing or something rubs, grinds or gets in the way that I hadn't anticipated. Many times, one of my accomplices in my crazy schemes, Rupert or Slim, will take a look and say, "If I was you I'd cut that back into a V, slot that grommet there, lengthen the noggin and slide the top bracket over that one and there you have it – perfect." Often they are right – they've created a Eureka! and I retort, "Why didn't you tell me that before I started the job and spent hours creating Frankenstein's monster?" Slim has a stock reply, one that I've heard many times, "It was only when I saw how not to do it that I came up with the idea of how to do it – but I could never have come up with my idea without seeing what you had in mind."

When trying to create a new supercharger drive tensioner or gearbox modification or an engine part I will look through catalogs, old photographs of other competitors' machines, magazine articles or even take my camera into the pits at race meetings and try to see what other racers have done before me. Many times my new component will consist of ideas and concepts from as many as ten other machines (and the biocomputers that built them) and then I will mix and match in my imagination, through my *visualizations* and let my biocomputer create my own unique part for my specific purposes.

Hot Tip! With a little imagination you can transport this story into the real world of stimulating growth in *your own* business and solving *your own* problems – or *whatever* your particular needs are. By trying, looking, asking, sharing, experimenting, being observant, studying what has gone before, you too can create Eurekas! for your own specific application.

KEY – GOOD USABLE OUTPUT IS OFTEN EASY TO MISS:

Some of your *output* may *seem* too obscure, small and incomplete to pursue. But remember, it's not only the Big Idea that will drive your success, but lots of smaller ideas and solutions, too.

For many years I had it all wrong. I was always waiting for the BIG break, the BIG idea – the BIG Eureka!, *the one* that would turn my life around and make me a million – overnight, right! It's a common delusion – there's even a television series called BIG IDEA. It took many years of research, working in the field, being an entrepreneur, conducting hundreds of seminars, listening to and interviewing hundreds of others in the same predicament and trying out numerous *keys,* before I cracked the success formula. Mind you, it was a BIG Eureka! when it did finally come – and it's this:

Most success comes as a result of thousands, if not millions of smaller ideas, sometimes a single big idea has no bearing on success whatsoever. The *key* is to listen for, capture and *act* on smaller solutions which make BIG IDEAS work, turning them into tangible reality – and cash!

Hot Tip! Duncan Bannatyne of Dragon's Den fame quipped recently, "I can't help thinking that if only young entrepreneurs would start working on a business, *any business,* and getting on with that, they would be a lot better off than trying to find a Big Idea."

!!! If Big Ideas come, great – but make up your mind to live *extremely* successfully with *a continuous stream* of smaller ones!

Hot Tip! It's fascinating to know that barren areas in America, South Africa and Australia where opulent gold deposits were found have been named *Eureka,* but it's also a fact that most of the gold mined from the earth comes out in grains, flakes and fragments, not whopping great nuggets. Whether you have a Gold Mine or a Goal Mind I can practically guarantee that the majority of your wealth that you mine from either will come out of small ideas and solutions rather than whopping great Eurekas!

Remember too that there are other types of output, besides Eurekas!, that can be helpful. Do not reject *output* just because it seems more like a tangled set of Christmas tree lights than a thousand-watt halogen beam. It may be showing you a circuitous path to success.

Remember our example of the biocomputer's *Enigma Output* in Chapter One? In a 24-hour period negative output can be overwhelming, and in the midst of it, little ideas and hunches are easy to miss. Remember our earlier example of typical *Enigma Output?* Here it is again, this time with a little glimmer of positive *Colossus Output* poking its head up through the dross:

I feel tired. I feel hungry. I feel sexy. I wonder what's for dinner tonight. How does everyone else have a credit card except me? I wonder if Fred will call me. I think I'll watch The Sopranos tonight… run an ad in the local paper advertising a new book I can write as a way to make more money – Wow was that a Eureka! I just had, one of those little ideas and hunches, nuggets of gold that get missed when they are mixed up with the base metal of my usual banal thoughts? It could have been – hey, I could write a book on Eurekas!, start my own motorcycle business, open a corner drug store, start a web TV company… (YAWNS)… *I'm so tired. I think I'll get McDonalds. What is the matter with me? I'm going home. I feel sexy. I feel tired. I feel hungry again. You're not going to believe this – I feel sexy again!*

!!! Listen for the faint whispers of shy inner voices!

KEY – EUREKAS! COME TO YOUNG AND OLD!

Turn Up, Tune In and Download. I am of course paraphrasing Dr. Timothy Leary, the 1960's counter-culture guru and advocate of LSD as the key to enlightenment. Leary also said, "Never trust anyone over the age of thirty." Indeed, young people can teach us old dudes a thing or two. They follow their hunches because they have energy, optimism, and *no fear* of failure. They don't chase that awful thing we call *security*, which, often as not is a ball and chain. Nowadays, when I'm sitting in my swish venture capital office in my tailor-made pin-stripe suit, and a young dude walks in wearing deliberately ripped jeans, sneakers and a baggy sweater with a skateboard under his arm, I immediately sniff the air. I'm not checking that he's washed – it's just I'm always on the scent for potential success, however jazzily or cool it's packaged!

Us old folks have our qualifications and our long resumes, our blue-chip investments and our *safe* pensions. We've been around the block and we know what makes sense – thanks kids. Or do we? A little learning can be a dangerous thing. In fact, by the age of 35, most of us know far too much for our own good. By this time, we already have various software programs securely installed in our biocomputers. Many of them are general in nature, we pride ourselves, for example, on having *experience* and *business acumen.* These programs remind us about the supposedly inalienable laws of profit and loss, supply and demand, the absolute necessity of capital to start any enterprise.

We are programmed to obey the code as it is written; we dare not, in fact cannot, deviate from its instructions. Yet it is precisely this sort of rigid, standardized software which can keep us on a treadmill. They are *commonsense programs,* and *commonsense* is a very questionable sort of wisdom. We assume it makes sense, but if Edison had followed its dictates he'd probably never have patented a single invention. If Leonardo da Vinci had been a commonsense guy he'd have forgotten about trying to build a hot air balloon, given up the sketches and paintings that are now worth millions, and taken a *proper job* as a mailman or shop assistant. A flippant speculation, I know, but my point is this: what we think of as solid, sensible programming is often the passive acquisition, over many years, of very limited, off-the-peg software. It is *safe option* software and, more often than not, it softens the brain. Remember, the road less traveled is usually less congested than the interstate highway. You may reach your destination faster by veering off the beaten track – and taking a lesson from the young'uns. So don't always trust the *output* that comes with maturity. The tired old bulbs that spell out *wisdom* may want replacing, with ones that spell out *risk* – and you have heard of *risk-reward* ratios – haven't you?

Hot Tip! Getting Big Idea after Big Idea is often a formula for disaster. You are frequently much better off coming up with just *One Big Idea* and then following through with hundreds and if necessary thousands of smaller ideas *and* solutions to see the *One Big Idea* through to successful conclusion.

KEY – EXPECT A DAILY STREAM OF COLOSSUS OUTPUT:

Here is your personal biocomputer forecast. There will be occasional bolts of lightning, followed by persistent long-term flashes; the general outlook is good! Expect large, turnaround Eurekas! now and again, but do remember that once your biocomputer is up and running on all eight cylinders (I love mixing up computer analogies and V8 internal combustion engines), hopefully within a short time of completing this codebook – you can expect a daily stream of profitable ideas, images, inspirations and hunches, both large and small and an equal number of solutions.

Let me give you an example of my own daily *Colossus* Output. Invariably I am working on two or three books at any one time, and for each of these I may receive between 100 and 200 hunches and solutions every day. These can vary from ideas for a whole new chapter, a fresh title, a turn of phrase, a complete (or incomplete) paragraph, a caption, an anecdote, a joke, a link, a reference, an example, choice or change of word or maybe a neologism of my own invention – coining a new word or way of describing something. In addition to the books, there will also be between 10 and 20 consultancy clients for whom I need fresh ideas, solutions and inspiration. For each of these clients I will get an average of five ideas a day – every day. That's a total of 325 ideas every single working day of the year. A lot of people don't believe me when I tell them this figure. How, they ask, do I ever get any actual work done, if I'm distracted by all these ideas every day?

The simple answer is that my ideas are my work and the *key* to my success. I'm an ideas man – this is what I do, convert those hundreds of single thoughts into tailor-made consultation material, publications and other business projects. The Eurekas! for any project are not isolated flashes. They are more like an intricate network of filaments, or an animated optical display, amounting to far more than the sum of their *visualized* parts.

!!! If you're not receiving **Colossus Output** on a regular basis – you're doing something wrong – or nothing at all!

KEY – CAPTURE OUTPUT AS IT ARRIVES:

Download your ideas before you lose them. For my books and my consultancy work, I need to capture the solutions and Eurekas!, download them onto paper and file them before they disappear out of my own head and into biocomputer cyberspace. Over the years I have tried Dictaphones, laptops, tape recorders, text on mobiles and other gadgets. However, I have always returned to good old-fashioned pen and paper. They're light, quick, fit in my pocket, don't run out of batteries or snap, crackle or pop. When an idea comes, whether I'm on a train, boat or plane, in bed or dining out with my family, I can discreetly whip out a small notebook and quickly jot down the gist of the idea, just enough to remind me of it later. I don't need Wi-Fi or wires, not even a keyboard.

Folk ask me, "Do you get Eurekas!, and good ideas all the time?" I answer, "Yes, but I *never* know when they're going to arrive." If I'm driving, I have a notebook in the glove compartment and I'll pull into a service station to take notes if need be. If I'm with my young daughter Kay in McDonalds, (an occasional treat) I'll often get a flurry of ideas, as Kay's McFlurry drips over the table, bless her! Time is of the essence with *output* and even if the idea seems half-formed or unclear, I write it down as soon as possible.

I have a series of notebooks stashed in little hiding places around my home, office and car, so I'm never caught out by a sudden Eureka! – and by definition that's what they usually are. I'd recommend you do the same; invest in a six-pack of spiral pads and place them in strategic positions throughout your home and office. Remember to stow a pen with each, and make sure it works. Otherwise, when those unexpected Eurekas! arrive, you might find yourself using a tube of lipstick or the children's crayons! And don't forget notepads for the more functional areas of the home, the workshop, garage, even the loft if you spend time up there. The washed-out pages in one of my notebooks remind me how many Eurekas! I get while taking a bath. Hey – it worked for Archimedes!

Even these days a lot of writers eschew modern mechanical means of recording their output and from start to finish of a manuscript stick resolutely to notebook and pen. Of course someone has to type it all up later, but at the creative stage of the process, authors who work in this traditional way recognize the special, direct link that handwriting makes between their mind and the ideas flowing onto the page.

There's a kind of ancient magic invoked when the human hand makes marks on paper. Incidentally, it's not for nothing that many corporations ask for handwritten applications from prospective employees; graphology is a respected art and many larger corporations have in-house specialists. There is a sense of immediacy in writing by hand, and this same uninterrupted gush of thought, consolidated instantly into the written word, is exactly what I get from transferring my Eurekas! onto paper whenever and wherever they arrive.

KEY – DISCOVER WHAT WORKS FOR YOU:

Everyone has to find their own route to generating *Colossus Output*; many times you have to go down a few dead ends before you find a path that really delivers the *Colossus Output* you require. While a beautiful environment, a garden view, a house overlooking the sea or an oak-paneled library provide inspiration for some people, in other cases it may do nothing at all for the biocomputer.

Sometimes, the charm of your surroundings becomes a distraction and the sought-after Eurekas! simply don't happen. Many a famous author has experienced this particular enigma, choosing the most minimal of workrooms over plush surroundings. Monasteries were built with the spiritual enlightenment of their interns in mind, and such buildings don't tend to be luxurious. The greatest polymath of all time, Leonardo da Vinci, who incidentally loved codes, and undoubtedly cracked his own, would stare at a blank wall for literally hours on end. You really should try this some time! This would eventually open the floodgates to a stream of Eurekas!, and he would then reverse the inertia with long and furious bouts of active creativity – producing highly intricate sketches, anatomical drawings, sculpture, inventions and famous paintings including *Mona Lisa, The Last Supper* and *Virgin with Child.*

!!! Make a point of never going straight to bed at the end of the day. Always sit quietly on a chair and relax for a few moments, to *listen* and *see* if the biocomputer has any ideas or solutions for you! It's just like checking on your e-mails – and how often do you do that?

KEY – EUREKA! CALLING:

I mentioned that my Eurekas! come in the form of a voice, usually a *small still voice* whispering an idea in my ear, though sometimes it's more of a bull-horn shouting "Do it now!" or it might be "Do nothing" or "Phone Mr. Kramer" or "Buy shares in this company" or "Put Fred Smith on the board of Newco, Inc." Whether whispered or bellowed, when it comes the voice is unmistakable. I *always* obey its instructions to the letter – immediately. Actresses have their Svengalis, poets their muses, and I have my *small still voice.*

Your Eurekas! may also come in flashes of light and voices, but there are other forms. My colleague Steve Cunningham and I have discussed this, and he laughs about my *small still voice.* But check this out: Steve's typical *Colossus Output* appears in his mind on a sheet of white A4 paper. The basic details are printed out like a lawyer's to-do list. Just like my *small still voice,* Steve's A4 Eurekas! never fail him. He, too, acts on his ideas *immediately.*

Another colleague of mine, Bob Morey, gets his *output* in words, and they frequently arrive at 3 or 4 a.m. Being a seasoned biocomputer programmer he has his pad and pen on the night table and, bleary-eyed, writes these Eurekas! down as they come. Bob's wife Liz is a talented musician and poet. As you might expect, her *output* is mainly in pictures, feelings and sensory impressions. She can convert this *output,* often very quickly, into word-based keys for songs, lyrics and verses. As long as she captures the initial images in word-based keys, she can return at a later date and build them into complete poems and songs. It's a bit like the old Pitman Script shorthand used by journalists to record interviews and events as they occur. Speed is of the essence, and the same is true of Liz's artistic inspirations – if she doesn't quickly cement them with her personal shorthand keys, then it's almost practically impossible to retrieve them at a later date.

Maybe your *output* will arrive on a post-it note, in the form of a gut feeling or picture, a computer screen, an order pad or a neon sign in Times Square. Maybe it'll be carved into Mount Rushmore or displayed across the Hollywood hills, embroidered on a pair of Levis or spelled out across the sky in a vapor trail. Or perhaps like Steve, it'll be a sheet of paper in your mind. The medium is irrelevant; it's recognizing the message and *acting* on it *immediately* that counts.

!!! Listen to and *obey* the *small still voice!*

KEY – GIVE YOUR OUTPUT A TRYOUT!

When you're starting out to crack your own code, it's hard to know if your *output* is intelligent *Colossus* material or *Enigma* garbage. If it's the former you should act on it, but how can you tell? The truth is, in your early days, you can't. The only thing you can do is take it for a spin and see if it's roadworthy.

One of my seminar delegates, Lisa, stood up and told an amazing story: by the age of 55 she had made and lost a fortune in business. After enjoying years of considerable success and wealth, she honestly admitted that she was now penniless. Her rent was overdue; she had no savings or disposable assets; and no bank would give her loans or credit. One *intangible asset* Lisa did posses, however, was *determination* – the desire to get her biocomputer up and running, to pick herself up and get back in the race. With nothing to lose, she was prepared to follow her hunches, start reprogramming her biocomputer and create a new future for herself.

First, Lisa made a list of all her skills and soon realized that many of them were marketable. She had knowledge, expertise and industry experience that she could sell. All she needed were those first vital customers to start the ball rolling. This meant advertising, so she approached the newspapers with a view to buying some space. Since she had no cash or credit cards she asked for terms on account. Alas, they weren't interested. Her credit rating was zero and it was either money up front or no advertisement. It was at this point that Lisa got a sudden, unexpected Eureka! She would ask one of the many fax-broadcasting companies (this was before the Internet and e-mail took off) to give her a fax advertisement on credit. As a newer type of medium, she figured fax-broadcasters may be more inclined to give her a chance and defer their charges until she'd earned some fees herself. The advertising wasn't exactly cheap – amounting to around $1,000 – but her biocomputer told her it was the way to go. Lisa was fully prepared to try hundreds of advertisers to get the necessary credit deal, but do you know what? The first one she approached agreed to fax her single-page broadcast to 30,000 recipients and grant her a 30-day credit period. The first part of the program had delivered successful output. Now, would it deliver that much-needed cash?

Within a few days of her fax broadcast going live Lisa had pulled in $400. Now, she could pay off 25 percent of her advertising bill and have some cash to play with – but what can you do with the $150 that was left? Maybe she should pay as much as possible off her advertising bill now. But that would still leave a shortfall of $600, due for payment in two weeks. Could she be certain further work would come in before that? Again, her biocomputer gave her the unequivocal answer – she should take the cash and use it to propel her business forward. She immediately ploughed the whole $400 into national press classified advertising. Wasn't this a little reckless? Wasn't a bird in the hand worth two in the bush? Perhaps – but what could she do with that bird? She figured it was better to go for broke and trade it for a bigger bird, preferably the goose that would lay the golden egg!

That may have been reckless if Lisa had just splashed out the money thoughtlessly. But she didn't. She *listened* to her biocomputer, programmed it for success, visualized, **INTERNALIZED** and kept faith in herself and the future. Very soon her national press advertisements were pulling in good profits. She quickly paid off her bills, recouped her investment and built a successful business. Though she hadn't been sure her original Eureka! was the winning one, she had to try it out, and this is what *you* must do. At every stage of the game, program your mind in *BasicVisual InAdvance. See* your desired outcome in the greatest detail you can imagine. That way, you won't be *taking* a gamble, you'll be *making* well informed and computerized decisions. There's a big difference!

Hot Tip! Over and above the money rolling in and satisfactorily turning Lisa's dire financial situation around, she also gained the valuable lesson of the importance of listening to even the *smallest* of ideas and hunches and *running* with them. Maybe you are *already* receiving *output* of an insignificant nature – that's not so *insignificant* after all! Once you start using *Output* it just gets better and clearer!

!!! I've kept the main point of Lisa's story for the end: it wasn't until Lisa reached her breaking point and was absolutely bust that she made a *decision* in her own mind to really start taking *mental effort* and *mind power work* seriously. That in itself enabled her to shut out everything and start *focusing* on *inner pictures* of where she wanted to go, *InAdvance.* Like I've intimated before, when you're without – you *must* practice within!

> "Lack of money is *no* obstacle. Lack of an idea *is* an obstacle."
> *Ken Hakuta*

KEY – GOOD SEX FOR GOOD OUTPUT:

Over lunch in a gastronomic restaurant in London's West End, Dr. Mohamed Arif Nun, a serious player in Malaysian business circles, introduced a number of thought-provoking ideas into the conversation. Mohamed is a talented mathematician and creative thinker and, like me, is interested in the whys and wherefores of biocomputer output. "Sex," he announced between courses, "is a driving force in the creation of mental output. Before sex, work hard programming your mind for the solutions you need. After sex, prepare yourself to receive the output. Good sex taps into the reptilian brain and all conscious thought stops. This is also good for output. In life we are *not* taught three things: how to think, how to make love and how to breathe – and all of them have a profound effect on *output*." Esoteric wisdom from the lips of a successful man cannot be ignored and may be a *key* for you.

!!! By regularly programming the biocomputer and diligently *using BasicVisual InAdvance* you become more able to spot synergies and understand fully how to take advantage of them.

KEY – CELEBRATE COLOSSUS OUTPUT:

Each time you recognize and successfully use *Colossus Output* to achieve a goal or solve a problem, celebrate the occasion. No matter how minor the *output* or the progress, marking the occasion will encourage your biocomputer to kick in more often, providing you with even more *output*. The celebration doesn't have to be over-the-top. You can light a candle, open a bottle, or take yourself out for the evening. I always make sure my biocomputer knows that I appreciate its efforts, and that I'm looking forward to more of the same.

My old friends Art and Bea Jordan told me that when they were down to their last $2, they decided to get goal-oriented and take mind programming and regular meditation seriously. Their ideas started to flood in! They had finally *booted up* their biocomputers! As the psychological tide turned in their favor, they still only had the $2, but they went out and bought some hamburgers, a few sesame seed buns, a red rose and a candle and had a celebratory feast (that was in 1963, of course, when $2 could buy more than a small coffee at Starbuck's)

!!! Art and Bea went onto make pots of money. When I had this conversation with them they were living in a coastal mansion – formerly owned by the Johnnie Walker Whisky baron – in Magnolia, Massachusetts. The dream house had a full-size organ, stunning spiral staircase, oak-paneled rooms, sparkling chandeliers and a magnificent outdoor swimming pool carved in solid granite that replenished itself each day with fresh seawater when the tide came in.

KEY – KEEP THINGS POLISHED:

Seamus O'Rourke, my early super-mentor, taught me how to make a fortune just by keeping things orderly. This was in the days of my motorcycle empire, and Seamus was a stickler for polishing bikes, sweeping up the yard and generally making everything look smart and tidy and even on empty boxes he'd write *MT* just for kicks. As he did these basic tasks, he'd generate ideas for window displays, promotions, sales drives and slashing our overheads. He never consciously sought these brain waves – they just arose as he pottered around the showroom.

I didn't realize it at the time, but Seamus had demonstrated a profound truth about the human biocomputer: turn down the volume on the left side of the brain (by engaging in hard physical work, for example) and the right side of the brain will perform prodigiously. He made me laugh one day with his unique explanation of the Second Law of Thermodynamics, "If you don't keep cleaning, repairing and improving things *all the time,* they will rapidly disintegrate." It's only in recent years that I have verified this to be true.

KEY – GO THROUGH THE MOTIONS – HOW I GOT MY FIRST ROLLS ROYCE:

Early in my career, I dreamed of owning a Rolls Royce. I concentrated very hard and used verbal affirmations for my goal. Affirmations were then in vogue for self-help, in this case, helping myself to a dream car. At the time I drove a tatty Ford Escort. I repeated my affirmations regularly. I recorded them on a tape machine, in the present tense and full of emotion, and played them for hundreds of hours in my car. Nothing happened! But I was determined to get my Roller, despite my totally inadequate financial *and* severely limited mental resources at the time. I took stock and realized it was no good just downloading the software title (*I Own a Roller*). I had to download the *actual* program, in all its vivid detail, in order to get the *output* I so desperately required. In actual fact, I *pretended* my Ford Escort was a Roller, only parking my tatty Escort if the gap was at least twenty feet, big enough for *my* Rolls Royce. Back home I'd go *through the motions* of polishing my imaginary car, lovingly burnishing every contour of the bodywork including the imaginary Spirit of Ecstasy on the imaginary Rolls radiator grill. My neighbor thought I was mad! I performed this Silver Shadow play for about three weeks. Still no *real* Roller – but the *imaginary* one was getting clearer and clearer. I could actually *see*, in my mind's eye, that I was the proud owner of a Rolls Royce. I widened the gateposts at the bottom of my drive because I knew I couldn't get a Roller safely through without scratching the sides.

Then, I had a hunch – a mini-Eureka! I phoned my PR agent, who owned a Rolls Royce. Would you believe this? He was desperate to sell it! We worked out a deal, and he even introduced me to a specialist financier who arranged a no-down loan! Eureka! – my first Rolls Royce, a bright yellow Silver Shadow with TV antenna on the trunk. I was moving up in the world – you could say I *saw* it coming, and it did!

KEY – NEVER STOP VISUALIZING *InAdvance* – HOW I LOST MY FIRST ROLLS ROYCE:

Have you ever wondered why so many cars and houses get repossessed every year? I have. And I've been on the receiving end in each case.

I obtained my first Rolls Royce by *visualizing* it in detail, by going through the motions of a Rolls Royce owner. I *acted* on a simple *idea* – which worked, so far, so good.

I had a lot of fun with that car. I showed off, dated girls, organized photo-shoots and all the other things you'd expect from a young tycoon with his first Rolls Royce. In fact, I was so wrapped up in the thing that I completely *forgot* the principles that got me the car in the first place; I forgot all about visualizing my continuing success, consolidating my business and my financial position in general. I didn't set new goals or try to increase my disposable income. I definitely didn't *visualize* making regular payments on the car and although I knew it was unwise, I didn't make *enough* mental effort to *see* good things happening for me **InAdvance.** I let the line of least resistance take its course – and failed to make crucial payments.

I could very clearly *see* it all coming down on top of me as the situation went from bad to worse. Now I started *mentally planning* escape routes, but it was too late, for once you start going down that road you automatically start to create a negative self-fulfilling prophecy. Just as I had *mentally* foreseen the Rolls Royce arriving into my life, 18 months later the *unchecked* downward mental spiral resulted in Mr. Repo Man winching up my beloved Rolls Royce and towing it away into the sunset. You could say I *saw that* coming – and it did!

!!! Now, when things go wrong – and they do *every day* when you have 10 early-stage or start-up companies all trying to raise money, I *always* mentally focus only on *positive* outcomes, *especially* if it looks like it's all going to end in a heap!

KEY – PEEL BACK THE LAYERS OF YOUR MIND:

During the times in my life when all I got from my biocomputer was *Enigma Output,* I found it very useful to relax in my special chair and imagine, just like Alan Turing used to, that I was peeling back layers of my mind, like an onion, and that I had to get *beyond* each layer to arrive at *Colossus Output.* Although, in my early days I confess I really didn't know or appreciate *exactly* what was at the core – although Turing swore there was nothing!

I would sit in my special chair and listen to the negative thoughts at each layer before discarding them. Layer two was usually overcoming the urge to get up for a coffee, B.L.T. or sticky bun or anything to take me away from my meditations. I knew my mind was playing tricks on me and had to get beyond this. Next layer of the onion was the urge to give up altogether and go to sleep, either in bed or right there in the chair. Again, I knew I had to resist. I was determined to reach my destination – which I have now discovered to be Nirvana!

There are many other layers blocking your deeper awareness and you have to push past all of them. There may only be two or three for you, or twenty or thirty. One thing is certain – if you stick with your meditations the cravings, impatience, restlessness and tiredness will *eventually* fall away and you'll reach that core – the place where *Colossus Output* is generated. Negative thoughts will disperse, the internal dialogue will stop, *Enigma Output* will dissipate and pure unadulterated *Colossus Output* will flow. This can result in the most *illuminating* of thoughts, that you couldn't have summoned up consciously or dreamed in a *million years,* and then you too will rapidly be on your way to fulfilling all your worldly wishes. It's at this exact point your cashflow will suddenly and deservedly exceed your outgoings and you'll be on *your* way to abundance and millions! – say it with me – millions!

CRACK THE CODE!

❖ Capture your Eurekas! at the point of arrival. Ink on paper is the *key.*

❖ Consciously acknowledge the difference between *ideas* and *solutions.*

❖ Aim high, program high. Using the biocomputer improves the biocomputer. Generate code that cracks code!

❖ There's a program for solving any problem, software for every type of success. Find *your personal keys* and write your own code.

❖ *Output* won't always be what you expect. More often than not, multiple small ideas and solutions will lead to great successes.

❖ Output requires trial, persistence and patience – keep experimenting with *input* until *Colossus Output* arrives.

❖ **Eurekas! on Demand** come as a result of precise *bespoke programming* and lots of relaxation. You can program specifically for solutions!

❖ Even a *little* output can light your way to a hidden fortune.

❖ Act on output *immediately* – the more you use the more you receive.

❖ Check for biocomputer output as often as you check your e-mail. Do this patiently, in Silence, Stillness and Solitude - $$$, remember?

❖ The calculator, machine or computer doesn't matter; it's only the *output* that counts.

THE SIXTH KEY

ACTION

THE MASTER KEY

I Act - Therefore I Am
— Ron G Holland

Enigma: The general public always hears about the Eureka! – the Big Idea – but they hardly ever hear about what *really* went into creating success, what it *really* took to turn a specific Eureka! into commercial reality. In my mind, that's an enigma, but it's only a *small* part of the extremely complex code that I really wanted to crack. Eurekas! are *always* intrinsically interlinked with *hard work* and *action* – sometimes even failure, as long as the person concerned got up and tried again – perhaps with other *keys*, but *always* plenty of *action!* Always! Consider both the hard work and the action required to bring these famous Eurekas! to life:

> When serial inventor and ideas man James Dyson created the world's first cyclone vacuum cleaner he had to make over 500 prototypes before he had a product that he could actually sell.

You can imagine how exasperated Dyson felt when a certain TV presenter said, "Now tell us all about your *Hoover*, James"!

Malcom McLean invented the shipping container in order to replace the method of shipping goods in the 1930s. Today, shipping containers and the ships that carry them have revolutionized the way products are moved around the world. This invention is considered by many, to have created a larger impact on the world than the Internet.

Lillian Moller Gilbreth was an inventor, industrial engineer, industrial psychologist, author and mother of twelve children. A pioneer in ergonomics, Lillian patented many kitchen appliances including an electric food mixer, shelves inside refrigerator doors and the famous trash-can with a foot-pedal lid-opener. Action-woman extraordinaire!

Originally called *mistake out* this was the invention of Bette Nesmith Graham, a Dallas secretary and a single mother. Bette worked extremely long hours, using her own kitchen blender to mix up her first batch of *liquid paper* or *white out*, a substance still used to cover up mistakes made on paper.

When Thomas Edison had his illuminating Eureka! about using carbonized cotton as a filament for his electric light bulb, he was already *actively* on the case – he'd failed 10,000 times before he finally succeeded. When questioned on his genius, his simple reply was, "Genius is 1 percent inspiration, 99 percent *perspiration*." You can replace the word *perspiration* with *action!*

When Louis Daguerre was congratulated on his invention of photography he was patently honest, "You must never forget that this discovery only happened after 11 years of discouraging experiments."

When Scottish genius John Logie Baird invented television way back in 1926 he had plenty of Eureka! moments – however, he put his brilliant success down to clever publicity, hard work, sheer stubbornness *and* non-stop action.

Eureka! I first talked about *Action is Power* in *Talk & Grow Rich* in 1981 and have always thought of action as a crucial part of success, but for some obscure reason or mental blockage I had not quite got my mind around how to address it in *The Eureka! Enigma*. Then I came across a book entitled *Action* by Robert Ringer, the author of a number of best-selling self-help books, including *Winning Through Intimidation* and *Looking Out for #1*. Action is as *profound* as it is *fundamental* and it was Robert's book that inspired me to write this sixth chapter. Robert's thesis is that *action* is the *key* to the brain's ignition – only I would take his statement to a *much* higher level. *Action* is not only the ignition - going back to my favorite internal combustion engine analogy - but also the accelerator pedal, fuel, supercharger *and* the drive shaft – it is in short the *Master Key!*

Action is the *Master Key* to getting the brain working, the Eurekas! flowing and success lighting up your life. A-c-t-i-o-n is the code that unlocks the biocomputer – and switches it **ON!** What follows is the most powerful chapter in the entire codebook. I have endeavored here to drive a series of subtle but vitally important points home in minute detail because I firmly believe that these *subtle* points of *action* are precisely what so many people fail to take on board in their own lives. By doing so, we soon begin to see that the phrase, "the harder I work, the luckier I get" isn't just a throwaway comment found in self-help books, but is the very *essence* of a successful, happy and fulfilled of life. Let the *action* commence!

Hot Tip! You can download the chapter *Action is Power* from *Talk & Grow Rich* for FREE at www.eureka-enigma.com

In the sections that follow, I'll give you a number of *keys* that you can use to unleash action in your own life. They might not all work for you, but who knows? Some almost certainly will. You have to try them out to see! Nothing ventured nothing gained!

Eureka! I had a small idea come into my head. This time I didn't dismiss it, I *acted* upon it – and *that* idea was the codebook you're reading now!

KEY - WORK "IN" YOUR BUSINESS AND WORK "ON" YOUR BUSINESS:

Dr. Ivan Misner, founder and chairman of BNI, the world's largest business networking organization, told me an inspiring story of his own Eureka! moment. Over twenty years ago, when Ivan was twenty-eight he lost a major client for his business. The resulting loss of income was a classic example of, "necessity is truly the mother of invention" and that led Ivan into figuring out how to very quickly fill the gap. His idea was to do a little networking of his own and it proved to be highly effective. Not only did he replace the shortfall in business but a couple of colleagues noted that what Ivan was doing was so effective they asked if he could build them business networks of their own, to allow them to increase their own businesses, which he did. The main crux of the idea was linking small groups of people together, that Ivan calls "Chapters", but ensuring at all times that there was only one person of each profession in each group. An extremely sound practice, that still holds fast in BNI today. Within weeks, the word got around and rapidly there were chapters springing up all over the place.

At the end of the first year Ivan was exhausted and decided to take relaxing break to do some "vision making" over the Christmas period and took himself up into the snow covered mountains at Arrow Head, not far from Big Bear Lake, California, where his retreat is today. As Ivan started to relax and unwind, the more he pondered on the fact that he had arrived at having twenty networking chapters in the business, more by accident, rather than by design! The more he thought about it, the more he realized that problems were heaping upon problems. Mostly issues to do with how people related to each other, egos, loyalties and many operations weren't as streamlined as they could be.

During this break, Ivan decided he must work not only "in" his business but he must work "on" his business and he started diligently writing down minute details of how everything slotted into place and why other things didn't gel properly. He then started to analyze each component of the business trying to make it more and more effective, with a view to making the next year in business run more smoothly and less stressfully. The more detailed the notes became, the clearer the picture became. The more Ivan *visualized* a smooth running network; the clearer became his ideas on how to actually accomplish this. *Colossus Output* had started to arrive by the bucket load; mini-Eurekas!, revelations, solutions, minute details, ideas and hunches flowed. The copious notes that followed were eventually turned into a *policies and procedures manual* and that was the very beginning of what has now become a 700-page bible that each chapter adheres to. He worked out meticulous training programs for his people, wrote up answers to frequently asked questions, created a cost-effective central marketing program, worked out how things could be made more effective and efficient, making sure no one had to go through his own learning curve by sticking to proven methodologies that worked best, every single time, based on his experience. Developing the credo "givers gain" and ensuring that by joining a chapter everything humanly possible would be done to ensure that each individual had an extremely good chance of increasing his or her business. Once and for all the guesswork would be taken out of networking. No one had ever done this before!

His whole enterprise was crying out for systems and that is exactly what Ivan started getting his mind around. However, when he did start drilling down, he realized he didn't have any at all, let alone robust ones. Not only that, he could now plainly see the way he had set up the business was problematic from the word go. What a wake up call! This was to dramatically change; Ivan decided not only to create systems, but robust systems for every single aspect of his business, that were highly effective and ultra efficient. The best! Simple replication was the order of the day. By the time Ivan had ironed out all the bugs and created foolproof systems for every aspect of his business, he was really proud and looking forward to the new year's trading immensely. It was at that exact point his major Eureka! moment hit him...Eureka! with the tools and systems he created over the break, he could now take his business nationally and globally. Wow! It dawned on him that he really did have a "tiger by the tail" and he now realized he had all the best tools, systems, vision and clarity of thought on how to accomplish the new goal of building a global network. Ivan changed the name from *The Network*, a name he couldn't trademark, to **BNI,** which he could, and the business has gone from strength to strength. Indeed, it is the most successful word of mouth networking organization in the world.

These sound but exciting ideas lead Ivan to form a board of advisers, one from each of most of the existing chapters. This was to be Ivan's mastermind group and he openly admits his reticence in going from a one-man-band to having a formal board. He laughed when he told the story of how, at that precise moment, he picked up a letter opener that was on his desk that his mother had given him as present, and he noticed for the first time it was inscribed: *Diplomacy is the art of letting someone have your way!* and he immediately realized everything would work out fine. He then decided to get a $10,000 bank loan (that was in the days when $10,000 actually meant something!) to enable him to invest in high quality printed materials: brochures, business cards and folders for the year's business. The roll out had begun – and continues to this day!

Dr. Ivan Misner's Top Tips for Networking!

1. Build quality relationships. Take time beyond normal business interactions to deepen your relationships with referral sources. Invite them to social functions, learn their hobbies and interests, and help them pursue their personal goals.

2. Network in new places. Other than your strong–and casual–contact groups, look for new areas to find partners with common interests, such as charitable organizations and professional support groups. Don't prospect right away; let the relationships mature.

3. Focus on others. Rather than having a, "What's in it for me?" mind-set, ask yourself, "What can I do for this person?" Continually look for ways to bring business and benefits to others in any group you're a part of. Make yourself known as the person who always has something for others. This is a powerful way to both deepen and broaden your network. Don't forget, "Givers gain." What will you *give* to enhance that relationship? A book, a DVD, a lunch, coffee, quality time, advice, a contact, encouragement, motivation?

FINAL FOOTNOTE:

The explosive growth of the Internet allowed Ivan to grow exponentially from 500 chapters to 5,000 chapters in forty countries and now the BNIConnect program is going to harness the power of all the online technologies including Twitter, FaceBook, Forums, Internet, WebTV, blogging, texting and podcasting. Ivan insists the core ethos of the business, which consists of weekly face-to-face meetings and only having one member of each profession in each chapter, won't change, but by harnessing these modern technologies massive growth will occur. In 2008, BNI passed over 5.6 million referrals in over 5,000 chapters with over 111,000 members in 40 countries resulting in more than $2.3 billion in business. All that from just one Eureka! and I have an overwhelming feeling the best is yet to come! And by the way, "vision making," is a term that I particularly embrace!

Very Hot Tip! Whether it's a solution, a hunch, an idea, a thought, a gut feeling, a notion, an inkling, an Aha, a ping, an epiphany, a full-blown Eureka! or even a "Veruka! Experience," (as my little girl calls it!) – act on it!

KEY - DO IT NOW!

I know so many people who *have a book inside them*. They've had eventful lives or have knowledge or expertise they could share with others – and in doing so make a tidy sum of money. I know it, they know it, and they have every intention of sitting down to start their book – *one* day. *One* day? How often have we heard those fateful words? The would-be authors say, "I'll write it when I'm retired" or "I'll do it after I've finished this project" or still vaguer, "When the time is right. . ." Listen: the time is *never* right, not until *you* make it so. For *anything* and *everything* you want to achieve, the only *right* time to begin is now. Action, Action, Action – simple as that! I ought, therefore I can! Do It Now!

Hot Tip! A simple formula for success: have an absolutely clear *intention and vision* of what you want to accomplish and spring into action – ready or not!

!!! "Only do the thing and you shall have the Power."

- Ralph Waldo Emerson

!!! Actions speak louder than words!

KEY - CONTINUOUS ACTION:

My own great action hero, Winston Churchill, once said, "I'd rather see a crooked furrow than an unplowed field." This is great wisdom and a philosophy that I *act* upon every day. Case in point: as soon as the Internet burst into life, I sprung into action and got my own website. It wasn't perfect by any stretch of the imagination – more like a holding page – but is was up and running with my address and contact details; and within 5 weeks that website had generated some $800,000. I'll tell you how...

My pager kept beeping and it was a message from someone whose name – Muna Pabari – I didn't recognize, urging me to phone him. I have to confess this went on for a couple of weeks and through this guy's absolute persistence and insistence, I eventually returned his call. I wanted to cut to the chase and asked him quickly but politely what he wanted to sell me. His reply was, "Nothing." Apparently he had come across me on the Internet after reading one of my books and tracked me down. "Could we do business together?" he asked.

A little light bulb went on in the back of my cranium and a *small still voice* whispered, "Success comes in the back door!" so I invited Muna to my office for coffee and the customary sticky buns. We met in my palatial boardroom and I shared with Muna at least six projects I was working on. My Eureka! was that he may be able to find investors or board members for my companies – who knows? I gave him the whole nine yards and off he went. After some days with no further contact I had second thoughts and didn't expect to hear from him again – but I hadn't taken into account that he was in *action* mode and he was getting Eurekas! of his own!

A few weeks later Muna phoned me again and wanted me to meet a colleague of his who had various investors lined up. I thought it was worth a chance so we met at the Connaught Hotel in Carlos Place, Mayfair. Over a delightful dinner, I met his colleague Charles and he told me about one specific investor who had recently sold his business and was actively seeking to make investments – Charles had already told him about one of my projects.

Charles agreed for me to talk directly to his investor on the phone – I did, and the investor was pretty excited about the deal in question, having already read the *Wow Factor* business plan. "How much money do you want?" he asked. I *immediately* replied, "$800,000," because I knew in a few days I was due to activate a formal option agreement that required $400,000 and I thought it would work really well if we had an *additional* $400,000 in working capital. His *immediate* response, "If you give me your bank details, I'll wire you the money." Simple as that! True to his word, the investor did wire the funds – they came in about three hours before we went to the lawyer's office to sign our option agreement and part with $400,000.

Important footnote: The lawyer acting for the other party had actually phoned me that very morning to make sure we really had the funds to consummate the deal – in other words, don't turn up unless you have the check. I assured him we did have the funds, knowing the investor's money might not arrive. It did however – just in the nick of time! My experience in business is that *providing* you spring into *action,* consistently striving toward your goal, the money will always come –*usually* at the eleventh hour and *always* in the last place you look for it.

Further Footnote: A few weeks later, again over dinner, this time at Claridges, Charles revealed that his investor had sold his company for $60,000,000. I said, "If you had told me that in the beginning, I'd have asked him for $1,000,000!"

Final Word: Winston Churchill, Prime Minister of Great Britain during World War II and a champion of the *Colossus* project, was in regular contact with Alan Turing at Bletchley Park. The distinguished Churchill – whose *Colossus Output* included over 40 books and 500 paintings, once stated, *"Continuous action,* not strength or intelligence, is the *key* to *unlocking* our potential."

!!! A funny thing happens when you don't act – nothing!

KEY - SEED-MONEY ACTION:

"If only I had the capital." "We failed because we couldn't raise the money." "The bank said No!" I hear these words at least three times a week – even more on seminar days! As a start-up entrepreneur or executive they're words you are going to have to live with, get over and move on.

How? That's what I hope to show you! The trick is that you have to do whatever it takes; and I do mean this most literally – whatever it takes. Most people go to the completely wrong sources for money. They try risk-averse sources like banks and venture capital companies – and they usually keep trying until they eventually give up.

Before we get ahead of ourselves, I want to make one thing clear; the grass is *not* greener on the other side. I have raised funds on both sides of the Atlantic as well as in Australia and Eastern Europe. Business people in the UK seem to think that raising funds in the U.S. is simple; it isn't. Many entrepreneurs in the U.S. are now looking to London in order to find an easier rulebook, a shortcut, easy money – which they won't find here either! When you're looking for money you do have to try every angle, it's true. Many times, you can rustle up the funds you need from family and friends. You may have to enroll a colleague or friend to come into your new business as your partner – with some cash. I know literally hundreds, if not thousands, of smaller enterprises have been bankrolled themselves using credit cards. (Recommended? No! – Do whatever it takes? Yes!) Could you clean out the loft, garage or spare bedroom and have a yard sale? Put stuff on eBay? Cash in some shares, sell your car, re-mortgage your house or your mother's house (only kidding!?)

Don't forget that I filled seven empty motorcycle showrooms by persuading Hell's Angels, Road Rats, demon enthusiasts and strawberry weasels to bring in their cherished Triumph Bonnevilles, BSA Gold Stars and Velocette Venoms and leave them in my showroom – on Sale or Return. It worked like a dream, and you know what, *creative financing* still works like a dream today! Remember this – sometimes there is no other way!

Sometimes you have to supply your own basic labor just to cobble together the tiny amount of seed money to start a business. *Seed* money is a very appropriate term because a small quantity of seed can reap a healthy crop of plants and eventually fill a whole field with produce. And a *little* seed money is often all it takes – that's why they say, "EMILY – Early Money Is Like Yeast." You take that tiny amount of EMILY and make it delightfully expand by *carefully investing* it in your business.

In the real world, no matter what the self-help books tell you, you really do have to do whatever it takes! Stop saying to yourself, "It's easy for you to talk, but others had capital or at least some resources." Nonsense! Research proves that at least 95 percent of entrepreneurs start with nothing other than large portions of *passion* and in *most* cases a *half-baked idea,* but they start – and it's usually only a small amount of *action* that often kicks in the power. Colossus power!

The secret is to do something, anything, to get hold of that seed money, even if it feels well below your station. I have done all sorts of jobs: dynamiting (crazy but true, with a guy we used to call Boom! Boom!), selling nuts from a stall, tending bar, stuffing envelopes, grinding boat hulls, painting houses, pumping gas, distributing leaflets – all the time thinking, "All I need is some seed money to get me up and running." Whatever it takes – right!

!!! "Fresh activity is the only means of overcoming adversity."

– Goethe

!!! "Action makes more fortunes than caution."

— Vauvenargues

KEY - BOOTSTRAPPING ACTION:

When engineers build a suspension bridge, they first throw a thin cable across the river or chasm. Sometimes this is done with the aid of a bow and arrow, rocket or mortar. They use this cable to hoist a slightly heavier one, which in turn hoists a third cable and so on, building up the structure until eventually it's strong enough to drive a Mack truck across. It's a process known as *bootstrapping,* and you can use the same principle to build success in any endeavor. Your first *cable* is any small task you *know* you can achieve, even if it is a mind-sapping struggle; achieving that first goal enables you to slowly consolidate your position, *cable by cable*. Like a suspension bridge, your biocomputer software must be tailor-made, built to the shape and dimensions of your particular challenge; it must be flexible and willing to change so it doesn't snap when the wind blows.

In business terms, bootstrapping is an infallible way of establishing an enterprise and a cashflow with absolutely *no* resources. The Invisible Entrapment code that says, "I could do it, but I don't have capital" or "I can't do it because the timing is all wrong" can keep you stranded forever – and forever is a *very* long time! I have bootstrapped myself into *fulsome* revenue situations many times, and met literally hundreds of millionaires – and even a few billionaires – who did the same thing, starting with nothing, some of them even in debt. Fire *your* rocket with a thin cable on it today! Create some powerful new code to bridge your own gap. Today – not tomorrow!

KEY - GO-FOR-IT ACTION:

Entrepreneurs these days are faced with a multitude of rules and regulations; following the letter of the law can be a headache in life and business. How long would you wait at a red traffic signal at 3 in the morning in the suburbs when the red light was obviously jammed stuck? Five or ten minutes, an hour, or all night until a policeman appeared to escort you safely across the road? The message here is that sometimes in your life, you just have to *go for it!*

That point was brought home to me on a recent trip to New Zealand. I ended up having an early breakfast meeting, one Sunday morning, in downtown Auckland. When we left the hotel, my host, who really was frightened of his own shadow, *insisted* we wait until the little green man came up on the traffic light before we crossed the road. We would have waited 20 minutes and quite possibly taken root if I hadn't *convinced* him that the streets were absolutely deserted and *insisted* we cross the road - *regardless.* Entrepreneurs do *not* buy into *Nanny Culture*, no matter where they are in the world – in actual fact they are quite rebellious about it! *You* will *need* to be, too, if you are going to succeed!

Now back to business. Governments actively encourage small businesses to start – they rightly figure that there can be *no oak trees without acorns.* Yet at the same time they unwittingly do everything within their powers to make it extremely difficult to start a small business. Here I am referring to the inordinate amount of red tape and bureaucracy that exists. Most small businesses simply don't have the time or resources to dot all the government's i's and cross all the t's – even if they had the *inclination* to.

Start-ups trying to raise funding are faced with an inordinate number of rules and regulations governing exactly how they finance their fledgling ventures and that dramatically slows the growth of companies. You will *have* to use creative financing techniques, especially if you are trying to create something out of nothing and are going to survive and ultimately win!

Final Word: The only time I'm frightened of my own shadow is when the shadow is wearing a hat and I'm not!

!!! "The way to get started is to quit talking and start doing."
– *Walt Disney*

KEY - TRIAL-AND-ERROR ACTION:

Multitudes of entrepreneurs go through life making the same mistakes over and over again. Maybe it's starting a new venture with the same undercapitalized game plan that collapsed the previous business or trying to make a business work with inadequate profit margins or ineffective marketing methods that cost far too much and deliver measly results.

It was years ago when I discovered that persistence and positive thinking are *simply not enough* to attain sustained success in any endeavor – there must be a whole lot more. Scientists write detailed reports on every experiment they carry out in order to have a record of where they have been. They constantly refer back to these reports and keep trying out new experiments or new methodologies until they reach their goal.

Most entrepreneurs, in contrast, blithely carry on believing that faith, positive thinking and persistence *alone* will get them to their target – and perhaps they will, but only *very* slowly. You must not give up! However, a far better course of action is to *dramatically alter* the *programs* in your biocomputer to ensure that your future action is *breathtakingly* different from action in the past – that alone will help you attract the resources you need for your new venture, before you even knock on the first door. Using the old software will guarantee you the exact same results of failure

– i.e. not reaching your target. Use of ***Basic Visual InAdvance,*** *combined* with *aggressive action* is the shortest route to any goal.

!!! "Don't be too squeamish about your actions. All life is an experiment."

— *Ralph Waldo Emerson*

KEY - TELEPHONE ACTION:

As we have observed, many people fail to get their projects off the ground because they think, "I haven't got the capital, people, skills, contracts, premises, office building, workshop, computers or the 101 other things that are required." This Invisible Entrapment program has brought more terrific ideas *grinding* to a halt than any other impediment.

My partner Bruce Snyder has a great antidote to that particular Invisible Entrapment program: telephone action. And it really works! At the start of any new entrepreneurial project – and I've started many exciting projects with Bruce, sometimes without resources – Bruce literally forces himself to get into some phone *action*. As soon as an idea was loosely formulated, he'd call just about everyone he knew and tell them all about it with great enthusiasm. In his own unique style, Bruce would engage friends and associates in conversation, very quickly enrolling each one, in spirit, as a champion of the project. He would then reiterate all the resources needed to bring the new scheme to fruition.

"Even if you can't come in with money yourself," he'd say, "maybe you have a friend or family member who might like to invest? Perhaps you can help on the admin side of things, or help keep the books. Perhaps you'd like to help us with sales or marketing? Tell you what – bring some of your colleagues over to the office for an informal chat and coffee, and we'll take it from there."

Of course, a lot of Bruce's phone calls fell on deaf ears, but you'd be surprised how much money, referrals, computers, copiers, office space, vehicles, investment capital, skills, advice, moral support and other resources he did manage to *attract* with his simple, direct approach. After five or ten calls, Bruce would often announce, "Would you believe it? Alex is coming in with two computers complete with printers" or "David can't let us have an office, but he can let us have a desk in one of his open-plan suites. It's only a desk for one, but he'll be happy to squeeze two chairs and two phones onto it. I took it, because at least we're up and running!" Bruce immediately picked up the phone to make his next call, but continued talking as he was dialing, "Now all we need is a little investment capital – so we can pay ourselves!"

The funny thing is, Bruce is not a born salesman – far from it. He's a scientist, physicist, mathematician. In actual fact, he *hated* making those phone calls, but – and this is the Big But – he did it anyway. He got into *action* and did whatever it took. He told me on more than one occasion that it's a little known law of physics that all difficulties *yield to action*. You *know* what you've got to do, once you've got the *vision* – smile and dial! Right!

KEY - CLASSIFIED ACTION:

While I was on one of my book tours, I was being interviewed on the radio and the interviewer asked me for a good tip to help start-up companies cost-effectively increase their revenues. I immediately replied, "Start a classified advertising campaign!" The interviewer's instant reaction was, "That doesn't sound very exciting to me" and he immediately moved on to the next guest.

I often wondered if anyone listening to the radio show was curious about what I was going to say – because I guarantee, it's a gem. Classified *action* can turn your life around; I've been recommending it to young and old entrepreneurs alike, for years.

Classified advertising is one of those mediums where you can reach a vast target audience for not a lot of money. It allows you the financial freedom to *test, test, test* until you discover just the right phrasing that will get your telephone ringing off the hook. The secret is to *visualize* the outcome you desire, give the biocomputer plenty of *Bespoke Input* and wait for your own magic words to pop into your mind when you're not thinking. Whenever business gets slack for me, I run my three magic words, *Venture Capital Alternative* and business floods in.

When I was contemplating creating audio versions of my books, my friend and record producer George Hargreaves arranged for me to fly to the Isle of Man, (where he lived at the time) because he wanted to introduce me to Mitch Murray, who had a recording studio there. Mitch, incidentally, wrote a string of hit songs in the 1960's including *How Do You Do It*, *You Were Made For Me*, *I'm Telling You Now* and *The Ballad of Bonnie and Clyde*. (George, a songwriter himself, wrote the blockbuster *So Macho* for Sinitta).

After the first hour of reading my book aloud in the studio, Mitch said to me, "Boy, you can write, you can talk, but you can't read – that's the worst book reading I've ever heard!" In the end, Mitch narrated the book himself and did a word perfect job. I guess it's one of those things that when I speak in front of a live audience I come to life, become supercharged, dynamic even, but because I *read* very deliberately it *sounds* as though I'm a halfwit.

At the end of the week I had dinner at Mitch's home and we started talking. Mitch wanted to know if I had any ideas on how to create cashflow from the Isle of Man – since he had become a tax exile and hadn't had a chart hit in a while, he wanted a way of generating some revenue. With his permission, I took Mitch into state of hypnosis that deeply relaxed him and I talked to him for about an hour. I told him there was plenty of money on the mainland UK and people would be happy to send over cash, checks and credit card payments. All he had to do was supply some simple product or service – and his biocomputer *already* knew what that was. All I was there to do was to help him connect the un-connectable. I told him that by placing classified adverts in *The Sunday Times* business-to-business section and other national newspapers and magazines across the country, money would come flooding in. I planted this *code* deep into every neuron in Mitch's biocomputer – where inevitably it would create trillions of computations. Trillions!

When I arrived back in London it wasn't long before George got into action promoting the beautifully produced audio version of *Talk & Grow Rich,* and we had great fun on a nationwide TV and radio tour. One day I was checking up on our publicity and marketing campaign and guess what caught my eye in the classified columns: *Britain's leading speech writer. Get no laughs, pay no fee. After dinner, weddings, corporate, etc. Visa and MasterCard accepted. Mitch Murray, phone: 555 12346789* – it's been running ever since!

!!! "Never, never, never give up." – *Winston Churchill*

KEY - ENTHUSIASTIC ACTION:

They say you can't fake enthusiasm, but *they* are wrong – very wrong. Not only can you fake enthusiasm, but you damn well must. I have seen a top-flight car sales person who had to switch car dealerships; she suddenly found herself selling the cars that had previously been competition. Do you think that sales person suddenly declared, "I can't sell these because I haven't got the enthusiasm for this brand of car?" Of course she didn't! Like any true professional she changed gear and *acted* enthusiastically about every car in her new showroom.

The same goes for motivation. I hear too many young people say "I can't get motivated" – consequently they do little or nothing. Lack of motivation and enthusiasm are two tricks the mind *will* play on you, especially if you don't take the initiative and play the opposite trick – plenty of motivation and enthusiasm – on your mind first. The *key* is always to *act* motivated and *act* enthusiastic, if need be forcing yourself to do things regardless of how you *really* feel internally. Genuine motivation *and* enthusiasm *and* ideas will follow – but it is *highly likely* you will have to *act* first.

Final word: "If you're passionate and *enthusiastic* about your work", just as my wild life action hero Steve Irwin said just before his untimely death, "You'll be a winner, mate!"

KEY - PHYSICAL ACTION:

Luxury can become tedious. After too much *soft living* the spirit yearns for a little privation; a windswept coastline in winter, a star-lit night under canvas, a grueling cross-country walk, or some hard physical labor – the kind that builds up a sweat and a real appetite, (not for food, but for life).

Look in *Who's Who* or at the *Fortune* 100 CEOs and see how many high achievers list sailing, climbing, fell-walking, or horse riding as their hobbies. These executives spend much of their time in air-conditioned limousines, offices and planes. They stay in the most sumptuous hotels in the world, with every luxury at their fingertips, every need catered for. Yet whenever they have a spare few days they put on a pair of hiking boots and head up the chilly slopes of Ben Nevis, or take a little dinghy bobbing out into the Bay of Biscay with zero visibility and a heavy squall blowing in across the Atlantic. Why? Because it reminds them they're alive, and it *stops* the internal dialogue. Physical labor provides a contradiction – a contrast – to the pampered world of sedentary work. And as oxygen floods the brain, so too can ideas…

Indeed, *physical action* can be a good way to quiet the internal dialogue that threatens to drown out your *Colossus Output*. The *key* to that may just be physical activity as a way to stop thinking – to let your subconscious biocomputer do what it's meant to do – generate *Colossus Output*!

Peter Ouspensky, whose lectures were published in 1950 (as *The Psychology of Man's Possible Evolution),* would invite his students to *hard physical labor* periods in the garden of his country house in New Jersey. As the rhythms of their exertions took hold, the students would be aware of a cessation in their debilitating internal dialogue. The *Enigma* machine, which had been scrambling their mental output, was confronted by the *Colossus* of the biocomputer, and each student heard, for the first time, their own clear messages – their personal Eurekas!

At the Betty Ford Center, recovering alcoholics are ordered to scrub floors and take out the trash – to find themselves by reconnecting with the necessities of real life. Eastern mystics have a saying, "What comes after cutting firewood, fetching water and cleaning pots and pans is enlightenment, and after enlightenment comes cutting logs, fetching water and cleaning pots and pans." I learned this to be true – and embraced it!

What really gets *me* in the zone – where *most conscious* thought stops – is when I start to tinker with my motorcycles and racing engines. Polydyne camshafts, noggins, nitro-methane, boost pressure gauges, superchargers, pop-off-valves, high-compression pistons – for me that's where it's at! I guarantee that when I'm welding a frame, milling noggins on the metal lathe or measuring a piston with a micrometer I am not thinking about any of the thousands of business problems that could impinge on my biocomputer, if I let them. When I ride my motorbikes that altered state is elevated further and *all conscious* thought ceases.

What works for you? It may be something equally as simple as riding motorbikes, but whatever your answer, *physical action* could be an invaluable *key* to unlocking your biocomputer.

Profound Footnote: If you indulge in hard physical activity without specific goals in mind, you'll just be doing *hard work* – and that's exactly what billions of *poor people* across the globe are unwittingly locked into. The more you link *absolutely specific goals* to meditation, visualization, bespoke programming in **Basic Visual InAdvance** and – of course – physical *action*, the more *Colossus Output* you will receive.

KEY – ACTION - BUT WHAT ACTION?

Let me share with you the most asinine conversation I have ever had in my whole career – and that's saying a lot because, believe me, I've had quite few. We'll call our story subject Mr. Lazybones and what he said went something like this: "I don't mind working hard. No Sir!

But what I am opposed to is not knowing what the end result will be. I must know that at the end of the day, I will have made $500,000 or $1,000,000 or $10,000,000; otherwise, what's the point of it all? I mean, you could set up a business or do a whole load of work and three or four years down the road find you've done all that work for nothing. Someone has to absolutely, positively guarantee the amount of money I will make – otherwise it's completely pointless doing all the work in the first place."

I actually learned quite a bit from Mr. Lazybones in our brief conversation – about how *not* to go about life. Imagine if our old friend Thomas Edison had gone about his 10,001-tries task of discovering the electric light bulb with the same attitude? We'd still be reading by candlelight! Mr. Edison couldn't have possibly known on his 5,000[th] failure that he was only halfway through the process of unlocking the secrets of the incandescent bulb. He just continued in a *step-by-step* endeavor to succeed in his quest. On his 10,000[th] failure he wouldn't be aware that he was just one more experiment away from success. For all he knew at the time, success may still have been months or years off. He was only concerned to *keep on keeping on* until the darn thing worked.

Hot Tip! Remember that every single paragraph in this codebook is designed to help *you* unlock *your* biocomputer. We have already decided that we *don't* know which *combination* of *keys* will work for *you*. If you find a *key* that works for you – use it, if not, move onto other *keys* that will work.

KEY – DISCIPLINE YOURSELF TO ACTUALLY DO THE MIND POWER WORK, PART I (OR, GUNTHER GUMSHOES IS STILL DESPERATE FOR SUCCESS):

Gunther Gumshoes has read all the books, he's past 40 years old, and he's still searching for success. He's treading on peanut butter every day – and we all know how that feels. He has witnessed a number of colleagues make serious money from network marketing and other business ventures and wonders if he too, could find some way to a larger income, if not the abundance he's convinced that is out there.

He has a charming wife and four children and, at present, a 9-2-5 direct sales job that barely pays the mortgage. There is no cash for treats or extras, and life is run on a very tight budget – not quite potato soup every night, but almost. Determined to create a better life, he devised a plan that will allow him to enter his mind and alter things from within.

Gunther gets up at 6 every morning and starts his visualization routine. Yet before his mental images of future success have time to form, the kids are bouncing off the walls; they need breakfast and have to be taken to school. Forced to break off his mind power work, he runs his screaming kids to school. After dropping them off he sneaks into the park for a quick visualization session before he starts his sales calls. Unfortunately, whenever he does this, it is either raining or cold, someone has a radio blaring, or a stranger starts talking to him. If it is warm, the park is full of noisy toddlers or the gardener is out with his high-powered lawnmower; in the fall there is always the leaf-blower man. Not ideal conditions for visualization.

Abandoning the park, he shrugs his shoulders and makes his way back home. While his wife is at the shopping mall he sneaks back into bed, puts his earplugs in, pulls the duvet over his head and starts to visualize. Now, in Silence, Stillness and Solitude ($$$) the pictures finally begin to take shape. All along he's known this is the only way, sensory deprivation is how we can all free the energy of our minds. But wait for it…

Inevitably, just as Gunther is deeply absorbed in building his images, his wife comes home and gives him hell. He protests that he's not just lazing in bed – far from it. He's engaged, he tells her, in vital *mind power work* which is going to dramatically improve their lives; generating vacations, cashflow, restaurants, a better home, a whole new exciting lifestyle, ad-infinitum. Gunther's wife is all for this, of course; she wants the finer things in life, too. If her husband were on the phone trying to make sales, working part-time as a cab driver, digging people's gardens, washing windows or even doing a home-study course to improve his qualifications, she would see the purpose of his efforts. But lying down with his eyes shut just doesn't make sense to her because there's nothing tangible being achieved. It's not that she lacks intelligence; it's simply that she hasn't investigated and bought into the whole concept of *Bespoke Programming* like Gunther has. Maybe he could explain, and she might get it. On the other hand, she might think he was losing his mind, rather than trying to re-program it.

By the time they've both calmed down enough to discuss things, he has to answer the phone. Before they know it, the children need to be picked up from school, and the whole ghastly domestic merry-go-round grinds on. Gunther's is a true story, and one I have heard repeated many times – the names change and sometimes the gender roles are reversed, but the nightmare scenario is usually the same.

Six years after our first meeting, Gunther turned up at another of my seminars, "How's it going?" I asked. "Well, not so bad, but I haven't made any quantum leaps yet," he replied. "It's hard to find a quiet place where I can get into my mind and carry out my visualization and meditations properly. I know this is absolutely essential so I do my best, but it can be so frustrating."

Gunther was making a living as a sales person, but he'd been making a living six years previously, and he was clearly still desperate for a breakthrough. There were creases in his suit, scuffs on his shoes and bags under his eyes and he was still driving the same old wreck – I mean auto. Despite his good humor and desire to succeed, he still hadn't dealt with the major bug in his biocomputer code – a lack of self-discipline required to do what he needed to achieve success. For Gunther, a lack of proper *visualization* space was something he tried to accommodate. He just wasn't seeing it as the *primary* obstacle to his success. It was, and still is, *his* Invisible Entrapment program that is stopping him getting into correct action - that of doing the necessary *mind power work* for success – regardless. And I really do mean *regardless!*

KEY – DISCIPLINE YOURSELF TO ACTUALLY DO THE MIND POWER WORK, PART II (OR, NORMAN BLOPAST SUCCEEDS AT LAST):

Norman Blopast was another one of my protégés and, like Gunther, he desperately wanted success. His family members, none of whom had ever owned their own home, had experienced a long succession of failures. Determined to break the mould, Norman had started his own construction business. But try as he might, he just could not get control of his mind – which is, after all, the starting point for everything and everyone. He was always tired, his children forever screaming, money tight and contracts short on the ground. He'd made a number of ill-judged decisions and things were going from bad to worse.

On the first day of the rest of his life Norman hit on a plan, after reading my previous book, *Turbo Success – How to Reprogram the Human Biocomputer*, and suddenly he knew what he needed to do. He was absolutely set on seeing the plan through. First, he sat his wife Linda down and had a long chat. He explained that he felt life was passing them both by. They never had any money, fun or vacations. He said he was fed up with living a hand-to-mouth existence and wanted them both to start really living. Linda agreed whole-heartedly with Norman's sentiments.

Norman's plan was simple: he explained to Linda that to move forward he would need his own space where he could develop and program his mind for success. He stressed that this was for the betterment of the entire family. Neither Norman nor Linda knew for certain what the outcome would be, but because of Norman's calm, clear outline of the plan, this is what they did…

Linda agreed to have the children in bed by 8 every evening, without fail. She would then retire at around 10. Norman needed an average of six hours of sleep a night. If he awoke at 7 in the morning he needn't turn in until well after midnight. With the rest of family tucked up by 10, this gave him three hours to set aside for regular *uninterrupted* mind power work. Bliss!

In those three hours of silent down time, Norman devoted himself to inspirational reading, meditation, listening to motivational tapes and CDs, *Bespoke Programming* and visualization in **Basic Visual InAdvance** – the groundwork for his future success. Knowing that he wouldn't be *disturbed,* he could slip into Alpha state, designing and

INTERNALIZING a picture gallery of successful images for himself and his family in the future.

A whole new world unfolded for Norman; now he regularly taps into a deeper level of consciousness. Ideas, solutions and possibilities well up from his biocomputer, guiding him towards avenues he would never have considered consciously. As he follows through on these new ideas to the letter, his switched **ON** biocomputer delivers even more *Colossus Output*. It's rather like having an ongoing conversation with his biocomputer. Sometimes the replies come immediately and sometimes a subject is put on hold for a while. But the quality of the conversation is always rich and often surprising.

Norman is now going from strength to strength, not just financially, but also physically, mentally, emotionally *and* spiritually, as well as being a better father, husband, lover and breadwinner. His confidence has gone through the roof! His relationship with Linda has begun to bloom in a whole new light. And with their new routine they find they now have *more* quality time for each other and the children, rather than less. They also have the cash to enjoy it – for vacations, outings, the theater, cinema and their chosen luxuries – his and hers, brand new, top-of-the-range Toyota Amazons. Such a remarkable renewal can only occur when you accept the importance of *mind power work* in your *daily* schedule – *and* combine it with *unwavering action*. Break free from money worries, get out of the rut of a hand-to-mouth existence and get your very own slice of the Good Life!

You have to pro-actively create *your* perfect environment for *mind power work*. You may have to buy wax earplugs, headphones, move to a quieter neighborhood or even change jobs. Like Norman, talk to your partner and anyone else whose co-operation is required. *Mind power work* comes more easily once you have created the right environment – so you really do need to spring into action and do this now!

‼ "Nobody knows how to form a pop group – you just *do* it."

– Keith Richards, The Rolling Stones

KEY – SMALL ACTIONS CAN HAVE A MIGHTY IMPACT:

I've talked about the mock-up books that I create *InAdvance* of a real book being published, and this technique can work wonders for any endeavor. Architects make prototype models, as do theater set designers, airplane, car and yacht builders – chiefly to show board members, clients, producers and manufacturers the finished product (albeit in miniature).

The key to success lies in creating some physical manifestation of your future goal – in this way you can jump-start an obstinate biocomputer. For example, if you have a money-making idea but can't see how to make the first move, print just a few business cards with your name and title – *Real Estate Broker, Computer Training, Piano Lessons, Photographer, Ghost Writer, Copy Writer, Mechanic, Interior Designer, Yacht Charter, Computer Repairs, Massage & Nails* or whatever you're planning. Who knows – it might be the *key* to jump starting *your* biocomputer. And, if you hand your business cards out at opportune moments, before long someone will ask, "Can *you* do *that* for *me*?" You get your business cards printed and then, as if by magic, you *are* in business. Simple as that! You will have invented your new self and released it into the world via a powerful talisman bearing your name, role and business. You see, it's all about overcoming inertia. Another tip, in addition to printing business cards, is to develop a website – at the very least a holding page. You'll need a domain name; that alone will stimulate your creative juices. Find an available name that works for your business. Then get a support team of real people to help you. The most effective way to do this is to join a professional networking group like BNI.

When you come up with a business idea, don't push it to the back of the mind, spring into *action,* hold your first meeting, put the word out that you need partners, capital or other resources. Send an e-mail to family, friends and past associates (even if you've forgotten all about them, they may be pleased to hear from you). I have used this technique many times and contacted people from five or ten years back who've ended up coming on board various projects – sometimes with a cash investment as well! Use your network, energy and *action* to springboard your great ideas into reality.

As soon as your business idea pops into your head, get your first client, even if you don't have your office or business premises; invest in a tiny amount of stock and sell it from your bedroom or kitchen table – like many other start-up entrepreneurs have done. Buy the stock even if you can't afford to! John Caudwell recently sold his phone company for some $3 billion and he delights in reminding people that when he started out his entire stock consisted of 26 mobile phones but by the time he sold the company he was selling 26 phones *every second*!

Make that first phone call, join that BNI networking group, send that first letter, ask that first person the first question, take that first action step. If you follow through with *action* every step of the way, more ideas and solutions will come along of how to solve the problems that face you on a day-to-day basis. It's all about adding more and *more imagination* to each new step, like pouring coals onto a fire and stoking it up – I feel another analogy coming on!

Final Word: My favorite guru Sri Guruji Pillai told me that the business card was the single most important thing in business – sometimes indeed the *only* thing that's necessary to create million-dollar deals. So make sure your business cards are an appropriate reflection of your business. If you ever change your address, e-mail or phone number, don't scribble it onto your existing cards; *always* and immediately get new business cards printed – they could be the *key*stone of *your* empire.

!!! If a butterfly flapping its wings in Samoa can cause Krakatoa to erupt, think what leaving your business card in the lobby of the Hilton Hotel might do. Small actions can have a mighty impact!

KEY – THE COLOR-BLIND ADVANTAGE:

I have been conducting seminars for the past three decades, and I'm pretty observant. Over those years – the past few in particular – I've noticed an increasing number of black people and other ethnic minorities coming to my seminars in the UK, U.S. and across Europe.

Often, we have a 50-75 percent non-white audience. (We even had one guy turn up who wasn't green - but he was from another planet!) And do you know what I've noticed? Everyone at my seminars is as color-blind as me as we strive in business and life to capture the same energy, share some fun and take great strides forward — together!

And while not everyone in my audiences may end up launching and growing a highly profitable fast food chain, many people – I am sure – can be inspired by Panda Express founders Andrew and Peggy Cherng. By solving problems day-after-day since launching their first Panda Express outlet in 1983, the husband and wife team are now well on the way to making fried tofu and orange chicken as popular as Big Macs and fries – by matching McDonald's pace of around 30,000 outlets worldwide in 50 years. The Cherng's mega-appetite for success took root in East Pasadena in 1973 when Chinese immigrant Andrew turned his back on a B.S. in applied math and convinced his dad to become the chef in his first restaurant. Today the Cherngs operate over 1,000 Panda Express locations, and are growing strongly as they live the American Dream – thanks to their persistence, hard work and action.

Other ethnic minorities like Tiger Woods, Venus and Serena Williams, Will Smith, and M. Night Shyamalan have proved that a person's racial origin, background or gender is no obstacle to achievement. Using and practicing ***Basic Visual InAdvance*** you can crush all obstacles in your path – regardless of your circumstances. Indeed, if you analyze the life stories of the wealthy, the influential, the famous and those who have achieved tremendous benefits for mankind, you will usually find that they have overcome poverty, financial restraints, disability, abuse, ridicule, prejudice, bigotry and a myriad of other personal and life problems. Those problems can affect your dreams and ambitions – only if you let them!

You may remember my good friend George Hargreaves who liked *Talk & Grow Rich* so much he bought the audio rights. George now has his own church, TV series and recording studio. I have had many inspiring conversations with George, but the one I had recently was the best. George was telling me all about his successes and how he uses his blackness to his advantage. George makes a point to keep pushing forward every day with prayer, action, positive goal-setting and thinking things through *InAdvance.* He meditates regularly, reads self-help books and – even more importantly – encourages other people to do the same, constantly! George pointed out to me that he has noticed a growing number of black people getting more and more serious about success, accomplishment and *mind power work* – and is doing everything in his powers to help make that happen on an even grander scale. I am convinced George is right and I can't tell you how pleased I was when Lewis Hamilton became Formula One champion in 2008 and Barack Obama was elected President of the United States – both achieving success thanks to their total focus, overwhelming perseverance and competence. Fantastic!

One of my business partners, Peter Brown, is a black guy and we do incredible things together and as the years go by we will continue to do things – bigger and greater things. I admire Peter's work ethic and we spark off each other – Peter, by the way, is part of my mastermind group and was one of those who gave me astounding feedback for the codebook that you're now reading! The other thing I like about Peter is that, like my Asian friend Muna, he asks and keeps asking, "Can I edit a book? Can I help write the brochure? Can I assist in any other way?" and on and on, never ending; and every time I add to his to-do list, you know what, he goes out and does it, over and over again! Performing! Brilliantly!

Like Peter, I do not believe there is any excuse – including skin color or lack of education or parental love – for not striving to be successful. Just consider the tale of Madam C.J.Walker, who despite being born the daughter of former slaves in poverty-stricken rural Louisiana in the mid-19th century and orphaned at the age of seven, she was the first known African-American woman to become a self-made millionaire! Walker's journey started when she suffered a serious scalp ailment and experimented with a number of home-made cures and other remedies that ultimately led to her selling her own product, called Madam Walker's Wonderful Hair Grower, a scalp conditioning and healing formula. Extremely ambitious and energetic, she promoted her products by embarking on a mind-boggling door-to-door sales drive across the southern and southeastern U.S. Her drive and ambition soon led to her build a national sales organization that at one time employed over 3,000 people and helped her amass a personal fortune within 15 years. And what was her work ethos? Surprise, surprise, Madam Walker's prescription for success encompassed perseverance, action and faith in herself and God. She is quoted as saying, "There is no royal flower-strewn path to success. And if there is, I have not found it – for if I have accomplished anything in life it is because I have been willing to work hard."

In many ways, Madam Walker reminds me of Oprah Winfrey – who I have heard many times make the point that she *created* her own success. *Creating* your future and your success is what this book is all about. When you start using **Basic Visual InAdvance** you too, like George, Madam Walker, Lewis, Barack, Oprah and Peter will start to create your own future – *exactly* as you *program* it to be.

Let's not forget that personal *vision* can also be a catalyst for transforming itself into community *vision,* business *vision,* national *vision* and even global *vision.* Just think what could be achieved with **Basic Visual InAdvance** taken to a *national level* which overcomes deprivation, poverty, race and any other obstacle you can think of.

Need evidence? Look at the past two decades where countries like China, India and Brazil have emerged as world economic powers transforming the perception of Asia as a region. Consider the *tiger* economies of Singapore, Hong Kong, South Korea and Malaysia. Look what they have achieved with a national *vision* of enterprise, innovation and determination. As they say, it all *starts in the mind*! Let's go for it – together!

!!! Don't Procrastinate – Activate!

Hot Tip! Eurekas! come to those who are involved in *action* – the more *intense* and *energetic* that action is, the higher probability Eurekas! and success will follow.

KEY – SET UP AN ACTION BASE:

All good superheroes have an action base; you should, too. In fact, you should spring into *action* by preparing your action base – whether you're ready or not. Make your base as comfortable as you can and as quiet as possible.

I'm lucky; I have seconded the entire top floor of my home where I have several computers, numerous printers, loads of bookshelves for books and research materials, filing cabinets, multiple phone lines and a white board. Framed magazine covers (featuring yours truly, of course) and dust covers of many of my books adorn the walls. One cabinet has my motorcycle trophies and on another shelf there are public speaking awards. I have a shower room, TV, radio and CD player. I have a profusion of potted plants: ferns, African violets and orchids, as well as fresh flowers delivered every week. I work hard to create an ambiance that is conducive to creativity. I have a small kitchen where I brew copious supplies of coffee and tea, and of course a refrigerator that is stocked with cold drinks, goodies and vitamins just in case I run an all-nighter – which I frequently do.

You may have better facilities than I do, or perhaps not, but *whatever* your situation, make your start creating an *action* base where you can lock yourself away and not leave or want for anything – then get yourself busy. Very busy!

KEY – LIGHTS, CAMERA, ACTION, SCENE 1:

I meet people on a regular basis that would love their 15 minutes of fame but aren't prepared to pay the price. Yet most people don't even know what the price is! So I want to share a story with you, from someone who has paid the price and is reaping significant rewards.

By sheer coincidence I met UK TV star Tony Robinson at a bash in Monaco a few weeks back. We were raising funds for an exotic speedboat manufacturer (a consultancy client of mine); Tony was invited along for the buffet lunch and I ended up having a chat with him. That was great because I'm Tony's #1 fan, in part for his hilarious role as Baldrick in *Blackadder*. Baldrick's catch phrase is, "I have a cunning plan" which, incidentally, I've adopted as my own.

Tony and I talked about lots of things, but the part of the conversation that really grabbed my interest was Tony's take on becoming a successful actor. He said, "Get into the part, passion, emotion and practice, practice, practice count for everything – and action, action, action." Of everything Tony said, he put the most emphasis on action; before fame and fortune comes your way you may want to *act* on meditation, by doing it and keep on doing it. *Act* on visualization by trying every combination of *images* until you get usable *Colossus Output. Act* on phone calls by making lots of them and returning calls promptly. Most importantly, immediately act on your ideas, large and small, when they come! Develop an *action*-oriented life; keep an *action*-oriented diary with daily to-do lists; work hard on morphing into an *action* man or woman today!

So what's the price of success? Action, action, and more action! Or is that too big a price to pay - for all the *fun* and *goodies* that you want out of life? Only you can answer that!

Final Word: Max Clifford, who probably knows more about getting his clients *and himself* in front of the lights and cameras than anyone else in the UK (I know because he was my PR consultant at one time), once advised me, "Devise an image and keep working on that image until you get it right. Make a point of getting into *action* at least ten times a day!" Max also gave me a lot of feedback personally, "Get your beard trimmed, invest in tailor-made suits, (from his tailor I hasten to add, and I feel sure he got a kickback!) polish your shoes *and* start *acting* like Top Biz Guru." (a phrase coined for me by Max himself, who is an *action* man).

Interesting Snippet: One fine spring day I was at Max Clifford's Bond Street office, when he was visited by a famous businessman – one who's on TV a lot. The mogul frantically told Max that one of the national newspapers was about to break a negative story about his private life – a story that, in all probability, would have destroyed his credibility. What happened next appeared quite surreal: Max *immediately* sprang into action and with the phone on hands-free dialed the journalist and asked him not to run with the story – and the journo agreed, saying, "Max, you owe me one!" Max clicked off and turned to the tycoon with a wry smile and said, "*You* owe *me* one!" I remember that day well because Max had just got me a full page article in the *Daily Mail* with the headline TALK AND GROW RICH, and that article was of how I introduced him to yet another client of mine, Lady Bienvenida Buck.

!!! "Success seems to be connected with action. Successful people keep moving. They make mistakes, but they don't quit." – *Conrad Hilton*

KEY – LIGHTS, CAMERA, ACTION, SCENE 2:

I recently attended a soiree at the British Film Institute to celebrate the works of the Maysles brothers – the godfathers of modern documentary film. I say that in a highly affectionate manner, since my first wife, artist Roz Kramer is their niece and the two of us spent much quality time with them. This included a memorable dinner at their Dakota apartment on West 72nd Street in Manhattan, the same fateful night in 1981 that their neighbor John Lennon was shot dead outside the building. The Maysles brothers, with Albert on a lightweight camera and David on the sound, used to run an incredible double act memorializing important events like JFK's Wisconsin Democratic primary campaign; the Rolling Stones' tragic Altamont gig in *Gimme Shelter*, which captured the off-stage stabbing of a young fan; the Beatles' first crazed trip to the U.S.; the decaying Bouvier family (reclusive cousins of Jackie O) in *Grey Gardens*; and the artworks of French artist Christo, who wraps buildings, creates giant water lilies and erected an orange nylon curtain across a valley stretching some seven miles, in *Rifle, Colorado*. Yet what always impressed me so much about Albert and David was their *relentless action*. Every week, it seemed, they would jump on plane or rush to the other end of town for a photo shoot or to the airport to meet a Russian dissident or some other celebrity, or take a train trip across the U.S., a motorcycle ride across Russia or a motor-scooter trip across Hungary and Turkey just for the hell of it. They always went with the flow and everything in their lives appeared to flow effortlessly. The Maysles brothers lived the dream – their dream – and as a consequence, because of their enthusiasm, energy and willingness to spring into *action*, the Eurekas!, ideas, contacts, work and opportunities literally flooded in; and as far as I can recall, they never once advertised!

KEY – LIGHTS, CAMERA, ACTION, SCENE 3:

I really do try to practice what I preach and just recently I was handed a DVD: *What the bleep do we know…*

A couple of things sprang to mind as I watched this fascinating film. The first was to make a DVD of my own, using graphics, animation and a brilliant story line to explain the workings of the human biocomputer, what could be more exciting - this was going to be better than a thriller! Within a day of conceiving the idea for the *Eureka! Enigma* film and as a result of springing into feverish action, a world class team had started to come together; producers, animators, sound technicians, film crews, script writers - really exciting! The more I got into action the bigger the snowball effect! Awesome!

The second thing that came to mind was this: very quickly I was introduced to some brilliant storyboard artists and a number of them showed me previous works and explained how they were necessary in the making of a film in so far as a storyboard could very quickly get the film crew and actors up to speed, as to what was expected of them. I could easily see that we were going to need the whole film and animation storyboarded, no problem. My Eureka! was that we could all use storyboards to create pictures for our own futures and I have already started to work on mine – when will you begin yours?!

For *The Eureka! Enigma* film, over the course of the next few months, we will be interviewing a number of people who I have helped become millionaires and world champions. I am also particularly interested in interviewing those who have created successes (either large or small) through the art and practice of *visualization*, combined with action, to be part of the film - any ideas? You can also register your interest in the film: www.eureka-enigma.com

KEY – MIND POWER COMBINED WITH ACTION UNLEASHES EXPLOSIVE POWER!

It is often when two elements are combined that enormous power is released. For example, when you're mixing car body filler all you need is a tiny amount of hardener to set off a half gallon of filler; the hardener acts as a *catalyst*. Combine Uranium or Plutonium with a catalyst and you'll get nuclear power – depending on which catalyst you use, you will either develop electricity or a nuclear bomb! When you consider that over 95 percent of most people's actions are spent trying to compensate for *Enigma Output* you see how vital it is to *combine deliberate action with concentrated mind power work. Action* is the ultimate catalyst!

Very Hot Tip! "By combining *massive action* with *massive mind power* you will become invincible." – *Ron G Holland*

Very, Very Hot Tip! In practical terms it means that you have to start your business, whether you are ready or not, or don't feel quite confident, or don't have sufficient funds, knowing that with action *and* visualization in ***Basic Visual InAdvance*** all will be revealed, as you start *and* as you proceed – but invariably *not before* the action button has been pushed!

CRACK THE CODE!

❖ You have to *proactively* create your own space for *mind power work.*

❖ The *key* to unlocking your biocomputer is *you* – get into *action* today and kick-start your biocomputer.

❖ Money, success, love and happiness all manifest themselves from the *action* of programming your biocomputer correctly.

❖ There is no one stopping you from springing into *action* but *you.*

❖ Eliminate *everything* and *anything* that stops you from engaging in *action.*

❖ When ideas present themselves, *act* on them. Doing so will generate even more ideas and solutions – alongside a lavish millionaire lifestyle, designer wardrobes, exotic cars, money, investments, first class travel, businesses, country homes, mega-yachts *and* V8 motorcycles, if that is your desire!

❖ Your biocomputer is a 24-7-365 loyal servant. *Program* it to lead a more action-oriented life. *Act* on it.

❖ Many of the things that can impede your *action* and block your success are Invisible Entrapments programs, be ultra-wary of them.

❖ Stop kidding yourself – and start getting into action!

THE SEVENTH KEY

Basic Visual InAdvance

THE ADVANCED MANUAL

To induce your brain to work like a computer, you must first program it like a computer.

– Ron G Holland

Enigma: Why is it that computer users install conventional software and work with it for an entire year before they eventually sit down to read the accompanying manual: *How to Install and Get the Most from Your Software*? As they say in computer parlance *RTFM* – which you'll probably want to Google.

Eureka! Our finest Eureka! moment has to be when we categorically accept that by intentionally programming our biocomputer for specific goals, in a *precise* manner, using our own unique *keys*, it will deliver powerful augmented *Colossus Output* that will greatly and unequivocally assist us in reaching our goals. Armed with that knowledge, further study and application is unadulterated joy.

Just when you thought we were nearing the end of the codebook, this climactic chapter builds into a dazzling crescendo as we assemble all the vital strands of the most powerful personal success philosophy in the world. In Chapter Two I introduced the all-important software, **Basic Visual InAdvance**. You'll need to understand intimately how to program your biocomputer with this software if you want to generate *Colossus Output* and achieve your goals. This chapter is designed as an advanced software manual for **Basic Visual InAdvance** to assist you in doing just that.

KEY – FIREWALL:

When computer programmers learn to write software, one of their first lessons is how to write the installation instructions in a simple, accessible form; the last thing a consumer wants is software that's difficult to install. Yet it's surprising how many good programs carry completely baffling directions for their use.

Just as there is an optimal way to download software for your computer, there's an optimal way to download software to your *biocomputer*. And I'm going to explain it to you in a simple, accessible way.

As I was writing *Turbo Success* in 1993 my extensive investigations led me to the Reticular Activating System (RAS), which is a crucial part of mind programming that is frequently overlooked. It was this remarkable discovery that became a major turning point in my life.

The RAS is positioned at the top of the brain stem; it's about the size of your pinky finger (but, as they say, big things come in small packages). It acts as the brain's firewall, controlling the information that flows into your brain's neurons. This area of tightly packed nerve fibers and cells contains nearly 70 percent of your brain's estimated 100 billion nerve cells, a total of 70 billion cells. But it can be deliberately deactivated to allow you to insert *Bespoke Input*, completely bypassing your intellect.

The RAS was discovered by two renowned physiologists Dr. Magoun and Dr. Moruzzi and I hope this brief explanation will lead you to find out more about it for yourself, and of course motivate you to *deliberately* invoke its use on a daily basis. It is the RAS that the stage hypnotist or the clinical hypnotherapist deactivates in their subject or patient prior to inputting suggestions. In the early 1980s I practiced hypnotherapy for a period of time in Boston, Massachusetts, working with a variety of patients – all facing problems they couldn't consciously resolve including tinnitus, insomnia and inadequate self-image. By taking my patients into a state of hypnosis, i.e. deactivating the RAS and thereby completely bypassing all their mental defenses, I was able to insert software to override many negative programs, including those causing excess weight, nicotine and alcohol abuse and drug addiction.

The RAS plays a fundamental role in reprogramming the human biocomputer. You may have heard the story of Edison and his method of visualization? He relaxed in his armchair and intuitively deactivated his RAS to allow his imagination free rein. He held a bunch of keys in his hand and if they dropped he would be alerted to the fact that he had fallen asleep. With practice, you will be able to emulate Edison and enter a state of ultra-consciousness at will.

The RAS is, in effect, the firewall to the human biocomputer. Most computers have firewalls and the more sophisticated the set-up, the more impenetrable that firewall is. Firewalls stop hackers, crackers and other users from penetrating your computer and stealing information or corrupting it with Trojan horses, viruses, worms and worse. If your firewall isn't working effectively, or is bypassed, your computer can be taken over and information manipulated or stolen, many times without your knowledge.

Like the computer's firewall, the RAS is literally the filter of the mind – it helps screen out anything that could potentially damage your biocomputer and its software, as well as all the information your biocomputer receives that's simply not relevant or important in your life.

Although it's only a tiny part of the brain, the RAS does a *Colossus* amount of work, making trillions of computations per second, simultaneously and continuously. Imagine, for example, driving along a busy road with cars streaming toward you, some at frightening speed. You register these cars one by one, assess the risk and are prepared, in all instances, to act if one car does something unexpected; the human biocomputer even processes an estimate of another driver's psychological makeup. Yet once that vehicle has gone past you and the risk has gone, you never give it a second thought. The RAS has filtered all the information that has no value to you, which allows you to get on with focusing on the next car and the next, all day long. Imagine if the RAS allowed all the cars to stay in your biocomputer; you'd have thousands of them to worry about and you'd probably go completely mad or, at the very least, the cork would pop out!

The RAS is the same mechanism that allows thousands of people to live under the flight paths of Jumbo Jets. The majority of people living there have their RAS filter out the *unwanted noise* and they never hear a sound. Friends come to visit and exclaim, "Gee, how do you put up with this!?" Truth to tell, if they lived there, within a few days *their* RAS will have filtered out the *unwanted noise* and they too would not hear the aircraft or be distracted by them.

As a firewall the RAS works brilliantly, but the problem is that it often works too well. For example, if you're studying a glossy brochure of a new auto that you want to be able to buy, you really need that information impregnated into the neurons in your biocomputer - to create a program - so you can come up with ideas and solutions on how to acquire it. Yet it is highly probable, unless you carry out certain actions, the RAS will filter out the information you take in from the brochure and stop the desired image from *sticking* in your mind – in the all important neurons. You'd only get a *superficial impression* of the dream car when you really want to download the *full impression* of it. Wow – that's profound!

You need to get past the RAS to get programs *embedded* into your mind. The *key*, when installing any new biocomputer software – whether it's running a scenario of moving into your 8-bedroom villa, a deal you are trying to close for $250,000 or the expansion plans for your engineering business – is to *totally* relax first, slip into Alpha state, deactivate the RAS filtering mechanism, bypass the intellect and *only then* install detailed *Basic Visual InAdvance* programs, *seeing* the completed goal and hundreds of options of how that particular goal could be accomplished – *Bespoke Input* – right!

Yet once you're relaxed, your RAS is deactivated and your main defense is down for someone to intentionally or unwittingly slip in corrupting, negative, de-motivating or otherwise damaging software into your biocomputer. So as soon as you're done inserting programs in **Basic Visual InAdvance,** it's critical that you *snap out* of the deactivated mode immediately, i.e. bring your RAS back into operation so it can then perform its very important filtering function – if you don't do this, you'll be susceptible to other people's negative suggestions and programs. The RAS is brilliant at keeping those at bay – *once* it is reactivated. You *reactivate* your RAS by counting yourself out of the altered state, jumping up and down, drinking coffee, slapping yourself around the face, taking a cold shower or whatever it is that you do when you get out of bed in the morning to bring yourself into a fully functioning state!

Installing software when you are completely relaxed is such an important part of the whole *Eureka! Enigma* system that some valuable additional material has been made available for readers of this codebook: visit www. eureka-enigma.com and here you can download for *free* the chapter entitled *The RAS* from my book *Turbo Success – How to Reprogram the Human Biocomputer.* In addition, there is also a *free* audio relaxation induction, the identical one that I use for taking *myself,* my *patients* and *clients* into Alpha state, which is *guaranteed* to deactivate the RAS. You can download this onto an MP3, iPod, CD, computer or other device, listen to it and relax yourself before embarking on any **Basic Visual InAdvance** programs – but whatever you do, don't listen to it while driving! (Bruce did and he went 150 miles past his turn-off on the freeway, before snapping out of the altered state!)

Hot Tip! Thomas Edison was thrown out of school at age 12 for his poor speech, reading and mathematics skills, but went on to patent 1,093 inventions and become a multi-millionaire. He got something *right* – his *right* brain!

!!! I'm Bristling With New Ideas!

KEY – WRITE DETAILED PROGRAMS:

When it comes to programming a conventional computer it is relatively easy to understand what kind of programs you require for the particular output you desire. Is the same true of the biocomputer? Let's first conduct an experiment. We're going to write a simple computer program, beta test it and see what we can learn from the results.

Let's imagine we own a family robot called *Freddie iRobot* whose job is to help you with household tasks, including run errands. Today we want him to do food shopping and we need a program for this. First we'll give the program a name: *Freddie Goes Shopping!* Now we write some lines of code for the program: Go to car. Get in car. Drive to store. Buy groceries.

What do you think will happen? Not a lot, I can assure you. We have only used four lines of code and *assumed* far too much. *Freddie iRobot* will come back and say, "Where is the car parked? How do I start it? Which store? What direction? What groceries do you require?"

We have what computer programmers refer to as *lack of functional specification*. What we must do – and this is the hardest part of programming – is break the task down into a detailed *step-by-step* process by using more lines of code. So, *Freddie iRobot*, try this:

1. *Go to the car, which is parked immediately in front of the house.*

2. *Open the car door and get in the driver's side, where the steering wheel is.*

3. *Find a small hole in which to insert the key, which is now in your pocket.*

4. *Turn the key and start the car.*

5. *Travel down the road for exactly one mile.*

6. *Go into the supermarket and buy three quarts of whiskey, two tubs of ice-cream and three magazines.*

What bugs might *Freddie iRobot* find here? Suppose the car doesn't start? We should include solutions in the program. Also, the store might be closed, or there could be a traffic diversion. And how does *Freddie iRobot* know whether we want Jim Beam or Jack Daniel's, Haagen-Dazs or Ben & Jerry's and *Time, Forbes* and *Fortune* as opposed to *The National Enquirer, Washington Post* and *New York Times?* And what does *Freddie* do after the supermarket visit? You've given him no further instructions so he might do anything from staying put to pushing on down to the coast for a spot of surfing – with *Nancy iRobot,* perhaps!

We might need to add another 200 or even 500 lines of code to the program to ensure that *Freddie iRobot* gets to the supermarket and returns with the groceries we require – and that's just for our playful *exercise.* In reality, a computer programmer would write tens of thousands of lines of code to facilitate this simple task. Every logistical detail of the operation would be covered, from finding the car to unloading the groceries back at home. And in between, the programmer must predict any likely pitfalls and provide ways out – contingency options (branches). If the program is not written in this comprehensive way, end users will inevitably experience problems as bugs crop up.

Of course, programmers can't always spot every possible bug, so beta testing of software is usually carried out by thousands of *guinea pig* users who get free or discount programs in return for their feedback – feedback that enables the programmer to *dramatically* improve the product prior to its public launch. You can simulate this test process with your biocomputer programs – give them theoretical test drives by asking appropriate questions such as, "What if interest rates rocketed / my supplier went bust / my best customer went to a competitor / I broke my leg / the stock market crashed / we don't raise the capital we need?" Worst-case scenario types among you may want to extend this cheerful list of lurking bugs!

What have we learned from *Freddie iRobot?* We find that even the simplest tasks are comprised of far more *detailed steps* than we first imagine. And if we are *imagining* ourselves creating a business, becoming a millionaire, writing a bestseller – whatever your goal is – then we need to think about *detailed steps* in the same way.

Moving from the program: *Get the car and go shopping* to *Becoming a millionaire* is a giant leap for mankind – womankind too! And as you know, simply affirming, "I am a millionaire" and *hoping* it will happen just *doesn't* work. That's not to say becoming a millionaire, or accomplishing anything else you desire to do, is impossible. It is to say that nothing less than a verifiable *Bespoke Programming* method can guarantee you success in your chosen ambitions. Just as we programmed *Freddie* to pick up our whiskey, ice-cream and magazines, you can program your biocomputer to fetch you your new mail order business, Beverly Hills dream home, Mercedes-Benz SL65 AMG, ocean-going Riva Duchessa and *still* leave you a million on deposit. *You can do it!* But you have to write the program first – then install it using *Basic Visual InAdvance.*

Many individuals have chosen; *I am a millionaire* as a program and endeavored to install it in their biocomputers – usually with little or no results. Having been in the self-help arena for over 30 years, I have met *thousands* of those people – we've grown together! To get your biocomputer to work like a computer you have to treat it like a computer, not a mailbox for sending your wish list to Santa! You want to become a millionaire? OK, you have your software title; now you must begin serious work on the *actual* program. If you're feeling fazed remember that you're in a perfect position to design a program for your biocomputer in the favored *top-down* tradition, i.e. with your overall goal defined first. Here are your top-down planning steps:

1. Define your overall goal

2. Work out the logic to get you there, but do not concern yourself with lack of resources – it's the biocomputers function to come up with all the missing links!

3. Write the program

You have already defined your overall goal as; *I am a millionaire* so you can go straight to stage two. But don't expect to complete this step in one attempt! It requires rigorous discipline as you evaluate your options and make some serious decisions. Think about the program you want to create and experiment with some lines of code, which you can begin to write as you answer various questions: Where will your million dollars come from? Working for someone else or starting your own business? Say you decide the latter. OK, what type of business? If it's a restaurant, is it up-market cuisine or fast food? Something tried and tested or a new concept? What locations? What kind of premises? Will your financing come from savings, commercial loans or family? Will the loan be fixed rate or variable? And those are just a few of the many questions you'll have to ask and answer in step 2.

This is far from rocket science, but you'd be amazed how many people try to make money or start a business without firmly answering *basic* questions first. As you answer them, you can begin to create a logical sequence of cause and effect and then go on to write *detailed* program code for your biocomputer to process – which will finally give you *Colossus Output,* filling in all the missing gaps such as where to obtain money and other resources, or showing you other *ultra-creative* ways to do it – perhaps without any money at all – remember how I filled my motorbike shops?!

The kinds of decisions I've mentioned are just the very beginning of those that you'll eventually have to make as you write a full program, detailing every step backward from your overall goal to where you are now. Step 2 is likely to be the longest if you're doing it properly. Forcing yourself to answer the how, why, where, what, who, which and when of every step of your future can be a sobering experience. If you get stuck, remember how Alan Turing helped crack the Enigma code – begin by eliminating millions of wrong answers first; if you can't think of a viable business idea, list *all* the ideas you *don't* think will work for you, and why, and then see what emerges. You will learn things about yourself in this planning stage, maybe discovering that your route to success is likely to be very different to the one you anticipated. These discoveries are all part of the exciting success-building process.

KEY – MULTI-SENSORY PROGRAMMING:

Attaching feelings and emotions to your visualizations is a *major* part of **Basic Visual InAdvance** but I also know a lot of people *don't* add emotion to their visualizations – perhaps because they have never had the concept explained in a manner that made complete sense.

Many self-help advocates think that it takes a long time to program a biocomputer. But that doesn't necessarily have to be true – when the programming is done correctly. To program your biocomputer correctly – and quickly – you have to infuse *vast* quantities of *emotion* into your programs.

Consider how most people become afflicted with phobias: they have an experience that's impregnated with tons of negative emotions of say fear, anger or hate (our most potent emotions). Ever after, any reminder of that initial experience triggers the phobia. Here's an example: a young boy picks up a loose trash-can lid from the deck and a snake strikes –writhing and hissing – and frightens the pants off the poor boy. (I have had this experience and it *is* quite scary!) Every time the boy is in a similar situation – facing the prospect of picking up a trash-can lid – he accesses the memory of his experience, which has been infused with eye-popping emotional content, and he's once again petrified. He may well have a phobia of snakes – and trash-can lids – for years to come. He now has a powerful program, *deeply embedded* in the neurons, a permanent track to run on – that took *fraction of a second* to install. This is a major *key!* We need to learn more!

Here's another example: a young girl is teased by her classmates, who threaten to drop frogs down the front of her blouse. She sees the frogs and accesses excessive feelings of fear, not really knowing what the frogs may do to her. Like the young boy's, her experience is likely to create a permanent track in her biocomputer that will affect her for years to come. Why? The exceptional amount of emotion she experienced was a powerful catalyst for burning that phobia program onto the neurons in her biocomputer. Even looking at pictures of frogs in a book or seeing frogs at an aquarium will likely have a traumatic effect on the girl.

These are examples of instantaneous biocomputer programming. The point being is that inordinate levels of *emotion* can impregnate neurons *permanently!* We want to harness that monumental power to write and install our biocomputer programs faster and more effectively – like we've never done before!

Let's take a look at the emotion of worry. Can you remember a time when you were worried? I can, and I assure you it wasn't pleasant. I have actually stood in front of a mirror at the start of the day feeling really nauseous. I suffered internal dialogue and endured unbearable mental pain and anguish – if you can relate to this and you are a *good* worrier that is *fantastic* news. But you can also verify with your own experience that if you *keep* worrying it has a habit of turning out to be self-fulfilling prophecy. Yet being a worrier *also* means that you know exactly how to access the part of the biocomputer we must now turn **ON** to feeling emotional – both negatively and positively, in the correct fashion.

What you have to do is become a *warrior* and not a worrier. What *warriors* do is absolutely know the *positive* outcome of the battle they are just about to *win*. They beat their chests, daub on war paint, punch the air, work themselves up into a frenzy, beat battle drums, shout and scream and literally psyche themselves up and tap into *all* their emotions at the *deepest* level, supercharging literally *billions* of neurons with positive *and* negative emotions. Believe me, for hours before their almighty battle they will be harnessing extraordinary measures of *negative* emotion aimed towards killing their enemy – with a view to *positively* winning on the day! Emotion is the rocket fuel that kicks in the turbo-power of ***Basic Visual InAdvance.*** Harness the emotion – all of it!

Hot Tip! Let your billion-dollar biocomputer do the work – that's what it's there for!

WHAT RON HOLLAND REALLY DOES – PART ONE:

I have already told you in great detail what I *visualized* for publishing this codebook: going into the publisher's office, smile on face, horns in pocket, absolutely *knowing* that I would get a deal and pick up a big fat check. *Seeing* myself on the *Richard and Judy* and *Today* shows which are tremendously popular in the UK and *seeing* books in warehouses - and also flying out of warehouses, by the truck load!

What I haven't revealed yet, is that I started getting *truly* emotional about *seeing* books flood across the country and across the world. I developed that *feeling* and *elation* about getting the book finished and a deal signed. I relished in the *joy* and *happiness*. The *feeling* and unbelievable *satisfaction* was immense now that I had completed my trilogy of *Talk & Grow Rich, Turbo Success* and now, *The Eureka! Enigma*. I could now speed-up the next book project - Yippee! I worked *hard* at cultivating and harnessing these emotions and impregnating billions of neurons.

I could actually *hear* myself talking to the publisher and actually *hear* her speaking back to me and asking *detailed* questions – all in my imagination, in the biocomputer: How much promotion was I prepared to do? Was I already on the seminar circuit? Would I be prepared to do a six-week author tour in the U.S.? Would I be prepared to dramatically increase my profile before I got there? I totally flooded my senses and all of these *questions* with emotion – and the more *emotion* I applied, the more stunning ideas started flooding out and those ideas led me to start a publicity campaign two years *before* I went to the publisher.

My *Colossus Output* also led me to secure a great publishing contract with audible.com and to start promoting MP3 downloads of seven of my previous audio books. It also led me to legally procuring all my book rights back from previous publishers so that I could be in a position to offer a 10-book deal revolving around *The Eureka! Enigma*. It led me to starting up my seminars, alongside *hundreds* of other promotional activities, so that when I finally made a formal submission of the *The Eureka! Enigma* manuscript, I had already significantly increased my profile and was already on a high and a fabulous roll. As they say, the rest is history! But it didn't happen by accident – I programmed for it!

Hot Tip! This really is a *mammoth revelation*: there was a *staggering* amount of *action*, work, energy and creativity that went on behind the scenes, actually implementing hundreds of solutions, ideas and Eurekas! in the two years prior to me even approaching a publisher – that's in *addition* to actually writing this codebook.

!!! Losers unwittingly visualize the penalties of failure.

!!! Winners *intentionally* visualize the rewards of success.

WHAT KAREN DID!

Flooding your *visualizations* with *emotion* is not easy, neither is it obvious! I want to tell you a story about Karen who came to me for some advice, only recently. Karen was a fairly successful businesswoman who had built a number of sizable businesses, but most importantly of all she recognized her weak points and wanted clarification on how to move forward. She could see, from previous talks, that she had often stopped short of putting the full code into her biocomputer, to take her way beyond the end game plan. She took that on board and she brought up the subject of *emotionalizing* goals. Funnily enough I had already *read* Karen as being *highly* emotional. I could also pick up immense energy of positive vibes and an *equally* large amount of negativity. What she asked me specifically, was how could she really harness all her *positive* energy and impregnate billions upon billions of neurons with it.

Karen was surprised as to what I told her next, and you may be too! Karen had a huge amount of anger, frustration, hate and bitterness. Karen was trying to use *Bespoke Input* with *only* positive emotions - as many of us try to do. I told Karen to harness *all* of her emotions, positive *and* negative, and charge her neurons with the emotion, get them excited, and switch them **ON!** - and do it in any way she could! I then related to her a story concerning a good friend of mine who was timidly selling bales of hay, goldfish bowls and cat food from her pet shop in South London. A mean bruiser of a guy came in and started looking around when a stray puppy crossed his path. He got his foot underneath it and kicked it across the room – and it went flying! She harnessed her emotions and charged him three times the amount she would have normally have charged, for the dog that he eventually ended up buying. Now, let's not get into the rights and wrongs – let's stick with switching the biocomputer **ON** and turning peoples lives around. The upshot of her story was from that day on she was a changed woman and went from strength to strength – big time! Harness both positive *and* negative emotions! Could this be a *key* for you? I bet it is!

When I finished the story Karen looked ten years younger, she was transformed and beaming. She was so excited! This is what she said, "Suddenly it all makes sense Ron. Now I know why Boudica, a tribal warrior Queen in Britain 2,000 years ago, failed miserably all her early life and only became powerful *after* she was brutally gang-raped, her children beaten with rods and many of her subjects brutalized by the Romans. I'd read the story many times, but never equated it to *harnessing negative emotions*. The ultimate in girl power!" Check it out!

WHAT RON HOLLAND REALLY DOES – PART TWO:

I try to harness all positive and negative emotions when I am visualizing. Sometimes I strut around the room shouting and screaming and punching the air. I know that I must alter my physiology, emulating a warrior, if I am to really get into a *sufficiently powerful emotional state* to have a *meaningful effect* on the neurons in my biocomputer – and switch them **ON!** I find it ever so difficult to get emotional if I am in Alpha state, so it is a delicate balance of doing some visualizing in **Basic Visual InAdvance**, then standing up and pumping myself up emotionally, then slipping back into Alpha to carry on with **Basis Visual InAdvance**. I also spend a lot of time trying to *feel and know* what it would be like to accomplish a specific goal. I exert myself to be *quietly confident* and *blissfully happy* and *just know* that I have arrived at my goal. This is a very difficult process to describe, but when you actually start practicing yourself, you'll absolutely know when you do start to get those *feelings of knowing*. The real *key* here is experimentation, trying all ways to access all *emotions* and see what works for you, in terms of *Colossus Output*.

!!! "Everything you can imagine is real." – *Pablo Picasso*

Hot Tip! Keep feeding in a *perfect vision* of everything you want in your life, become a mental magician, and soon you will be living your dream – because your biocomputer will burst forth with brilliant creative ideas, like a desert in bloom after its first rain. Remember – it's all in the code!

KEY – THINK & GROW SLIM:

What a title for a book – try and beat me to it! Anyone who has been caught in the diet trap, trying each new system and yo-yoing around on the scales knows the frustration of trying to lose weight. There's always a plethora of healthy eating books out there, all making oodles of boodle for their authors. But I haven't come across one yet that really gets to grips with the fundamentals of creating *permanent* change. They all talk about food and exercise and serve both topics up in a variety of tasty ways. But every single book about diet is written in **BASIC WORD** – and incidentally so is every self-help book in the market place! If ever there was a conspiracy theory it's that all diet book authors have ganged up and made a pact to never release the real truth about losing weight – so they can go on selling more and more books!

What the vast majority of slimming books and systems fail to tell you is that the *only* way to lose weight *permanently* is to *first* install in your biocomputer a powerful *mental* weight loss program in ***Basic Visual InAdvance.*** It is imperative not only that you *visualize* yourself as slim, but also *visualize getting* slim and *keeping* slim – by inserting *hundreds* of different options of *eating* and *exercising* in a disciplined fashion. It is vital to run *numerous* mental scenarios through your biocomputer and thus create a permanent track on which to run – in the neurons. Skinny code – right!

See yourself at different times – entertaining, under stress, wining and dining, snacking and eating comfort foods – and then *visualize* the kind of healthy eating behavior you want to achieve. *Superfluous eating* – when you eat *not* out of natural hunger, but out of habit, tension, anger, frustration, boredom, craving or obligation – is the curse of those with a weight problem. Friends like to be hospitable and offer food, and it can be difficult to say "NO!" without feeling you've given offence. Create suitable programs for new, healthy behaviors – ways to keep out of those kinds of traps – and play them out, *in your mind's eye,* regularly.

Input the correct *bespoke software* program for your biocomputer when you're totally relaxed, i.e. with the RAS deactivated, *weeks, even months before* you even start your diet and exercise routine. Keeping to an optimum weight may seem trivial compared to those concerned with making their first million, but don't forget how easily the former can impede the latter. Good health and fitness can do wonders for your career and business success; if you're not healthy and fit you're not going to be able to get to work and keep up long hours and do extensive meetings and traveling – you'll be tired, flagging and not be able to concentrate. And good health and fitness – like anything else – can *only* be achieved through the use of *Basic Visual InAdvance*.

Let's take as an example the program: *I will lose weight.* From this simple affirmation you can move on to consider the following. Exactly what do I have to do in order to lose weight? How do I *look* when I have lost the weight? What do I say and how do I behave when others offer me food or drink that I know I should decline? How should I behave when everyone around me is eating sumptuous three-course meals, plying themselves with mouth-watering deserts and consuming vast quantities of sugar-loaded alcohol? Where, when and how will I exercise without feeling self-conscious? *Picture* these scenarios and decide on the most desirable image and effective behavior on your part then modify each picture accordingly and keep inserting this program until it takes hold in the depths of literally billions upon billions of neurons. The *key* is to visualize *InAdvance* healthy behaviors – drinking water and eating lots of fruit before every meal, for example. Work out literally *hundreds* of suitable options that will work *specifically* for *you* and then **INTERNALIZE** those options.

I am often in awe of the number of patients I have worked with, many under hypnosis, who have told me in no uncertain terms that their *bad* eating programs are intrinsically tied to a *partner* or an *event* that makes them angry, unhappy, sad, de-motivated, frustrated or some other emotion that forces them to eat unhealthily. The astounding thing is this *partner* or *event* could have occurred many years ago, but had affected their biocomputer at a cellular level. Programs such as: *He came home late again last night, I'll eat a gallon of ice cream* or *she upsets me so much and makes me so angry, I'll have a beer* – or *coffee* or whatever negative emotive programs have embedded themselves into billions of neurons and are now *unwittingly* controlling your *output*.

You will of course notice that none of those programs have anything to do with *hunger* – people are eating themselves to death because of an *emotional* program that has been installed, which they have managed to *link* or *anchor* in some perverse way to food. With some simple, straightforward, honest analysis you will be able to go *inside yourself* and discover what your programs are, *and* correct them internally – *before* you start your diet. Once you have imbedded a sound program into billions of neurons at a cellular level and given yourself a *permanent* track to run on, I promise you faithfully it won't make an iota of difference as to which *specific* diet you choose to go on.

I remember numerous occasions having a Chinese luncheon with Max Clifford, (UK's top tabloid PR man) and various journalists he introduced me to. Max would be in his jogging suit and he'd make sure there was a good selection of exotic dishes on the table. Yet Max would never eat a thing – not even a fortune cookie! He would ease the conversation along and make sure the journalist captured the full story, or at the very least, Max's embellished interpretation of it.

These days I go to parties, clubs and business lunches and never touch alcohol. I order Coke, fruit juice or Red Bull and am quite happy with my *programming* and *behavior* and I have met all sorts of people who carry out similar behaviors that they are extremely happy about. They are in the *disciplined zone* that they installed weeks or months beforehand, and when they are in live, *under pressure* circumstances, they don't miss food or drink or revert to whatever destructive behaviors that were holding them back previously. They run *effortlessly* on the new software program. *Extraordinary power* is in those billions of tiny neurons – nowhere else! Nowhere!

KEY – MULTIPLE STREAMS OF REVENUE:

This is a topic I know quite a lot about, having revenues coming from a number of sources, including: royalties from many separate publishers, mobilization fees, success fees, seminar fees, consultancy fees, cashflow from book sales, subscription revenues from the *Debt-Free Club* and the *Eureka! Confidential Newsletter,* fees from mentoring and coaching, Internet revenues from various web sites, revenues from books, manuals and CDs, high-interest accounts, rental income, shares and options. (And I nearly forgot the day job – but of course that's only a joke!)

And *none* of that happened by *accident.* A considerable amount of planning and *mental effort* and *action* went into making all of those multiple streams of revenue actually happen. I started by writing up an action plan in **BASIC WORD** and then transmuted that plan into *Basic Visual InAdvance.* I really did *see* multiple streams of revenue in my imagination first, came up with the ideas, the *Colossus Output,* and then sprang into *relentless action,* turning it all into reality, and if *you* really desire multiple streams of income – I suggest *you* do the same!

So you want more? I'm happy to give it to you – after all, you paid me for this book, you are one of my income streams and I hope you remain a happy customer of mine for many years to come. I don't know where you live – USA, United Kingdom, Russia, India, China? Welcome aboard! Maybe you are in Canada, New Zealand, Australia, Denmark, Bulgaria or Hungary? My products sell in 32 countries *and* on the Internet, so I guess I have *global* revenue streams – just like I programmed for!

To build multiple revenue streams I create a plan or plans in **BASIC WORD**. I have four books on the go at any one time so I create four box files, one for each book. I have ten consultancy clients at any one time, so I create ten box files for them. As I start to *visualize* the success of each project in *Basic Visual InAdvance,* each book and each client starts shaping up in my mind. I get assorted ideas and hunches, as a result of *mind set* and *Bespoke Programming,* which I jot down and stuff in the appropriate files. I get *drawn* to books, magazines and trade directories, all of which are clipped or photocopied and stuffed in corresponding files. As each file gets bigger, the projects become clearer, and I start to hone the vision, which now includes all the new materials, angles and the direction the project is shaping up in.

That's why you must visualize *every day,* because life's plan is changing daily, it's a movable feast that is just getting bigger and better. The more you develop each project, the more the biocomputer delivers. The more you *visualize* your goals **InAdvance,** the more the *compounding* effect kicks in. In other words, the more you visualize, the more the images of your goals are *burned* on your neurons and the more *Colossus Output* you receive. When you get ideas that are a *result* of *Bespoke Programming* they come *packaged with motivation* and you will feel *compelled* to put them into action. If you want to be minted, if you want multiple streams of income, then start programming! Today!

KEY – REMOVE FAULTY LOOPS:

Programmers use looping for recurring lines of code, rather like writing the words *repeat chorus* between the verses of a hymn. Looping makes a program quicker to write and to use. But faulty looping can block the program by returning the user repeatedly back to one particular point. This inability to move forward can plague biocomputer programs, too. I recall a period in my Boston office when things were not going at all well; I was repeatedly blowing out deals and couldn't seem to break the negative loop pattern.

I wrote down all the words *and* pictures going through my mind. I was shocked to discover I had some damaging bugs, faulty loops which repeatedly threw up images of my past failures – from companies that had gone down the gurgler to folk that had wronged me. As soon as I picked up the phone, my biocomputer would churn these negative pictures past my eyes, forming hyper-links to grim future possibilities – another blown deal, mounting debts, the oppressing shadow of bankruptcy looming. No wonder my sales calls would yield nothing; loops are self-perpetuating and mine was a real showstopper!

I needed to rewrite my program and remove the faulty loop from my software. I immediately wrote a list of all the good, positive, exciting things that had happened in my life. Despite my failures, I had closed deals, made money, had many successes, made lots of friends. I had accomplished literally hundreds of positive things in my life. I wrote down all my past successes in **BASIC WORD**, translated those words into pictures in **Basic Visual,** and then into *Basic Visual InAdvance* for inputting into my biocomputer. I then installed a *mental film* of all those previous successes *combined* with successes I desired to happen in the future and also *amalgamated* them with *many* alternative ways I could possibly make those future successes happen. Then I ran that *film* over and over again in my biocomputer, diligently installing the *bespoke program **InAdvance.*** Very soon after, I felt I was in a completely different space, the deeply imbedded failure program dissolved in a growing mood of optimism and well-being. Within a single month I had closed more business than in the previous twelve and I found myself, with the aid of *Colossus Output, automatically* saying the *right* things at precisely the *right* time to potential customers.

Another powerful *key* is that even if you haven't had hundreds of small successes that you can make a mental film out of, *it doesn't matter.* The human biocomputer cannot tell the difference between a real experience and a vividly imagined one – so create a film made up of imagined successes – success stories that never actually happened! And run *that* mental film – the *output* will be the same – and it'll be *Colossus!*

KEY – GOAL SETTING THAT ACTUALLY WORKS!

I have had the advantage of leading many hundreds of seminars over a long period of time and it is a great privilege to learn the innermost secrets of thousands of ambitious people as they go through life's troughs and peaks of failure and success. It is encouraging to see how many people setting out on a path of personal development have Big Ideas – or is it? Consider one serious young man who arrived at my biocomputer workshop, and told me his list of goals:

> ➢ To have $100,000,000 in the bank within three years (Yes, that's right, a *hundred million* dollars!)

> ➢ To own an island in the Caribbean

> ➢ To own a Bell helicopter and Gulf Stream jet - and learn how to fly

> ➢ To own the biggest, baddest, meanest 550-foot Mega-Yacht, with disco, helicopter, mini-sub and four 30-foot tenders. (You're talking of much more than $100 million here – but I admire his ambition!)

> ➢ To own an offshore bank

Nothing wrong with these goals *per se*. However, the guy arrived in a beaten-up pick-up truck, was dressed like a tramp and when I drilled down on him I discovered his thinking was not quite as sharp as it could have been; and he exuded tremendous frustration and lack of creativity – and I'm being diplomatic! On a scale of one-to-ten this lad was at zero when it came to receiving *Colossus Output* from his biocomputer. It wasn't even switched **ON!**

A list of goals that would have probably served this young man much better is:

> ➢ By the end of the year, my current business will be kicking in and generating $100,000 a year with good profit

> ➢ I instigate an aggressive expansion scheme and my cashflow triples

> ➢ I own a new Ford pick-up truck and, in my second year, a new BMW as well

> ➢ I concentrate on *harnessing* the power of my biocomputer and program twice daily for small goals

> ➢ I work diligently on programming my biocomputer so that I can verify with my own experience that I am really accomplishing my smaller goals with *reliable* regularity

➤ I monitor the *output* I am receiving from my biocomputer to ensure that it is compatible with the goals I have set for myself

➤ I fully grasp the principles of the biocomputer and faithfully use *Basic Visual InAdvance.* Once I have harnessed the awesome power of my biocomputer and it is delivering *Colossus Output* and **Eurekas! on Demand** I will then be ready to move up to larger, more ambitious goals

➤ Once I have managed to create a good living and an acceptable lifestyle for myself, I will actively begin to work on biocomputer programs that will start aligning me for much bigger goals such as having $100,000,000, owning my own bank, island, helicopter, airplane and mega-yacht

With *these* goals in place *and* extremely diligent programming, this young man would find himself shooting up the ladder of success, merrily, no frustration, overcoming all obstacles, creativity clicking in, accomplishing various and numerous smaller goals on the way. When he got his biocomputer clicking in fully, he would then be heading towards much larger goals, abundance and financial freedom – hey, why not?!

Hot Tip! I have never known *anyone* to accomplish the *larger* goals in life until they had *fully* harnessed the faculty of their biocomputer *first* and got it delivering usable, *Colossus Output.* This is one heck of a powerful principle – and it may be a *key* for you.

!!! If this *key* doesn't unlock *your* biocomputer – find one that does!

KEY – BE YOUR OWN LIFE TECHNICIAN:

With the human biocomputer you can't look in the yellow pages and call an expert to sort out your bugs and download new software. Although, of course, people do try the equivalent. They engage life coaches and visit shrinks – often for years and at considerable expense. I *guess* you can get comfort and support from such services, maybe make a little progress. But if you want to manage and permanently maintain your own biocomputer, the sooner you wean yourself off outside interference the better. Freudian, Jungian and other systems of therapy, together with most types of self-improvement, use single *keys* cut to a set pattern. *The Eureka! Enigma* equips you with a fantasmogorical machine for cutting your own unique *keys* – any number or combination of them.

KEY – WYSIWYG:

The subject of personal happiness is usually at the top of the agenda at my biocomputer workshops. Recently in a London workshop I met a great guy by the name of Howard who was desperately trying to create a happy life for himself. For Howard his *happy life* consisted of getting married, white-wedding style, having a couple of kids, creating a nice home and enjoying a stable, blissful future as a family man. But so far, he'd only managed one-night stands. What Howard wanted was not what Howard was getting, though it wasn't for lack of trying – he'd long been doing loads of *visualizations* of his desired family-life scenario, or so he thought.

Yet when we delved deeper into his ***Basic Visual InAdvance*** programming techniques this is what we discovered. Howard would relax on his bed and basically fantasize about making love. In his mind's eye he would be meeting a lovely lady, introducing himself, buying drinks, chatting, inviting her back for coffee and finally the clothes-off and sex scene. And it worked – great! As a result of his *visualizations* he could boast of a long series of one-night-stands and short-term relationships. Trouble is, he wasn't boasting. He was depressed that his brilliance at getting from the *bar to bedroom* in a few swift moves hadn't landed him a long-term partner.

I asked Howard if he'd ever run a *complete **Basic Visual InAdvance*** program of courting a woman, taking her on holiday, really getting to know her, wining and dining together and eventually popping the question. Had he actually *seen* the white wedding? Had he *heard* himself say "I do" and his fiancé replying and becoming his wife? Had he *seen* their lovely marital home, babies arriving and growing up, observed them enjoying a vacation together as a family? From the way his jaw dropped when I asked those questions it was obvious to everyone in the auditorium that he had visualized *none* of these things. Time had arrived to install the complete program, *happy family* code – right!

Howard blushed, "I can now see this is a classic case of having my ideas and thoughts in the left side of my brain in *words* but not converting them *correctly* into *pictures* – as Ron is always reiterating; a classic case of lost in translation and what you *see* is what you get!"

Hot Tip! The brain circuitry starts rewiring itself the moment you start *applying* creative visualization, ***InAdvance!***

KEY – WORLD CHAMPIONS VISUALIZE TOO:

I usually help people accomplish goals like starting a new business, raising expansion capital, finding innovative cost-effective marketing methods, writing a prospectus, or other business-oriented goals. But I once helped a fisherman program his biocomputer for championship success and I want to share the story with you here…

The fisherman in question is an affable Welshman by the name of Clive Branson. He came to me after hearing that I help people accomplish their goals; he wanted to be world champion fisherman. He had come second, third and fourth in numerous tournaments but the world championship title had always eluded him – how could I help? We agreed on my fee and I took him into a state of hypnosis, having previously informed him that I knew absolutely *nothing* about fishing – but *lots* about biocomputers.

With Clive under hypnosis, and his RAS completely deactivated, I graphically described his living room back at his house and told him, in no uncertain terms, creating very strong *mental* images in his biocomputer, to swipe clean the mantel above his fireplace. Whatever was there – an old clock, postcards, nick-knacks, Christmas cards, a vase – wipe it all off and let it *crash* in a big heap on the floor so the mantelpiece was now completely *empty.* The next task was to sit back in an armchair and totally *relax* and stare at the empty mantel and start to *visualize* the magnificent trophy he *was* going to win. I got him, still under hypnosis, to *feel* the *glory* and *fun* and *excitement* and *satisfaction* of winning. I now told him to go deep into his mind, to the world fishing championship and *see* the trophy and himself as the winner.

I then inserted a program of *all* the things he would *really* have to do in order to win the championship. Not just being there on the day and pulling out the largest fish, but *all* the things – I made a point of it – *all* the things he'd have to do in the year leading up to the championship in Portugal. I implanted a complete chain of *pictures*, wrapped up with mega-doses of *emotional* content, and inserted those *feelings* and *pictures* deep within billions and billions of neurons in his biocomputer, inserting world beating code – if you will. I talked for about an hour, making sure he really was accessing sounds, pictures *and* emotions. I then *snapped* him out of the altered state – i.e. reactivated his RAS.

I had forgotten all about this magical session until one evening, about a year later, when I was just about to get up on stage at an *Apprentice Millionaires Club* event at the Rubens Hotel in Victoria, London. We had a full house of about 200 people and this guy with a strong Welsh accent came up to me and said, "I don't know if you remember me boyo, but my name's Clive Branson and thanks to you I am now world champion fisherman and I wonder if I could get up on stage and say a few words, before you go on." Sure enough, he stood up on stage and held up his solid gold medal on a red ribbon flash and a large gleaming trophy, proud as punch, letting the delighted audience know how I helped him attain the championship using extraordinary mind power techniques – the same ones I am teaching you here in this codebook!

Later that evening, we went for supper and he revealed in detail the ideas that started to come to him as a result of our session. He already knew he was a great fisherman, but what he didn't realize, to actually secure the championship, were all the *other things* he'd have to do – finance a new vehicle for travel to all the events leading up to the final and fund the cost of accommodation at those events. He actually had to sell his house to finance everything himself – no sponsorship then, although once he was world champion the offers flooded in. For once, Clive had put together a *complete success package* – not just concentrating on the fishing, but finance, travel, admin, tackle and *everything* else related to ultimate success. And like they say, the rest is written in the record books. That's the remarkable story of the one that didn't get away!

SCIENTIFIC KEYS

CONVENTIONAL COMPUTERS ONLY THINK IN 1s AND 0s

"Conventional digital computers operate on a binary (meaning 2) system, i.e. 0s and 1s. It is highly likely that the biocomputer operates on a tertiary (meaning 3) system, i.e. Acid, Alkaline and Neutral and that is where the biocomputer's super processing power comes from, which is the *key* to thinking in *words* and *pictures* and *concepts*. In this area we are still within the realms of speculation – though informed, I hope."

Bruce Snyder, scientist, physicist, mathematician and Ron Holland's business partner for nearly twenty years.

KEY – A FAMILIAR REFERENCE POINT:

This entire codebook is dedicated to *visualization* because it is the *key* to inserting powerful *bespoke programs* into your biocomputer, giving you a permanent track to run on, leading you to your goals and generating a never-ending supply of *output* that actually works. I want to have one final shot at driving home exactly how to *visualize* – this may be particularly handy if you're still struggling with the concept. I like to start with a *reference point,* one that you're familiar with and can relate to and will immediately access *all* of the faculties that you will need to turn your biocomputer **ON!**

An imaginary beach – but a real one that you already know

My reference point is a beach scene that you know particularly well in the real world and I'd like you, in your *imagination,* to walk along that beach right now. Insert a clear blue sky and *feel* a gentle warm breeze coming in from the ocean. *Feel* the sand squelching between your toes and *feel* the hands of your lover and the sun baking down on your back. *Hear* the waves crash and seagulls calling as a distant boat sounds its horn and a nearby buoy rings its bell. *Taste* the frozen-banana, snow-cone or fiery-hot L'Atomica pizza that you're merrily munching on as you enjoy romantic and *emotional* conversation. Skip over the seaweed that's washed up, squeeze your partner's hand, giggle at a silly joke that doesn't make sense, get romantic with your lover as the sun begins to go down, catch a hint of her perfume or his cologne. Tiny *detail* is a crucial aspect of embedding code into your biocomputer, indeed it is the *accumulation* of all the *little things* that make a difference. Make it *real* in every sense of the word – but all in your imagination. *Feel* elation, happiness, fulfillment, zest for life – like you're really there!

Before we move on to the next scene I would like you to go back to all those *emotions* and *elevate* them to the highest pitch you can muster – until you couldn't possibly be more emotional. Hopefully by using a familiar reference point to start your *visualization* you have managed to get yourself not only *visualizing* but also accessing extremely important emotions that are really going to help you impregnate billions of neurons that will be crucial for you to actually accomplish your goals in the real world.

You walk around the corner of the beach and see your dream home

Now continue along that beach and start to turn the corner and look up and now *see* your dream home. *See* the *visual projection* in the exact same detail as your beach scene and insert a high content of emotion. Transfer that vivid visual content to the home of your choice and actually *see* in your imagination the detail in the marble tiles, carpeting, wallpaper and soft furnishings. Take your *emotion* into your home gym where you *see* yourself working out; then taking a dip in the cool guitar-shaped pool. Go into as many rooms in your dream home as possible and *see* them without furnishings and then view them fully furnished – exactly as you would like them. *See,* in your imagination, gold leaf around a mirror, gold-plated faucets in the bathroom, draperies that glide back and forth at the push of a button in the master bedroom, cut glass brandy goblets from Poland in the smoking room – if you have one! As you stroll nonchalantly into the immaculate gardens you smell freshly mown grass and you *hear* the steak and jumbo prawns sizzle on the Bar-B-Q and then *taste* Maine lobster with garlic butter and sip Brut Champagne and *smell* freshly brewed coffee. You *hear* animated conversation of friends in the background. The more *visual* and *auditory* detail and the more *emotion* you insert into your biocomputer programs the more neuronal pathways you create and by *visualizing* your goals over and over again you allow the biocomputer to start functioning at that level – to come up with ideas of how to help you to attain your worldly desires. This is *Basic Visual InAdvance* – and here's more…

We go from our dream home to our dream business

Let's not forget where we are and where we have just come from. We created a beach scene that we were already *familiar* with in the real world and used that as a reference point that was rich in *visual* and *auditory* detail. We then dramatically charged that image by adding an enormous measure of emotion – at every level. We walked around the corner of the beach and took that detailed impression with us into our dream home and now we must *see* in detail, many *practical* and also *impractical* ways (non-solutions) of actually accomplishing that magnificent dream home in the real world. This is exactly what most people *don't* do – they *don't* give their biocomputers *sufficient material* to work with, which will *help and assist* in creating an algorithm to actually solve the problem! This is the area where we must diligently apply our imaginations – to build the kind of business that will be required to buy and sustain the home of our dreams.

Establishing the *crucial link* between owning a dream house, flashy auto and other nice things *and* being *able to pay for them* escapes thousands of *Apprentice Millionaires*. We don't want to make that mistake again because this time around we really want to achieve our goals in the shortest time frame. We must now continue our *visualization* in the same mode of the pleasant walk down the beach and the guided tour through the dream home into a profitable business that will be able to sustain the lifestyle of our dreams.

Walk into the premises of your new business; maybe the first thing you *see* is the receptionist – exactly as you envision her! Continue now into the back office and *see,* in detail, a number of employees, what computers they are working on, what equipment they have, what exactly they are doing. Are they sending out mails-shots, entering up incoming orders complete with checks? What are you selling? Where are those products coming from and who are they being sold to? Perhaps you have sourced products in a *Hong Kong Trade Directory* or on *Google* or *eBay.* Perhaps you have started a consultancy business and you have made yourself busy networking, attending trade shows, breakfast meetings and handing out freshly printed business cards - by the dozen.

As you walk around your imaginary business premises *see* in your imagination various detail in smaller everyday items. Where did those coffee mugs, mouse pads or filing cabinets come from? What inspirational pictures are on the wall? Can you think of where these will come from? The *minute detail* is the *fuse that fires* the imagination for a fuller and bigger picture. You start with *detail* and the biocomputer will add much more detail and fill in missing links to allow you to complete the jigsaw puzzle. You need to give your biocomputer many lines of code so it can start assimilating and computing success formulas on your behalf. Even if you can't answer these questions you need to be *visualizing* things happening and products or services being sold. Operating at trillions of computations per second, simultaneously, it can and will do this for days or weeks on end, your biocomputer literally consumes data and your *Bespoke Input!* It often needs *gargantuan* amounts of *input* and *stimulation* to compute with, before it will deliver *Colossus Output* – in the form of usable formulas, solutions, good ideas and Eurekas! that will show you step-by-step the way of generating the *real money* that you need in order to pay for a *real house* in the *real world* - not a dream house in your imagination!

!!! "Imagine" - *John Lennon*

Hot Tip! Constantly remind yourself that you need to program far into the future and well ***InAdvance*** of arriving at your destination. The minute you accomplish one goal set others and start *Bespoke Programming* for them – ***InAdvance***

KEY – SWITCH YOUR BIOCOMPUTER ON!

The human biocomputer consists of over 100 billion neurons known as cells and these are all interconnected in a dense and intricate network - this you already know! Heretofore, you may have had a vision, a mental analogy in your mind, like I did, that to turn our biocomputers **ON,** we have to throw a single switch. However, this is far from the truth. A neuron is a kind of switch, a very simple one that has two positions, **OFF** and **ON.** The position this assumes, depends on what kind of signals are transmitted from other neurons - via electro-chemical activity. Now, coming back to our 100 billion neurons; this equates to 100 billion switches to be thrown and that is going to be a formidable task, one not to be undertaken likely I would suggest, especially if you are following this philosophy with a view to attaining *Colossus Output* leading to the material rewards you are entitled to. Having this major *key* revealed is so important, because it now becomes patently obvious why I have been so pedantic in driving home the protocols of how to reprogram the human biocomputer. To throw a goodly number of those switches from **OFF** to **ON** means you have to *excite* those neurons. Yes! Neurons respond to stimulation - they really do. Great portions of it! Once you start programming in your goals and aspirations in your best Technicolor ***Basic Visual InAdvance*** combined with as many solutions *and* non-solutions as you can possibly think of; fused with highly charged levels of emotion, amalgamated with many other *keys* described in this codebook; you really will turn your biocomputer **ON!** But nothing short of full *Bespoke Inputting* ***Basic Visual InAdvance*** will do the trick.

!!! I've *finally* switched my biocomputer ON!

Hot Tip! It was the *full range* of *emotions, gazerkle* and *exuberance* that supercharged ***Basic Visual InAdvance*** to ensure my *Colossus Output* in every case. Emotion excites the neurons and switches them **ON,** and don't forget, you have a hundred billion of them!

KEY – GENETIC DIGITAL-ANALOG ALGORITHMS:

I love getting feedback from children and this was no exception. A good friend of mine, Belladonna, asked her ten-year old son Jason, what was the difference between the brain and the mind. Jason said, "The brain is the box inside the head and the mind is the information inside the box." The answer was good, but not quite correct.

In a conventional computer, computations are done in a closed-box, i.e. within the four walls of the computer. Fortunately the biocomputer is *not* a closed box – far from it. Every biocomputer is continuously processing a stream of *input* dynamically generated by the environment. For example: the bank said "Yes" or "No"; $100,000 came into the business; the car broke down; the check bounced; the deal failed to close; our best salesperson walked out; we employed ten new salesmen; we lost our Internet connection; a big deal closed; and this process is repeated *forever* – and we haven't even started! As your biocomputer is processing the problems you have set for it, (i.e. the goals you are trying to accomplish) it is carrying out trillions of computations per second concurrently, yet at the same time it is also receiving vast quantities of *additional input* and data from your ears, nose, eyes, possibly a nagging partner, TV, radio, media, the Internet, input from any number of six billion other biocomputers, your environment and the daily, even hourly changing game plan of whatever it is you are trying to accomplish. Each new piece of *input* will throw a completely different light on the equation.

By far the biggest challenge that faces mankind is to get our brains to work like a computer. We must find a way of encouraging the words and pictures, the analog and digital to communicate with one another, and come up with a process of solving our personal problems – an awesome task in anyone's language!

We must find a *key* to unlocking all of this data and find a way of accessing it and processing it quickly and efficiently and convert it into usable solutions. You may have heard about Google's secret *algorithm* that allows rapid searches of its gigantic database locating just the right information in seconds. If you have used Amazon you will have witnessed their incredibly powerful algorithm that allows each individual customer to experience their own personal buying preferences and buy books so quickly, that many times they arrive before you've even ordered them - now there's an enigma! It is algorithms that allow all the 0s and 1s in your computer to make sense of just about everything you do on it. It's also an *algorithm* that is going to *unlock* your goliath database of pictures, words and concepts in your own biocomputer! In his time, the legendary mathematician Alan Turing talked about quantum, exponential and indeed genetic algorithms and the more I think about it, the more I realize that the human biocomputer generates its own brilliant genetic digital-analog algorithms to help you solve each specific problem that you request it to compute - in the most expedient step-by-step process.

Put simply an algorithm is formula. In mathematics, a formula is a *key* to solving an equation with variables. You probably will not get a more complex equation or one with more variables than that of *unlocking* each individual human biocomputer. In computing, linguistics, mathematics and related topics, an algorithm is a sequence of finite instructions, used for calculation and data processing. It is an effective method using *well-defined instructions* for completing a complex task. Some algorithms, known as probabilistic algorithms, incorporate randomness – and this is going to be crucial in creating algorithms that will unlock the stupendous biocomputer effect – i.e. that of getting the two hemispheres of the brain, the biocomputer, communicating with each other and generating ideas, solutions and **Eurekas! On Demand!** Your biocomputer will create its own genetic digital-analog algorithm, and the good news is that you do not even need to understand the algorithm – all you need to understand is the rules of the game – and it's this *protocol* that I hope I have conveyed to you in this codebook.

An algorithm can be developed for every conceivable problem. And by *Bespoke Inputting* you turn this from a useful *key* - into a significant *key*. This is your next high-level paradigm shift – and you've already had a few of those! You can see now why I have taken great pains to go into the detailed level of *Bespoke Programming* that we have talked about. You will now see that if you are *affirming verbally* that you want a Rolls Royce but are *visualizing* a Ford, the biocomputer will create a totally ineffective algorithm. Whereas if you are *affirming* a Rolls Royce and also *visualizing* a Rolls Royce, that particular *Bespoke Input* will create an extremely efficient algorithm. Likewise if you assist your biocomputer by telling it two hundred different things that could *possibly* be done in order to get your Rolls Royce and two hundred different things that *definitely won't work for you, for one reason or another* i.e. non-solutions, (in your humble opinion – don't forget the biocomputer will weave its own creative magic) as opposed to telling it six things that could *possibly* work and two *non-solutions* that is going to be a very different sort of algorithm. You need to create your own state-of-the-art search abilities and the only way you can do that is to create the most effective and most powerful algorithm you can – by giving as much detailed *Bespoke Input* as you can conceivably think of. If what you are doing is not working, spend even more time breaking down your goals into smaller and smaller steps that cannot be broken down further and consciously coming up with many more ways of how the goal *may or may not* be accomplished. Algorithms are only as good as their instructions, and the end result will be incorrect if the algorithm is not properly defined. Alan Turing advocated making the hardware as simple as possible and putting the whole of the complexity into the software - and that in effect, is what we have mirrored here in *The Eureka! Enigma* success philosophy.

SCIENTIFIC KEYS

Alan Turing, computer and biocomputer genius, often said, "A computer can do anything we know how to order it to perform" and then added, "The computer must first split up the algorithm *into simple operations* which are so simple that it is not easy to imagine *them further divided."*

The exact combination of *keys* that work to unlock your biocomputer is your personal algorithm and it's *that algorithm* that will induce the biocomputer effect to kick in – Big Time! – and once it does you'll never look back, believe me!

KEY – OUTPUT = INPUT²

Here's another major paradigm shift for you as we begin to realize that the expression Input = Output, (*especially* when it comes to human biocomputers) is completely erroneous! If you have been *Bespoke Programming* your biocomputer correctly the *output* you can expect will always be *Colossus Output,* which is eminently greater than the *input* you feed into your biocomputer. If Input = Output, you'd get out the exact same volume that went in – and that just wouldn't be an effective formula for *Colossus Output.*

That's certainly the case with conventional computers. Output may come out in a more useful form – the computer may compute answers, it may re-arrange stuff, it may save you a lot of time – all very clever, but it will not *create* anything. You don't want to be *inputting* into your biocomputer just to get the same *output* – what you want is something *extraordinary, mind blowing, earth shattering* and that's exactly what you get when you combine *mind power work* with *action.* The correct formula should be **Output = Input²** at the very least.

So what does all this mean? If you like, you can give your *input* a numerical value – 100, for argument's sake. Once you are satisfied that your *Bespoke Inputting* is complete, having used all your own particular *keys*, the *Colossus Output* created will be $100^2 = 10,000$. This is the order of magnitude that you should expect every time you program your biocomputer in **Basic Visual InAdvance** to come up with Eurekas! In simple terms it really does mean that a Eureka! is *massively* greater than the sum of its visualized parts.

Very, Very, Very Hot Tip! When you combine **Basic Visual InAdvance** with Action you trigger the world's most powerful success formula: Output = Input^2

KEY – THE REAL KEY IS ALREADY IN YOUR POSSESSION, YOU SIMPLY HAVE TO TURN IT:

Perhaps, like thousands of others, you have been searching long and hard for the secrets of success in books, tapes, CDs and at motivational seminars. The real *key*, however, will be something that you and you alone *do, deep within your mind*. It lies in every single cell within your biocomputer, and using your biocomputer to create code that cracks code, you must now begin to find your own individual *key* and turn it. Take a reality check right now, and ask, "Am I *really* visualizing – *really*?" Start today, by *visualizing* and **INTERNALIZING** everything you wish your future to be. Continue using **Basic Visual InAdvance** *every* day and soon a whole new exciting world will open up before you.

I have given you all the other *keys*. Start using them, and very soon you will unlock your own, unique billion-dollar biocomputer. It is yours to program and command and is waiting to serve you. Now armed with all the *keys*, including *Action – The Master Key*, and the knowledge of *how* to use them, and the *exact* reason *why* you should use them, there is no need for me to wish you luck. With *The Eureka! Enigma* system at your disposal, I instead congratulate you, **InAdvance – Basic Visual InAdvance!** – on your forthcoming success!

!!! Even when you find the right *key*, you may find the door opens inwards!

Hot Tip! In the simple step of starting and driving your car a few hundred yards on a busy street your biocomputer handles and processes more information than all the computers on the planet and the sooner you start to *harness* the power of your own super biocomputer, the sooner you too will accomplish your dreams and goals – whatever they are!

Final, Final, Final, Word! I hope you have enjoyed this codebook and that it is instrumental in helping you crack your own personal code. I sincerely hope that it has a *profound* effect on your life. It is designed to!

Now, being a consummate salesman, I am going to ask you to do something for me, *today* if you can. If you enjoyed this codebook, please buy at least *two* additional copies and *give* them to your nearest and dearest. Also, please recommend the codebook at every available opportunity *and* post a five star review on Amazon! In this way you will be helping to spread a very positive message for the whole of humanity. Then, when we meet – as I feel sure we will – you can tell me not only how *The Eureka! Enigma* has worked its magic for you, but how you've helped your most valued friends and colleagues turn their lives around, too. I'll be looking forward to reading your stories at: www.eureka-enigma.com

So, ladies and gentlemen, boys and girls, it's time to throw your hats in the air, shout "Hip, hip, hooray" and get cracking.

Onwards and Upwards,
Ron G Holland
London - New York 2009

P.S. Would you like to receive a <u>$500 DISCOUNT VOUCHER</u> for one of my workshops? All I am asking in return is that you really do follow up and follow through and purchase at least two extra copies of

The Eureka! Enigma for your friends – *before you forget!* While you are at it, please get *Talk & Grow Rich* and *Turbo Success* and then you'll be able to see the logical progression that enabled me to arrive at the powerful conclusions in this codebook. When you have done that, log onto www.eureka-enigma.com and tell me where you bought the codebooks and the receipt # and I'll email you a $500 discount voucher for one of my workshops – easy as that!

P.P.S. Give Books!

CRACK THE CODE!

* The RAS needs to be deactivated every time you program your biocomputer.

* You need to reactive the RAS once programming is finished.

* You need to be thinking in pictures, ***InAdvance,*** every day for the rest of your life.

* You have a hundred billion neurons and each one of these is a switch. You have to program with gigantic volumes of *negative* and *positive* emotion to turn these **ON!**

* The more precisely your words and pictures *match;* the more ways you can think of how to achieve your goal consciously; the more non-solutions you can create and program in - the more efficient the genetic digital–analog algorithm.

* If you find it hard to visualize use a familiar reference point to start from.

* Cultivate the habit of *seeing* not merely *looking.*

* If your goal setting isn't working try to set goals that are accomplishable and start proving to yourself that you can get your biocomputer to function effectively and delivering useable *Colossus Output* before setting larger goals.

* Output = Input^2 and that's awesome – putting it on par with Albert Einstein's famous formula $E = MC^2$ which is basis of nuclear science!

* See you real soon at: www.eureka-enigma.com – I look forward to it!

AFTERWORD

EUREKA!

When I started out on *The Eureka! Enigma* project I was well aware of other books that had been written on similar subjects, so I deliberately steered clear of them. I didn't want my thinking to be guided, swayed or contaminated. In one way I knew what I was looking for, and in another way I didn't. I did have a strong hunch that if I followed my intuition and worked hard, I'd get the answers I was seeking. The title chapters came to me quite easily, especially *Bespoke Input*, *Computation & Gestation* and *Colossus Output* because for centuries, books on idea generation have all talked about those three themes, in various guises. *Cracking the Code* came because of my breakthrough at the *Enigma Tavern*, which led me to Bletchley Park and *Software for the Brain* – well that was a no-brainer.

The problem that was bugging me was Chapter Six. At the start of the project the chapter was entitled *Invisible Entrapment*. Yet even when the book was finished –save final editing and polishing – something kept drawing me back to that chapter. For five months at least, I pondered, tinkered and rewrote bits of it – but it never really flowed or felt right. I was really struggling because part of me was saying, "submit it to the publisher" and another part, a *very* strong part said, "no, keep reworking it, you're not done yet." Every day I addressed the problem and still it never quite clicked - no matter how hard I wrestled with it.

One day I had two meetings to attend, both in the delightful market town of Melton Mowbray in the county of Leicestershire, some 130 miles from where I live. In the morning I planned to go to the Pera Headquarters where I was introducing a client to some potential advisers. In the afternoon I was to meet Muna Pabari, a long-time friend and business associate of mine, who lives 10 minutes down the road from Pera.

I have already mentioned that most people spend inordinate periods of time in meetings that are totally unproductive and I am acutely aware of this. That day, there was really *no need* for me to physically go to Pera Headquarters with my clients; I knew they would be looked after extremely well. I certainly didn't *need* to meet Muna – we go back at least 15 years and most of our business is conducted over the phone or by e-mail. I toyed with the idea of wriggling out of the two meetings and getting on with *The Eureka! Enigma* manuscript - in actual fact I had already picked up the phone to make the first call, but this *small still voice*, one I've heard many times before, said, "Go the extra mile, put in the energy and effort and attend the meetings" so I put the phone down and *immediately* justified a whole day out in Leicestershire. I *always* try to follow my hunches, even if my *intellect* is shouting, "Waste of executive time!" My overriding thought now however, was *just do it!*

My immediate thoughts were about Pera, a large and extremely successful consultancy that had been founded just after World War II by Winston Churchill, to assist British industry get back on its feet. They employ literally hundreds of scientists and have full access to 35,000 others across Europe. The company now specializes (among other things) in securing EU grant funding that can be used by SMEs to develop products and technology, giving them a quantum leap. They lead in innovation and I wondered if I would meet a genius or two – perhaps find a breakthrough I didn't even know I was looking for, but subconsciously sensed I needed.

I left early on the morning in question and arrived at Pera Headquarters in good time – in actual fact I got there early, so I had a cappuccino and my customary sticky bun in a small coffee bar around the corner as I read the *Financial Times* – and *Motorcycle News!* On the due time I drove into Pera's Headquarters and my clients were already waiting in the car park. We spent an eventful morning meeting directors, exploring opportunities, looking at many innovative products and technologies that were being developed and discussing in great detail what Pera could do for my client – all of which was incredibly exciting and re-affirmed in my mind that UK companies shouldn't try to compete on cost – but on innovation.

At about 2 p.m. Muna arrived at Pera's headquarter and I bade farewell to the directors and also my clients. Muna and I sat down for coffee, we had lots to talk about. After about an hour, he invited me back to his home as he wanted to show me a few things. Over tea and more sticky buns, we looked at a number of web sites, (with great interest I hasten to add) and as always, he showed me his latest reading – piles of books on computers, website development, e-commerce, copywriting and of course, self-help books – dozens of them.

The one book that grabbed my attention was Robert Ringer's *Action* – only because I knew Robert from my years of living in the U.S. and once had the great pleasure of gifting him a solid gold tortoise. I mentioned this to Muna and he *insisted* that I take the book with me. It wasn't really necessary; I skimmed it and got the gist of it while I was there. However Muna *insisted*. We had a great afternoon that extended way into the evening, culminating with dinner in a superb Indian restaurant, and I didn't get home until the small hours of the next morning. On the way home, I did notice on numerous occasions, Robert's book sitting there quietly on the passenger seat, and on arriving home I took it in with me and put it on my office table.

The next morning I awoke at five, as per usual (despite arriving home at two), and went into my office. Before starting my morning meditation, I had a perusal of Robert Ringer's book, which was still on my table where I had left it a few hours previously. My intention was to skim it one more time and then orderly shelve it, but what happened next was *truly startling*. I opened this 80,000-word book at random and certain words *literally jumped off the page* – SCREAMING at me, "*Action is the key to the brain's ignition.*" Eureka! *Immediately* I had the *entire*

Chapter Six of my own book – in one fell swoop – like a symphony. I felt like Beethoven, Bach *and* Tchaikovsky, all rolled into one, all of whom were renowned for their Eureka! moments – seeing *complete* compositions in one *insight* and then writing them up in one sitting. Eureka! I changed the name of Chapter Six from *Invisible Entrapment*, which I had been struggling with for five months, to **ACTION** – *The Master Key*. The chapter, as a result of *Colossus Output*, furiously wrote itself over four days and nights of intense, non-stop work and is the most powerful section in the entire codebook. I hope you like it - a*nd* act on it. Genius is the ultimate state of creativity and it is *accessed* via the door of action!

Penultimate Thought: The shining star of *The Eureka! Enigma* is the legendary Alan Turing, and although you have heard it before it would be remiss of me not to mention his extremely powerful words just one more time. "The computer, calculator or machine doesn't matter – only the *output* counts." I want these words above all others to *ring* in your ears!

Ultimate Thought: When you combine **Basic Visual InAdvance** with **Action** you trigger the world's most powerful success formula, Output = Input^2 and when you do, you too will succeed. Enjoy the *journey* and the *destination*. Now off you go – and don't forget to enjoy a few sticky buns on the way!

www.eureka-enigma.com

BUY A SHARE OF THE FUTURE IN YOUR COMMUNITY

These certificates make great holiday, graduation and birthday gifts that can be personalized with the recipient's name. The cost of one S.H.A.R.E. or one square foot is $54.17. The personalized certificate is suitable for framing and will state the number of shares purchased and the amount of each share, as well as the recipient's name. The home that you participate in "building" will last for many years and will continue to grow in value.

Here is a sample SHARE certificate:

HABITAT FOR HUMANITY

THIS CERTIFIES THAT
YOUR NAME HERE
HAS INVESTED IN A HOME FOR A DESERVING FAMILY

1985-2005
TWENTY YEARS OF BUILDING FUTURES IN OUR
COMMUNITY ONE HOME AT A TIME

1200 SQUARE FOOT HOUSE @ $65,000 = $54.17 PER SQUARE FOOT
This certificate represents a tax deductible donation. It has no cash value.

YES, I WOULD LIKE TO HELP!

*I support the work that Habitat for Humanity does and I want to be part of the excitement! As a donor, I will receive periodic updates on your construction activities but, more importantly, I know my gift will help a family in our community realize the dream of homeownership. **I would like to SHARE in your efforts against substandard housing in my community!** (Please print below)*

PLEASE SEND ME _____ SHARES at $54.17 EACH = $ $_____

In Honor Of: _____

Occasion: (Circle One)   HOLIDAY   BIRTHDAY   ANNIVERSARY

         OTHER: _____

Address of Recipient: _____

Gift From: _____ *Donor Address:* _____

Donor Email: _____

I AM ENCLOSING A CHECK FOR $ $_____ PAYABLE TO HABITAT FOR HUMANITY <u>OR</u> PLEASE CHARGE MY VISA OR MASTERCARD *(CIRCLE ONE)*

Card Number _____ Expiration Date: _____

Name as it appears on Credit Card _____ Charge Amount $ _____

Signature _____

Billing Address _____

Telephone # Day _____ Eve _____

PLEASE NOTE: Your contribution is tax-deductible to the fullest extent allowed by law.
Habitat for Humanity • P.O. Box 1443 • Newport News, VA 23601 • 757-596-5553
www.HelpHabitatforHumanity.org

Lightning Source UK Ltd.
Milton Keynes UK
UKOW051816200911

178989UK00001B/218/P